What is Slavery?

Brenda E. Stevenson

polity

First published in 2015 by Polity Press

Polity Press
65 Bridge Street
Cambridge CB2 1UR, UK

Polity Press
350 Main Street
Malden, MA 02148, USA

ISBN-13: 978-0-7456-7150-5
ISBN-13: 978-0-7456-7151-2(pb)

A catalogue record for this book is available from the British Library.

Library of Congress Cataloging-in-Publication Data

Stevenson, Brenda E.
    What is slavery? / Brenda E. Stevenson.
        pages cm. – (What is history)
    Includes bibliographical references and index.
    ISBN 978-0-7456-7150-5 (hardcover : alk. paper) – ISBN 0-7456-7150-0 (hardcover : alk. paper) – ISBN 978-0-7456-7151-2 (pbk. : alk. paper) – ISBN 0-7456-7151-9 (pbk. : alk. paper)   1. Slavery–United States–History. 2. Slavery–History. I. Title.
    E441.S88 2015
    306.3′620973–dc23
                                                                    2014047151

Typeset in 10.5 on 12 pt Sabon
by Toppan Best-set Premedia Limited
Printed and bound in the US by Courier Digital Solutions, North Chelmsford, MA

For further information on Polity, visit our website: politybooks.com

Contents

Figures and Tables

Figures

Tables

Acknowledgments

This book is drawn from my studies in slavery taken up since I was a young college student. I am thankful, therefore, to so many people who have instructed and guided me in this ever-fascinating topic, particularly John W. Blassingame, David Brion Davis, Robert F. Thompson, Sylvia Boone, D. Barry Gaspar, Joseph Miller, Leon Litwack, Darlene Clark Hine, V. P. Franklin, Deborah White, Nancy Cott, Edmund Morgan, Catherine Clinton, Elizabeth Fox-Genovese, and Paul Gaston. Of course, the support of colleagues is always invaluable. I would like to thank especially Stephen Aron, Ellen DuBois, Ronald Mellor, Teo Ruiz, David Myers, Scott Waugh, and Sharla Fett. I am grateful to my external reviewers as well as Elliott Karstadt and Andrea Drugan at Polity Press for solid and essential advice regarding how to contain and organize such a huge topic in such a small book. Ellen Broidy assisted with editing the first draft of this work. Kaitlin Boyd served as an excellent research and editorial assistant, for which I am very thankful. Finally I am, as ever, thankful to God, my parents, James and Emma Stevenson and to my husband James Cones and our daughter Emma.

Introduction:
What is Slavery?

What is slavery? It seems a simple enough question. Most people believe slavery was the condition that black people in the United States lived in before the end of the Civil War. In my college classes, for example, celluloid images of *Gone with the Wind*, *Roots*, *Sankofa*, *Uncle Tom's Cabin*, *Quilombo*, *Amistad*, *Beloved*, *Burn!*, *Belle*, and the 2014 Oscar winner for best film *12 Years a Slave* mesh, mingle, and struggle for dominance as my students try to answer the question on the first day of lectures. What most of them do not know is that the institution of slavery is one of the most common in history *and* also one of the most diverse. Almost every civilization has had some form of slavery – whether it was in Europe, the Americas, Africa, Asia, or Australia. As such, almost every ethnic/racial group alive today has been touched, at least ancestrally or geospatially, by the institution. Moreover, slavery still exists in most places. Indeed, an estimated 20–30 million people worldwide are still considered enslaved – either as chattel, debt peons, sex slaves, or as forced laborers. These enslaved workers come from, and are enslaved in, both poor and wealthy nations, although certainly the poor and politically dispossessed make up the majority of the enslaved in contemporary society. So, too, do women and children. Keep also in mind that the legacies of past slavery regimes remain among us. Many of those enslaved during the eras of American "discovery," colonization, and early nationhood have descendants alive today who are located on the margins of their societies, particularly economically, socially, culturally, and even politically; some who can even be counted among the millions still designated as slaves.

Despite the long history of the institution and its widespread use around the globe, most people in the United States associate slavery with the enslavement of Africans in this nation for good reason. While the area that became the United States did not import many Africans through the transatlantic trade (only about 4–5 percent of those Africans who actually came to the "New World"), the United States became the largest slave society in the Atlantic world in the mid-nineteenth century. No other colony, state, or nation in the Americas held more than four million black slaves at one time, as did the United States in the early 1860s.

Most scholars agree that the first Africans arrived as laborers in British North America sometime between 1607 and 1618. They were late arrivals to the New World since the Spanish and Portuguese had been importing slaves to their Central and South American colonies and to the Caribbean since the early sixteenth century. Slowly, their numbers increased in the British mainland colonies – at first in single or at most double digits per year – and then, as the seventeenth century entered its third quarter, as a steadily increasing flow. By the middle of the eighteenth century, thousands were arriving annually. Elsewhere on the continent, the Spanish and the French in Florida and other places along the Gulf of Mexico already had established colonies that included black, and indigenous, slave labor. The Africans' presence, and their economic, political, social, cultural, legal, and psychological impacts on North America, were enormous.

This book chronicles this presence and its evolving influence through a detailed scrutiny of the lives of the slaves and the institution of chattel slavery that shaped them. The topics that garner special attention in *What is Slavery?* include: demography; legal structures; African cultural change, exchange, and resilience; material culture/material support; resistance and accommodation; marriage and family; labor and leisure; and abuse, punishment, and rewards. These topics are brought to light by weaving together descriptive narratives that are placed within a broader context of the developing slave presence in the Atlantic Chesapeake, Lowcountry, southern Piedmont, Lower South and Southwest, as well as in the middle and northern seaboard before the Revolution. In these diverse colonial locales that became the United States, gender, generation, race/ethnicity, class, and political consciousness or moral ideologies all shaped the perspective of the enslaved, the slaveholder and the majority of North American residents who were neither.

The objectives of this book are ambitious, particularly so given its mandated brevity. It provides its reader with a sweeping description, synthetic in nature, of one of the most significant experiences in American history. It is not meant to be a research monograph with groundbreaking new analysis, although some of it has drawn on my research and analysis that have not been published previously. Instead, *What is Slavery?* has largely drawn on the published work of generations of slavery scholars, including my own, that has collectively taught us much about this mammoth topic. *What is Slavery?* is a chronologically and topically driven narrative. Still, there are some fundamental experiences of the American slave, and characteristics of the institution of slavery, that are emphasized throughout these pages and form the book's underlying themes.

Slavery for Africans and their descendants in the United States, as throughout the Americas, was brutal. Slavery fundamentally meant a loss of control over the vital aspects of one's life and the lives of one's loved ones. It often meant physical and psychological abuse. For slave women, and to a lesser extent men and children, it meant sexual abuse. By today's standards, the average slave was not treated humanely, or even humanly, by their owners or governmental powers. This inhumanity shadowed every aspect of the slave's life – marital and parental relations, labor regimens and working conditions, material support, medical treatment, privacy/intimacy, intellectual/cultural expression, punishment, and representation in law.

Slavery was a brutal exercise of exploitation by the individual and state of the bondsman and bondswoman, *and* it was extremely profitable. Even though popular ideas about slavery in the United States today are framed by a belief of regional (southern) importance, slave-produced wealth shaped the economies, both directly and indirectly, of most of the original thirteen British colonies, as well as those of the Spanish and French territories that would become part of the United States in the nineteenth century.

Slavery's influence on the economic wellbeing of the new nation did not diminish over the decades before the Civil War. This wealth, which was concentrated in the hands of a small white elite, was of little benefit to the slave. Slaves received only the most menial and minimum material, medical, social, and psychological rewards for their labor. Indeed, America's free white society's regard for the slave hardly increased over time, despite the continued profitability derived from slave labor. Instead, there was an increase in popular, and even "scientific," notions of "racial" inferiority that justified both slavery and the slaves' brutal treatment. Few did not experience this racial prejudice and it was this prejudice that so distinguished New World slavery when compared to forms of bondage in earlier periods of time and in other places. Thomas Jefferson's 1781 "suspicion only that the blacks, whether originally a distinct race, or made distinct by time and circumstances, are inferior to the whites in the endowments both of body and mind," became an accepted "truth."[1] Even President Abraham Lincoln, the "Great Emancipator," carefully explained to voters publicly in 1858 that: "There is a physical difference between the white and black races which I believe will forever forbid the two races living together on terms of social and political equality. And inasmuch as they cannot so live, while they do remain together there must be the position of superior and inferior, and I, as much as any other man, am in favor of having the superior position assigned to the white race."[2] It was, indeed, this stigma of racial inferiority that colored the slaves' lives, followed blacks out of slavery, and frames their "freedom" even today. "Racial ideologies undergirded the terror and coercion fundamental to keeping slaves at work," historian Lisa Lindsay notes. "In every slave society, masters and overseers whipped, maimed, raped, humiliated, and deprived enslaved people – tortures they would have considered unthinkable for (most) fellow whites."[3]

Regardless of their brutal economic exploitation and denunciation as racial inferiors, enslaved Africans and their descendants managed to survive their enslavement physically, psychologically, culturally, spiritually, and intellectually. This "survival," to be certain, was not a perfect one. It was borne out of resistance as well as accommodation, acculturation and even, in some instances, assimilation. Even so, there were some who could not endure their harsh circumstances. "It's bad to belong to folks dat own you sol an' body," admitted Delia Garlic, who was enslaved in antebellum Virginia, Georgia, and Louisiana. "Dat can tie you up..., wid yo' face to de tree an' yo' arms fastened tight aroun' it'; who take a long curlin' whip an' cut de blood [with] ever' lick."[4] Historian Nell Painter's brilliant thesis of the "soul murder" of the slave opens up our imagination and intellect to the question of lingering generational trauma among these persons and their descendants.[5] And there certainly were persons who did not survive at all. A significant minority of enslaved men and women committed suicide, suffered insanity, became demoralized and dehumanized, never recovered from physical abuse, badly treated or untreated illnesses, or were murdered by masters or agents of the "law," with the state's blessing. Still, the records of natural increase, long-term marital relations, vibrant cultural expression, unrelenting and diverse challenges to white authority, and creative and courageous acts that led to self and sometimes group emancipation document the slaves' determination to assert their agency[6] against tremendous odds in order to control important aspects of their private lives, working conditions, and human expression. Brutality, profitability, the evolution of a racist ideology on the one hand, and the slave's insistence on physical, psychological, and spiritual survival as manifest through family and community, resistance and cultural expression on the other, are the themes of this synthetic narrative.

The first chapter of *What is Slavery?* is meant to introduce the reader to the "history" of slavery. Certainly this work cannot describe, much less discuss, every example of slavery that we now know existed across time and place. Likewise, the remaining chapters take on no small feat in their attempt to describe the developing landscape of slavery in the United

States and the lives of its ever-expanding bound laborers. *What is Slavery?* necessarily moves back and forth from the "macro" to the "micro," or at least from the regional to the local. Readers are made aware of the broad design of US history, which is so shaped by this institution, and they may hear clearly the voices and stories across the generations of enslaved men, women, and children. The audience will be introduced to some of the scholarly sentiments about key elements of the slave's life and the structures that shaped it. Not only have these opinions evolved over time, but many are just being incorporated into the bulging historiography that is slavery studies. The most important intellectual debates related to slavery in the United States, and the Atlantic world more generally, have centered on: methodological approach (what sources to use; what voices to hear; what questions to ask and answer), as well as interpretations of the slave's relationship to Africa (cultural retention, extension, recovery, or loss); the slave's relationship to his/her owner (paternalistic or antagonistic and resistant, expressions of dependency or agency); the relationship of legal and religious structures to the quality of slave life (Catholic vs Protestant; French and Spanish colonial legal codes that were relatively comprehensive vs the piecemeal laws of states and locales in the United States; and the extension of slave legal codes from the British Caribbean to North American colonies); stereotyped slave personality type(s), including Sambo, Jack, Nat, Mammy, and Jezebel; slave social organization as opposed to disorganization (slave community vs disunity and allegiances to masters); the nature of the institution (paternalistic vs economically driven; benign vs brutal); the nature of the black family (nuclear vs extended and abroad); and the economic ramifications of slavery (profitable vs unprofitable); Clearly, there is much – undoubtedly too much – to try to squeeze into this short book. Nonetheless, *What is Slavery?* attempts to provide its reader with a sound synthesis of this essential experience in American history.

1

Slavery across Time and Place Before the Atlantic Slave Trade

"From the first written records in ancient Sumeria, the concept of slavery has been a way of classifying the most debased social class."

David Brion Davis, *Inhuman Bondage*[1]

Slavery has existed across time and place as one of the most enduring institutions and conditions found among peoples. Many of the examples of enslavement, bondage, unfree labor, debt peonage, concubinage, and so on that will be surveyed here, however, occurred in a society that one would not define as a *slave society* – that is, one in which the presence of slaves had a defining impact on one or more significant societal characteristics that influenced the lives of many, if not most, of its inhabitants. These affected societal traits typically protected the rights and privileges of slaveholders and others invested in the institution, not the slaves. As one will quickly conclude from perusing this chapter, the numerous forms of slavery found around the globe were, and still are, quite varied, not just between political boundaries, but within them as well. Slavery rarely has remained the same in any particular area. Its means of implementation, the characteristics of those who could be enslaved and those who could enslave, its influence on political, social, economic, and cultural structures and customs, the "rights" of the enslaved, the measure of state support, the ways in which the enslaved gained freedom and, indeed, what that "freedom" meant for the emancipated and their descendants produced an impressively diverse institution. Still, the reader will also quickly come to understand that some characteristics of slave status carry across time and place, or at least often repeat themselves. Noted slavery scholar David Brion Davis is absolutely correct in his association of slavery with social "debasement." The hierarchies that slavery helped to created, and operated within, situated the "slave" at the bottom, with rare exception. This is a fundamental similarity hereby persisted across an array of power relationships labeled as slavery. Other similarities include the means whereby persons came to acquire this status, the kinds of labor they performed, and the impact of slave ownership on a master's status. The most singular characteristic of the slave in post-contact America was that he or she was "black"; therefore, a racialized basis for slavery was quite unique previous to the New World institution coming into its own. Before, persons were much more likely to be enslaved because they were impoverished, war captives, criminals, kidnap victims, or were of a specific religion than because they were "black" or African.

Slavery in the Ancient World

In the ancient world, Egypt, Mesopotamia, Greece, Palestine, Rome, and Asia had slaves. So too did early societies in the Americas, Europe, Africa, and the Pacific. There were slaves in Babylon as early as the eighteenth century BCE and in Mesopotamian cities by 6800 BCE. The Babylonian Code of Hammurabi (c. 1790 BCE), for example, contains numerous guidelines related specifically to slavery. Slaves in Mesopotamia typically originated as war captives, criminals, and debtors, and they worked in agriculture, construction, and as domestics. Slave ownership there reached its peak in the first century BCE.[2] Documentation of slavery in Greece indicates that it existed at least from 1500 BCE onward, but was particularly important during the Hellenistic period (332–330 BCE) and especially in Athens, Delos, and Delphi. Fifth-century BCE Athens had more enslaved residents than free people; and Greece employed tens of thousands of slaves in its silver mines during the same era. Slavery in the Roman Republic was fully institutionalized by 450 BCE, and was incorporated into the Twelve Tables legal code (451–450 BCE). Indeed, close to 700,000 prisoners of war were enslaved between 297 and 167 BCE in the Roman Empire.[3] Altogether, millions of slaves inhabited ancient Rome, claiming 15–25 percent or even 35 percent of its population.[4]

What did it mean to be a slave in the ancient Greco-Roman world? Slaves had to be away from their original "nation" and "cultures" – an "other" in the society where the "free" did not regard him or her as a "person," and certainly not as an equal. A slave had no recognizable ties to nation, state, or lineage.[5] Roman slaves, for example, arrived from across Rome's vast empire that included Germany, Italy, the Balkans, Britain, Syria, Spain, Greece, Turkey, Somalia, North Africa, Jewish territories, and even India.[6] Slaves were chattel or property, and provided their masters with labor and status. It was understood, by slaves and their owners alike, however, that they still were human and, therefore, capable of emotion and even intelligence.[7] Nonetheless, a slave belonged physically and, at least outwardly, emotionally to his/her owner who could choose to use, clothe, feed, punish, designate an occupation, or have sexual relations with him or her largely at will. The vast majority of Roman slaves had few privileges and their status was passed on to their descendants. As enslaved people, they could not own property, marry, or have a family over which they could claim control.[8]

The origins of this status – inherited, war spoil, purchased chattel, kidnap victim, debtor, and orphaned, abandoned, or sold child of an impoverished family – also led to enslavement in China, Egypt, and other places in both the ancient and early modern world. Enslaved persons in the Roman Empire were found in all realms of society and were essential, in many ways, to various sectors of the economies of the ancient world. The largest numbers were domestics or agricultural workers. Indeed, although wealthy slaveholders could have hundreds of domestic slaves, most had much smaller numbers. Slaves also worked as skilled artisans, gladiators, in mining, and in administrative positions. As in societies throughout the western ancient world, domestic and skilled slaves had higher status than agricultural workers.[9] Slavery in the ancient Greco-Roman world meant, as it did in the Americas, that enslaved men, women, and children did not have control over their bodies. Physical and sexual control of a slave was a given right of owners and anyone the owner allowed access to his property. Owners also could choose to punish their slaves as they pleased, usually without state interference. Punishments could range from whipping and branding to imprisonment or even death.[10]

There was a consensus regarding the alienated social and political status of slaves, but there often was visible status diversity among the slave population that affected their labor and treatment. In the Greco-Roman world, certain prized slaves belonging to wealthy and powerful masters, therefore, had relatively significant power vis-à-vis other slaves, as well as some low-status free men and women.[11] As such, some enslaved persons actually found themselves on the border between "slave" and "free," due to their owners' great status. Others gained status, and some useful "freedoms," if they acquired important skills or an impressive education. A few, no doubt, actually could inspire the envy of very low-status free people. Freedom, after all, could be replaced with slavery if a free man or woman found themselves in dire economic straits or on the wrong side of the law. Likewise, the enslaved could become free.

Still, once enslaved, the condition typically was one for life and, for many, could be passed on to future generations. Interruption of this flow of propertied status came when an owner freed his slave or the slave managed to earn enough money to buy his or her freedom – that is, if the master allowed him or her to do so – since the right to buy one's freedom usually was not guaranteed. Even after gaining freedom, the stain of slavery often followed a person into freedom, even obligating the former bondsperson to a previous master.[12]

In the Roman Republic, for example, formal manumission did render the former slave with a limited type of citizenship. Freed people could legally marry, make contracts, and own transferable property. Males had some limited voting capacity, but they could not hold public office, although their freeborn sons could. In ancient Greece, slaves could seek manumission either through religious or civil means. Freedom meant that former Greek slaves had control over their movements and the right to earn income, but they still were tied to former owners or owners' heirs. Practically, this meant that masters or their families could call on emancipated slaves to provide some type of service or compensation. Those who refused to do so could be punished and, in extreme cases, re-enslaved.[13]

Just as slavery was not an unusual institution in the ancient world, nor was resistance. Slaves fought their bondage in many ways, including armed rebellion, such as in the uprising led by Spartacus in Italy in 73–71 BCE that involved thousands of slaves.[14]

Others committed suicide, escaped, murdered their masters, stole from them, burnt their crops, businesses and homes, and, of course, continuously designed passive forms of disobedience whenever they believed they might get away with doing so, for, as historian Keith Bradley notes of slavery in ancient Rome, a "game of psychological warfare [...] always existed between master and slave."[15]

Many ancient texts captured descriptions of slavery. Slaves and slavery, for example, are depicted in the Old as well as the New Testaments of the Bible. These persons typically inherited their status or were reduced to it as debtors, prisoners of war, criminals, or concubines. In the Old Testament, Jews, and other ethnic/racial groups, both held and were held as slaves. The Apostle Paul spoke of the plight of slaves and Peter instructed slaves to obey their masters in the New Testament. Of course, one of the most popularly referenced chronicles of slavery found in the Bible is in Exodus – the story of Jewish enslavement by Egyptians and their eventual release under the leadership of Moses. Jews, however, were hardly the only slaves found in ancient Egypt.

Given the longevity of the civilizations found in Egypt, it is not surprising that slavery presented itself somewhat differently in the Old Kingdom (c. 2700–2300 BCE), Middle Kingdom (c. 2134–1785 BCE), and New Kingdom (c. 1560–1070 BCE), as well as under Roman control (30 BCE–640

1.1 Slaves working in a mine in ancient Greece, 440–430 BCE
Source: Wikimedia Commons

CE). The largest number of enslaved were found during the era of the New Kingdom. Regardless of the era, most were military captives. During the fifth dynasty of the Old Kingdom, for example, there is evidence that at least 7,000 Nubians and 1,100 Libyan slaves were captured. Others during the ancient eras came from Syria, Canaan, Ethiopia, or, internally, were Egyptian criminals or debtors. Many labored in the agricultural lands, in mines, as soldiers, and in the domestic sphere.[16] Toil in the copper and gold mines was deemed the most brutal, with many fatalities. Most slaveholders only had one or two slaves, but certainly wealthy persons had more. Slaves who worked in palaces for royalty were believed to be the most fortunate because of the relatively high level of material support and because of the opportunity to acquire favor and, therefore, privileges that other enslaved persons would not experience. Moreover, at least by the time of the New Kingdom, some particularly privileged slaves held property and could inherit. Likewise, there is evidence that some bondspersons could testify in court and were educated in Egyptian culture. Slavery in Egypt, as throughout the ancient world, was hereditary. The New Kingdom will of Amonkhau (c. 1100 BCE), for example, stipulated that his second wife should receive "two male servants and two female servants and their children," along with an additional nine slaves.[17]

Slavery in the Middle East and Asia

Beyond Egypt, slavery flourished in other parts of the Middle East and vast trading networks brought persons for sale from across the region and beyond. Even though the institution was in place before the spread of Islam, the Qur'an, as the Bible, speaks of, and to, the institution of slavery, both assuming its existence and offering some guidelines. Shari'a law, for example, prohibited Muslims from enslaving one another. They could, however, enslave non-Muslims and there was a lengthy history of slave-capturing raids on non-Muslim communities and pirated ships throughout the Mediterranean, North Africa, the Middle East, the Iberian Peninsula, and the Balkans.[18] Most of the enslaved worked as domestics or were used as military personnel. The Qur'an also allowed male adherents to have sexual relations with female slaves, even if both were married; and many women were forced into concubinage relationships. Once a concubine had a child by her master, however, she was to be freed upon his death and the child was to be free upon birth.[19] Since a slave's status was determined by the status of his/her master, a hierarchy did exist among the enslaved. Many soldier slaves, for example, eventually were freed and then allowed some rights.

Central Asia, an enormous area of the globe that extended from Mongolia to the Caucasus Mountains and from Kazakhstan to Afghanistan, was not exempt from the institution of slavery, with some bondsmen and women also shipped to the Middle East. Indeed, slaves were a common and important item of exchange along the Silk Road. Most of the male slaves, especially Turks, became soldiers, while the women, as typical, were concubines and domestics.[20]

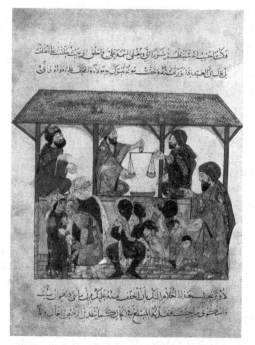

1.2 A slave market, from "Al Maqamat" (The Meetings) by Al-Hariri (vellum), Al-Wasiti, Yahya ibn Mahmud (thirteenth century)
Source: Pictures From History/Bridgeman Images

In various parts of Asia, including China, Japan, Korea, India, Cambodia, Malaysia, and Indonesia, the enslavement of war captives, debtors, and criminals persisted beyond the ancient eras. For example, an Indian treatise, "Arthahastra," written by an advisor to the Emperor Chandragupta around 300 BCE, noted that persons could become enslaved by selling themselves to someone, through inheriting the status, as a punishment for a crime or because of their war-captive status. Masters employed their slaves in numerous occupations, including service as messengers, domestics, interpreters, concubines, eunuchs, craftsmen, warriors, and rural agricultural workers. Although slavery thrived in the urban arena, South Asian masters used large numbers of slaves for agricultural labor during the Vedic period of 600–321 BCE. Chinese slaves helped to build the Great Wall and the tomb of Emperor Shih Huang Ti in the third century BCE. In ancient Japan, until the ninth century CE, male slaves were known as "yakko." During the Taika Reforms of 645 CE, specific rules regarding the "nuhi," or slaves, were created. More extensive laws were established in 701 CE that distinguished "public slaves," or "kunuhi," from private slaves, or "shinuhi," and provided for the improvement of status for the former. The ownership of large numbers of slaves in Southeast Asia, as elsewhere, brought a master social prestige and economic might. International and domestic slave trades operated between 206 BCE and the fourteenth century, providing slaves to China from as far away as Africa.[21] As late as the sixteenth century in Sumatra and New Guinea, as well as in the Philippines in the seventeenth and eighteenth centuries, significant slave-trading businesses operated.[22]

Slavery in Africa

Slavery, of course, existed in much of Africa beyond ancient Egypt and the continent's northern regions.[23] Various forms of the institution flourished across Africa from early periods onward. Arabs controlled the coastal East African slave trade from about 200 BCE. Young Ethiopian men used as warriors, and women and girls who were valued for their beauty and enslaved in harems, were especially important. By the twelfth century, even Chinese historians were writing about the enslavement of East Africans in the Middle East. Chou Ch'u-fei, for example, noted in 1178 that "there is an island in the sea on which there are many savages. Their bodies are black as lacquer and they have frizzled hair. They are enticed by food and then captured and sold as slaves to the Arabic countries, where they fetch a high price."[24]

Enslaved western Africans also were traded throughout the Arab world. Trade routes that carried gold, ivory, salt, and slaves eventually connected peoples across the vast continental expanse. By the eighth century CE, for example, a thriving Muslim slave trade, much of it reliant on violent kidnapping and raiding, was moving bondspeople from sub-Saharan African north and east to the Persian Gulf and, in

the tenth century CE, to Asia.[25] Much of this trade operated
out of the city of Zawila in the southern Libyan Desert,
moving along the important slave routes through Timbuktu,
Kano, Bornu, and Wadaj.[26] This trade flourished for more
than a millennium.[27] Some were eventually sold in parts of
medieval and early modern Europe. The majority were
females and typically used as domestics and concubines. At
some locales, Jewish traders preceded Islamic ones.[28] The
important West African kingdoms of Ghana, Mali, and
Songhai also practiced some forms of bondage.[29] By the mid-
nineteenth century, Muslim traders traveled as far inland in
Africa as the upper Congo and Lake Victoria to acquire
human property. They shipped these men, women, and
youths via Zanzibar, east to Turkey, Iraq, Iran, and Arabia.

In the western central area of the continent, among the
Kongo for example, slavery had been practiced since the
fourteenth century.[30] The same can be said about slavery in
Hausaland, located in northern Nigeria and southern Niger,
where military conquerors employed war captives in agriculture, construction, as concubines, eunuchs, and domestics,
and traded them for valuable items such as horses.[31]

At the time that Europeans arrived in fifteenth-century
sub-Saharan Africa, therefore, slave-trading and slavery

1.3 Slaves being exported from central Africa to eastern Africa,
c. 1866
Source: New York Public Library

existed in varied locations and was practiced by many ethnic groups. In Igboland in southeastern Nigeria, from where large numbers of enslaved persons were forced to reside in North America (particularly in Virginia and Maryland, for example) in the later seventeenth and early eighteenth centuries, persons could be enslaved for a number of criminal offenses including murder, incest, sorcery, and theft. Others derived their status from warfare with political or "foreign" enemies or because of debt.[32]

War captives held as slaves, or those recently enslaved who had not been incorporated into kin groups, typically were those who were sold, along with other valuable items such as gold, ivory, and cloth to the Europeans – the Portuguese, Dutch, Spanish, French, British, Swedish, and others – who traded along the Atlantic coast from Senegal through Angola and inland toward the central African region of Zaire/Congo from the fifteenth through the middle decades of the nineteenth centuries. European traders quickly came to understand that they could benefit from the existence of internal and external (moving north and east across the Sahara) slave-trading caravans and outposts. As historian John Thornton notes, African political and economic elites controlled much of slave property because enslaved persons produced substantial wealth and prestige for their masters and because they often were drawn from the ranks of captured military enemies in the hands of these elites. Slaves were especially important as "economic units" because they were transferable property, unlike land, which typically was held communally.[33]

Slavery in western and central sub-Saharan Africa, as in ancient European, Middle Eastern, and Asian societies, placed bondsmen, in particular, in a vast variety of occupational roles, including court administrators, soldiers, merchants, miners, craftsmen, agricultural workers and supervisors, musicians, and human carriers.[34] Women and children, who were the majority of those enslaved in Africa, had predictable roles in the domestic sphere, but women could also be used as miners, water carriers, midwives, and healers. In Dahomey, females could even be enslaved, under certain circumstances, as soldiers, commanders, traders, and governmental advisors. Most enslaved children were domestic workers, providing household labor in the form of cleaning, helping to cook and garden, taking care of livestock, and serving as companions for free children. Women also provided domestic labor and cloth production, and were especially important as agricultural laborers and, to a lesser extent, as concubines and sex slaves.[35]

Control of an enslaved woman's productivity included, of course, control of her production of future slaves. Males within the households of these enslaved women sometimes married them. To do so meant that they did not have to pay bridewealth, since these women usually were not part of a recognized kin group that would have required this obligation. Once enslaved, women were married and part of a kinship group. They gradually became assimilated into the society in which they had been slaves. Their children born of this marriage were free. Relatedly, those who were enslaved as children often were treated similarly as members of the household, although the tasks they were assigned to perform typically were lowlier. A slave's status within the same household tended, however, to improve across the generations.[36]

Women were enslaved, but they could also be slaveholders. Both as the wives and concubines of powerful African and European men, as well as on their own, a small minority of females acquired slaves, most of whom were other women and children. Some enslaved women also held slave property in their own right, particularly if they were close to gaining their freedom and were given the right, by their masters, to do so.[37] Some free African women, who gained substantial control in trading towns along the coast of western Africa from the Upper Guinea region to Luanda, held substantial numbers of slaves that they used in domestic, agricultural, and commercial sectors of local economies.[38]

Europeans who arrived in sub-Saharan Africa in the fifteenth century were from societies that not only had a history of an African slave presence due to Arab trading connections, but which also had a long history of "European" enslavement within and beyond their polities. Slavery existed, for example, at least in England, France, Italy, Spain, Portugal, Ireland, Hungary, Sweden, and Iceland. European slaves were not only taken and traded in Europe, but also in locales in the eastern Mediterranean, mostly through Spain and Italy. Norsemen, for example, raided and enslaved people from present-day Ireland, England, Scotland, and the continent, taking their captives to Greenland, but also overland to the Middle East and Central Asia.[39] Some estimates suggest that, by 950 CE, slaves comprised 15–20 percent of the English population.[40] Southern Europe, particularly Spain and Portugal, was the site of notorious slave raids, bringing Christian men and women as bonded persons into the Islamic world from the medieval period onward. The Barbary Coast, notably Morocco, Tunisia, and Algeria, was known for producing slaves taken by pirates – many from Europe (Italy, Spain, France, Ireland, England, Scotland, and Portugal) during the seventeenth through the eighteenth centuries, and some even originating from the United States in the first decades following the American Revolution.

Slavery in Europe and the Ottoman Empire

The Ottoman Empire reached its peak in the sixteenth century, and that part of it which included Eastern Europe witnessed widespread enslavement of Christian men and young boys who were converted to Islam and used as slave warriors. Many became imperial administrators throughout the empire, which spread from North Africa through the Horn and also included southeastern Europe, the Caucus, and western Asia. The men, members of the *kul*, were not treated as typical slaves. They had significant power, lived well, and usually married well. While theoretically they were slaves of the sultan, it was rare that they were dehumanized, treated with disdain or disrespect, or found themselves powerless to control their labor, bodies, or families. Women and children were domestic slaves, but usually in the households of the elite. Many of these lived in harems that functioned as a separate gendered sphere of activity and spatial location. Enslaved women in harems, particularly those from Europe, like their *kul* brothers, sometimes had elite positions and were trained by elite women in the household in a manner that would allow them to comfortably marry, or serve as the concubines of important men.[41]

The Crimean Khanate (Ukraine, southern Russia), a tributary state of the Ottoman Empire, also had an extremely vibrant slave trade from the fifteenth to the eighteenth centuries. Millions were enslaved as a result of raids into lands that form modern-day Poland, Lithuania, Romania, and Serbia. Those taken were usually sold to other parts of the Ottoman Empire, the Middle East and Asia, such as Arabia, Persia, India, Syria, and Turkey. They worked as agricultural laborers, in galleys, and as sex slaves.[42]

Slavery in Pre-Contact America

Slavery of various forms also existed in the Americas before European, or African, arrival in the fifteenth century. Indeed, the earliest explorers, such as Francisco Vasquez de Coronado and Hernando de Soto of the sixteenth century, and Spanish and French missionaries of the seventeenth century, provided some of the first written documentation of indigenous slavery in North, South, and Central America. In the Pacific Northwest of North America, for example, slavery was a part of many societies, although not all. Slaves were considered property and sold as part of a wide-ranging trading network. They inherited their status and also acquired it as prisoners of war and victims of slave raids. Slave raiding was particularly prominent among some groups, including the Tlingit of southern Alaska and the Chinook at the base of the Columbia River. The treatment of slaves, as elsewhere, could vary tremendously. Some were able to purchase their freedom; others could be killed for disobeying their masters; women were often used as concubines; and children could be adopted. Since most slaveholders were not agriculturalists, but rather fishermen, foragers, and traders, slave labor ranged from helping with the widespread, and essential, salmon industry to domestic labor.[43] In the Southwest, among the Navajo for example, most did not own slaves, but those who did had the right to punish them to the point of death. Slaves, who typically were captives of warfare or inherited, could hope to gain their freedom and even eventually become socially accepted or, in rare cases, prominent.[44]

Further east on the North American plains, slavery also thrived among some indigenous peoples, such as the Comanche, Sioux, Pawnee, and the Illinois. Slaves, as typical throughout the continent, were captives of war and the status could be inherited. Some, however, were used for ransom or trade for other items. Plains peoples not only were slaveholders and traders, but were also the victims of raids from eastern groups like the Sauk and Ottawa.[45]

Native groups in the Southeast and the Northeast were not immune from using captive and purchased slave labor in various capacities within their economies and social structures. Many women were concubines, children often were adopted, and men were used as low-level laborers. Some killed slaves to avenge the death of a group member who might have been killed in, or as a result of, warfare with the slave's affiliated or natal group. The Iroquois of the northern regions, for example, converted some war captives into slave labor, but killed others. They too adopted some, particularly children, into clans.[46] The Cherokee, located from North Carolina to Alabama, had a traditional form of enslavement known as the *atsi nahas'i*, meaning "one who is owned."[47] They occupied a precarious position in Cherokee society because, although members of that society, they were excluded from clan membership and, therefore, outside of the kinship system from which persons derived their rights and privileges. *Atsi nahas'i* had to rely entirely on their master's protection. These prisoners of war principally worked alongside women in their domestic and agricultural labors, work that included clearing fields, cultivating and collecting crops, and helping to prepare meals and clothing. These slaves sometimes also accompanied men on the hunt as carriers, and labored as messengers, collectors of firewood, and helped to build their temporary shelters.[48]

In pre-contact Central America, slave ownership, or being a slave, was a major determinant of status in the Aztecs' hierarchical society. These slaves, the *tlacotin*, were drawn from war captives as well as debtors and criminals, and their treatment could vary tremendously. Tens, if not hundreds, of thousands were used as sacrifices as part of religious rituals. The much more fortunate ones had the right to marry, did not pass on their status to their children, could own some property, buy their freedom and substitute others for their slave status. Since many slaves gained their status through debt, it was not necessarily a permanent condition if they were able to bargain for release once their debts were paid in full. Aztec slaves typically worked in agriculture, mining, and in numerous municipal construction sites for Tenochtitlán.[49]

Until the arrival of the Europeans, other Central and South American societies also exercised bondage relationships, what anthropologist Neil Whitehead terms "captivity and obligatory service" that did not center on the property value of the "captive."[50] Among the Tupi of Brazil, for example, war captives were meant for cannibalistic death as part of indigenous religious rituals. Still, this destiny was not an immediate one for these *kawewi pepicke*. Until the time of their demise, they were working members of households and many married members of their captors' communities.[51] Moreover, the Caribs of northeastern South America traded bonded neighbors, marrying the women and selling the men.[52] Captured children, and those born of captive and captor, seem to have been assimilated into their captor societies. These *poito* were like the *maco* of the Arawak – they could be slaves, but they also could be persons of much more elevated status, as in the case of those considered via a captive/captor marriage as a brother- or sister-in-law. The work that they performed in agriculture, construction, hunting, fishing, and in the domestic sphere contributed greatly to their associated communities and households. Still, many were not necessarily "slaves,"[53] in the sense of the kind of slavery that Africans endured once they began to in the late fifteenth century.

Slavery, therefore, as practiced across time, place, and peoples, could vary tremendously or have striking similarities. The variables which contextualized and shaped slave experiences and institutions of slavery included, but were not limited to, the degree of importance slavery had to the foundational attributes of a society's perceived wellbeing, especially its economic growth and political stability. In most instances, acquiring bonded persons through warfare was meant to punish and weaken a military and, perhaps, economic rival. Such enslaved war captives sometimes became members of conquerors' households of various statuses. Their contribution as laborers typically brought wealth and prestige to that household. In those societies in which slaves were merely property, their commodification usually meant a diminished social identity with few recognizable human rights. Their lives were harsh, often brief, and with little hope of freedom. Still, the existence of slavery also usually meant that there were avenues, even if rarely trod upon, for emancipation. The enslaved took advantage of religious, legislative, and judicial opportunities and participated in close, sometimes intimate, relationships to gain freedom. They also left behind a legacy of struggle to purchase themselves and family members. Resistance, too, forged similarities with common cases of flight, revolt, suicide, and passive forms of resistance frequently found in the slave record, despite the historical era or geographical location.

Further Reading

Campbell, Gwyn, Miers, Suzanne, and Miller, Joseph (eds) *Women and Slavery: Africa, the Indian Ocean World, and the Medieval North Atlantic.* 1 vol. Athens, OH: Ohio University Press, 2007.

Chatterjee, Indrani, and Eaton, Richard M. (eds) *Slavery and South Asian History.* Bloomington, IN: Indiana University Press, 2006.

Davis, Robert C. *Christian Slaves, Muslim Masters: White Slavery in the Mediterranean, the Barbary Coast and Italy, 1500–1800.* Basingstoke, UK: Palgrave Macmillan, 2005.

DuBois, Page. *Slavery: Antiquity and Its Legacy.* New York: Oxford University Press, 2010.

Glancy, Jennifer. *Slavery in Early Christianity.* New York: Oxford University Press, 2002.

Patterson, Orlando. *Social Death: A Comparative Study.* Cambridge, MA: Harvard University Press, 1985.

Rodriguez, Junius P. (ed.) *The Historical Encyclopedia of World Slavery.* 2 vols. Santa Barbara, CA: ABC-CLIO, Inc., 1997.

Rodriguez, Junius P. (ed.) *Chronology of World Slavery.* Santa Barbara, CA: ABC-CLIO, Inc., 1999.

Shaw, Brent D. (ed.) *Spartacus and the Slave Wars: A Brief History with Documents.* Boston, MA: Bedford/St Martin's, 2001.

Spicer, Joaneath (ed.) *Revealing the African Presence in Renaissance Europe.* Baltimore, MD: Walters Art Museum, 2012.

2

African Beginnings and the Atlantic Slave Trade

"Brought from a state of innocence and freedom, and, in a barbarous and cruel manner conveyed to a state of horror and slavery."

Ottobah Cugoano, a Fanti free boy enslaved in Granada[1]

The evolution of the trade in African labor to the Americans from the fifteenth through the nineteenth centuries, known as the Atlantic slave trade, marked a significant change in the definition and practice of slavery. The sheer volume of the trade itself – in terms of the millions of Africans enslaved; its four centuries length; the numbers of slave-trading institutions, industries, professionals, and skilled laborers responsible for the multiple attributes of the business of slavery; the geophysical space of the continent of Africa and the continents of North and South America affected; the global mercantile implications; the destruction of vast expanses of western and central western Africa; the numbers of European countries engaged; the immense wealth that the trade produced; the new crops advanced that became household necessities for some and markers of elite status for others – made certain that the Atlantic slave trade would have tremendous impact on creating, and shaping, the modern world. This is to say nothing of the creation of "race" as a category of social, economic, political, cultural, and "biological" significance upon which some of the most basic human interactions would, and still, depend.

Trade Numbers: African Origins, American Destinations

While there has been an ongoing debate among slavery scholars regarding the actual numbers of Africans who came to be enslaved in the Americas, most now agree that, of the 28 million Africans who were enslaved and sold during the period from the fifteenth through the nineteenth centuries, approximately 12.5 million left for the Americas and the Caribbean.[2] About 16 million purportedly were traded, not across the Atlantic, but rather to North Africa, on the coast of the Indian Ocean, and throughout the Middle East. But the 11 million or so who arrived in the Americas did not account for the millions, some believe at least four million, who died as part of slave-raiding warfare, during the forced marches to the slave-trading coasts or who perished in the Middle Passage – the ocean trip from Africa to America – as a result of scurvy and other diseases, dehydration, starvation, harsh treatment, or suicide. Nor does it measure the millions who lost their homes and families, and who were physically displaced as a result of the trade.[3]

The exchange of persons, along with other precious goods from Africa to Europe and later to the Americas, began simply enough – with the arrival of the Portuguese, under the guidance of Prince Henry the Navigator, in the middle of the fifteenth century. His mandate was to acquire gold, not slaves. Indeed, the Africans who initially became part of the trade from Africa to Europe really were more or less "bonus" items. From those first few hundred sold annually from the west coast of Africa to Portugal and Spain, starting in about 1470, the numbers grew dramatically over the next two centuries. While the Portuguese, and soon the Spanish, wasted little time in converting African coastal islands, including the Azores, the Madeiras, and Cape Verde, to economic imperialist outposts where they employed African slave labor in developing agricultural economies, primarily sugar plantations, it was increased colonization and economic development efforts in the Americas, via mining and agriculture particularly, that meant increased European slave-trading with Africa for labor. By the late fifteenth century, the Portuguese were exporting approximately two thousand Africans per year. This rough estimate continued through the sixteenth century. Many of these slaves did not go directly to Brazil or to other colonial outposts, but rather first arrived in Europe where they were used primarily in the cities as slaves and servants. It is estimated, for example, that Lisbon's sixteenth-century population was 10 percent black, some of whom were able to acquire their freedom.[4]

By the seventeenth century, the number of enslaved Africans purchased by European traders had increased tenfold to an average of ten thousand exported bondsmen, women, and children annually. Most went directly to the New World. In the eighteenth century, when 51 percent of all those enslaved during the Atlantic trade were shipped to the Americas, approximately 50,000 Africans a year were leaving the continent for enslavement in the American colonies controlled by the Portuguese, Spanish, Dutch, French, British, and Danes. Not only did these Europeans receive slaves shipped from Africa, persons from these nations, along with the Swedes, also organized much of the trade from Africa to the Americas.[5]

Stretching from the Senegambia region on the Atlantic coast, downward through the Bights of Benin and Biafra, and still further south along the coast to Angola and inland through Zaire, around the tip of the continent to include Madagascar on the Indian Ocean, the Atlantic slave trade would come to encompass, minimally, the modern-day African nations of Morocco, Senegal, the Gambia, Guinea, Guinea Bissau, Ghana, Sierra Leone, Ivory Coast, Liberia, Benin, Nigeria, Burkina Faso, Mali, Cameroon, Gabon, Congo, the Democratic Republic of Congo, Zaire, and Madagascar. With so many persons moved over such a long period of time, it is no surprise that some inconsistencies remain in the demographic record. Still, out of the documented 192 points of embarkation, historian Paul Lovejoy notes, the trade seems to have been concentrated out of five important ports, three in western central Africa alone (with Luanda being the largest overall, followed by Benguela and Cabinda), Ouidah in the Bight of Benin, and Bonny in the Bight of Biafra.[6] Even though the exact percentages of the distribution of the slave population recruits will probably never be completely known, many scholars now agree with Lovejoy's summary account that the largest numbers of enslaved came to the Americas from western central Africa – Congo, Angola (40.8%), and the Bights of Benin – Togo, Benin, southwestern Nigeria (19.7%), and Biafra – southeastern Nigeria, Equatorial Guinea, Cameroon, northwestern Gabon (14.3%). Lesser numbers arrived from the Gold Coast – Ghana (10.1%); the Senegambia region – Senegal, the Gambia (4.7%); the southeast – Madagascar (4.6%); Upper Guinea – the Gambia, Liberia (4.0%); and the Windward Coast – Ivory Coast, Liberia, and Sierra Leone (1.8%).[7]

They arrived in locales in the Caribbean and Americas as geospatially diverse as those from which they had come. The majority came to Brazil (4 million) and to the wide-flung Spanish-American Empire (2.5 million). Lesser numbers arrived in the British Caribbean (2 million); the French Caribbean (1.6 million); British North America and the United States (0.5 million); the Dutch Caribbean and Suriname (0.5 million); the Danish Caribbean (28,000) and Europe (200,000).[8]

While slavery in Africa had existed over the millennia, the investment in European commodities used in the Atlantic trade expanded tremendously the traditional trade routes and numbers of persons enslaved. Spain was the first to begin to send Africans to the Americas, taking black slaves to join indigenous peoples enslaved in Hispaniola in 1505. Important African export goods in the growing commercial contact between western and southern Europe and western and western central Africa, other than gold, were ivory, dyewoods, pepper, and other spices. Other trade items, used in more localized or intra-/interregional markets, included kola nuts and textiles. Commodities of particular value to seafaring merchants who needed to stock their ships before taking another lengthy voyage comprised certain food items such as salt, rice, palm oil, nuts, yams, gum, and fish.[9] By the beginning of the 1600s, the increase in the trade in slaves to accommodate sugar and tobacco production, as well as gold and silver mining, also meant an increase in the numbers of persons in Africa, Europe, and the Americas involved in the trade and the numbers of New World locales where African workers arrived. Sugar, alone, accounted for the labor of 70 percent of the African imported slave labor in the New World over the centuries.[10]

The expansion of sugar cultivation beyond Brazil in the mid-seventeenth century, particularly to British and French islands in the Caribbean, was especially important in the development of this crop's dominance and the corresponding growth in the numbers of Africans imported to cultivate it. These locales included Jamaica and Saint-Domingue – with planters who dominated the world market – along with the British islands of Barbados, St Kitts and Antigua, and the French colonies of Martinique and Guadeloupe. Other crops, especially cacao in Brazil and tobacco in Barbados, also fed this early agricultural boom. By the eighteenth century, coffee and indigo were also important slave-produced exports. While agricultural work was what occupied most enslaved people, they also worked in other sectors of the early colonial economies. Those in the first centuries of the Atlantic trade who came to reside in Brazil, for example, were also miners, herders, domestic servants, carpenters, wheelwrights, fishermen, and lumbermen, or performed other skilled and day-labor work. In Spanish-speaking colonial America, particularly Mexico, enslaved sixteenth-century Africans, many like the Akan who were from the gold-mining regions of Ghana (Gold Coast), worked in gold and silver mines.[11] By the seventeenth century, the British had started to establish northern colonial outposts in Virginia, Maryland, and the Carolinas that helped to create the tobacco boom. While much of the labor used to create these foundational agrarian societies of British North America was white indentured servants and to a lesser extent indigenous peoples of the Americas, by the last quarter of the seventeenth century, southern mainland colonies too were beginning to claim larger percentages of the African trade.

British North American Slave Imports

The origins of the enslaved who arrived in North America, particularly by the beginning of the eighteenth century, were no different from those sent to the British Caribbean. The

Portuguese controlled the trade in the sixteenth century, providing slaves for the sugar plantations of Brazil that became important as early as 1520. Beginning in 1590, the Dutch dominated the forced movement of Africans. Still, by the eighteenth century, and overall for the entire trade, British slavers delivered the majority of Africans to New World destinations. While there were some decadal fluctuations in the regional domination of the slave exports, the majority of African slaves departed from western central Africa, followed, in number, by enslaved persons from the Bight of Benin – also known as the slave coast – the Gold Coast, the Bight of Biafra, and the Senegambia. Slaves from these areas, who constituted the lion's share of the entire Atlantic trade, represented numerous cultural and/or linguistic groups and were procured in various ways.[12]

The continuous wars that occurred during the seventeenth and eighteenth centuries in western central Africa, particularly in the kingdom of Kongo, greatly contributed to the vast numbers of persons who were fed into the trade. Portuguese involvement with state and local politics in Angola, along with their creation of localized slave-raiding stations, added to the dominance of persons in the trade coming from this region. Overland routes and rivers allowed traders to transport their human cargo from the interior to slaving vessels on the Atlantic coast.[13] Small inland states often supplied slaves as a form of tribute to larger ones, such as the Luanda and Kazembe, or were themselves the victims of slave-trading raids. The Portuguese in Angola, however, were not the only European slave traders of importance there. The Dutch and the English also controlled the flow of slaves from north of the Congo River and north of Luanda. Moreover, European traders often had to cooperate with powerful African polities, such as the Katanga and Matambe of the Mbundu who dominated the interior trade in Luanda, to insure trading arrangements ran smoothly. Scholarship indicates that the first Africans to arrive in the colony of Virginia probably were derived from the Mbundu trade. Western central Africans eventually became dominant in the numbers of enslaved brought to British North America.[14]

In the second most important region of exportation, the Bight of Benin, European traders had a smaller degree of

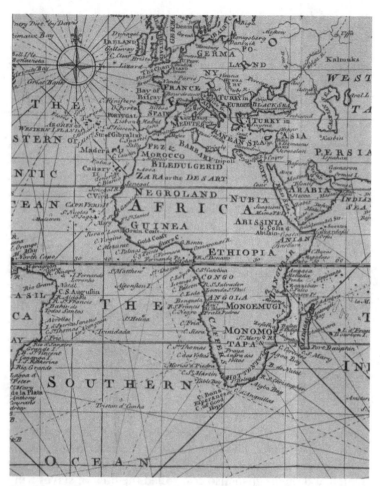

2.1 Late eighteenth-century Africa
Source: Courtesy of the Mariner's Museum and Park

influence and typically were confined to the coastline, rather
than allowed to penetrate into the interior. The Bight of Benin
slave trade benefited, instead, from the profit that local political states derived from the trade organized in competing port
towns created along the lagoon that drained into the Bight.
Allada controlled the lagoon trade at the end of the seventeenth century. Warfare, as in western central Africa, flared

2.2 Artistic traditions were important cultural attributes of the Africans imported to the Americas. L–R (top): Kongo Fetish; Mende Sowo mask. L–R (bottom): Seated Igbo Princess; Yoruba belly mask.
Source: Cones Collection

up in the Bight in the 1720s, reaping large numbers of captives who became enslaved.

The Yoruba of Oyo state, largely known for its effective cavalry, benefited significantly from these military clashes. Dahomey, to the south, also raided peoples in the Bight in the 1720s. Both Oyo and Dahomey eventually dominated the trading port of Ouidah, the major center of eighteenth-century Bight of Benin slave trade, although Oyo traded through other locales as well.[15] Islamic traders, not present in the western central Africa trade to the Atlantic, were instrumental in the Bight of Benin, acting as intermediaries with internal suppliers and trading networks.[16]

To the east of the Bight of Benin and encompassing the Niger delta and the Cross River Valley, the Bight of Biafra contributed large numbers of Igbo and Ibibio from 1600 onward. Many were enslaved in Virginia. Relatedly, the Bight of Biafra began to produce large numbers of slaves at the same time that Britain's Royal African Company (RAC), chartered in 1672, began to work effectively on this coastline. Despite the RAC's attempt at monopoly, most of Britain's exported slaves in the eighteenth century still found themselves on the ships of other trading companies and privateers. The largest centers of slave trade in the Bight were Elem Calabar (New Calabar), Old Calabar, and Bonny. Boats brought slaves from the densely populated interior down the many riverways that fed into the Niger Delta. According to historian Paul Lovejoy, the swampy delta discouraged European coastal trading settlements as existed in other parts of western and western central Africa. Here, Europeans did not venture inland as the Portuguese did in Angola and Kongo. Likewise, they had very limited interaction with Muslim traders. Instead, the slaves who arrived on the coast destined to be shipped to British New World colonies were drawn from village raids, as forms of tribute payment, or were victims of kidnapping.[17]

The Gold Coast, northwest of the Bights of Benin and Biafra, was also an important locale for the slave trade in the seventeenth and eighteenth centuries, but had been an important site of European trade of gold for previous generations. Warfare in the early years of the eighteenth century involving the Baule, Asante, Senufo, Guro, and Akan peoples provided a constant stream of slaves from the slave-trading "castles" of Elmina, Cape Coast, and Anomabu.[18]

Further north along the African coastline in the Senegambia region, Islamic trading networks were quite influential in the slave trade to the Americas. These traders provided slaves from the interior that came via Sierra Leone, Ivory Coast, and Liberia. Others arrived from the valleys of the Senegal and Gambia Rivers and from the forested lands nearby. Islamic jihads, which occurred between the late seventeenth and early eighteenth centuries, supplied many for the regional and long-distance slave trades both west and north. Lesser numbers of slaves derived from the Upper Guinea region, which was not substantially affected by Muslim traders, but which, through other means, supplied close to 5,000 slaves annually at the peak of the trade during the end of the eighteenth century. This number seems small, however, when compared to the 15,000 annually hailing from the Bight of Biafra, the 13,500 per year from the Gold Coast, or the 35,000 annually from Kongo/Angola during those last decades, or the 20,000 annually exported from the Bight of Benin in the 1720s.[19]

Slave Trade Organization

Up and down the west and the western central African coastline, European traders built fortified towns or "castles" that provided them with the protection, services, and some of the comforts necessary for a long-term investment in the Atlantic slave and commodities trades. These castles housed not only the traders themselves but also company factors and officials, soldiers, doctors, lawyers, accountants, craftsmen, clergy, and fort slaves who were used as concubines, domestics, and day laborers. Usually, African-owned farms were nearby, providing foodstuffs for fort inhabitants and for the long-distance voyages. Some of the best-known forts were found on the Gold Coast, where there were twenty-eight, including Swedenborg, Elmina – the first such castle, built by the Portuguese in 1471 – and Cape Coast. Others included: James Fort on the Gambia River; French forts at Saint Louis and Goree in Senegal; Bunce Island in Sierra

Leone; and numerous others in Nigeria, Benin, and Togo. The "ownership" history of Cape Coast Castle suggests its strategic military and economic importance. The Swedish erected a fort there in 1650, but the British took it in 1662. The British invested in the fort's rebuilding and enlargement, but the Dutch captured it in 1663. The following year, the British recaptured it and completed the expansion. In 1681, the fort's townspeople rebelled and attacked British authorities there. The French fleet bombarded it in 1703 and again in 1757. The Royal African Company gained control of Cape Coast Castle in 1757.[20]

These forts were of all sizes, but usually included a dungeon space, or baracoon, where captured slaves were kept until ships arrived for their departure. There, traders separated the men from the women and children, as on the ships to the Americas. Conditions generally were very harsh, filthy, and fearsome, contributing to the 20 percent of enslaved Africans who died before they reached the Americas. Slaves were subjected, as they often were on the overland and/or boat trips to the coast, to physical, emotional, and sexual violence. Food, water, and medical attention were minimal. Resistance was rewarded with corporal punishment, brandings, and sometimes death, although there were numerous escapes and attempted revolts on the way to the coast and in the forts as well.[21]

Organization of the trade beyond the use of fortified towns included the companies and business enterprises whose work was directly the acquisition of enslaved Africans for sale abroad. The earliest of these organizations were joint stock companies, some closely associated with, or chartered by, the royal houses of Europe. These companies received permission, usually in the form of a royal charter, and paid, in return, dividends derived from the profitable sale of goods traded under their titles, including slaves. The Dutch West India Company, chartered in 1621, the French Company of the West Indies (1634), the Company of Senegal (French, 1673), the Royal African Company (British, 1672), and the Portuguese Company of Cacheo (1692) were particularly important early entities. As the trade increased in importance at the end of the seventeenth century, however, many European monarchs suspended these monopolistic charters, preferring instead to tax the multitude of private companies and individuals who hoped to, and generally did, profit mightily from participating in the trade.[22]

Africans and the Atlantic Slave Trade

Europeans traded with Africans for slaves, gold, ivory, spices, foodstuffs, onyx, exotic animal skins, and leather. What did Africans receive in exchange from the Europeans? And what were the average prices of enslaved persons, especially during the peak of the trade in the eighteenth century?

Those Europeans invested in the African slave trade typically had to negotiate with African slavers or political and/or military leadership in order to successfully remove the millions of slaves that ended up on the ships destined for the Caribbean or the Americas. These negotiations included prices, preferred currencies, the numbers of slaves sold, and their demographic characteristics. The amounts of additional monies or items, sometimes called a "dash," used to initiate European negotiations with African traders or authorities, or to complete negotiations in the case of an impasse, also had to be determined. These business transactions typically included merchant/company representatives, known as factors, and envoys of the local or state African leadership, as well as translators on both sides of the bargaining table.

Africans were as pragmatic and particular about the imports they received from European traders as the Europeans were about the goods received from Africa. They exchanged their goods for cotton textiles originating from Europe, Asia, and other markets in West Africa, particularly: cloths of certain aesthetically pleasing and ritualistically important colors; metal objects of brass, pewter, and copper; iron bars; gold from Ghana; ivory from the same-named coast; Venetian-made glass beads; cowrie shells from the Indian Ocean that served as a form of currency up and down the west coast of Africa; firearms that became increasingly important in those areas of the trade, such as in western central Africa, the Bight of Benin, and the Senegambia where warfare and military campaigns were prevalent; rum made from Caribbean sugar, brandy, wines and other liquors; and grains, especially rice, from Sierra Leone and Liberia. The items that Africans were willing to trade for, therefore, illustrate the local, regional, and global exchange of commodities for bonded labor that characterized the Atlantic slave trade.[23]

Not surprisingly, the costs of a man, woman, or child sold to the Americas varied with their place of origin, age, gender, health, and skill, but also were subject to the overall demand for African labor. Generally, prices increased with external increases in demand in the late seventeenth and throughout the eighteenth centuries. The average prices for slaves, for example, rose by four to five times during this period, while the numbers of slaves shipped increased between two and three times.[24] The prices of slaves, calculated in the costs of goods traded for them, as such increased from £4 sterling at the end of the seventeenth century to as much as £18 sterling a hundred years later. At the same time, the numbers of Africans shipped as slaves to the New World rose from 30,000 annually to 80,000 or more over that century.[25]

African males from the ages of mid-teen through thirty were the most highly prized and priced for the American markets. Approximately 65 percent of all those shipped to the New World were males. This statistic, however, reflected not only the desire for male labor by Europeans in the colonies, but also the desire of Africans to maintain enslaved women in their home societies. Enslaved women were the most sought-after bonded laborers through much of western and western central Africa since, as agriculturalists and domestic workers, they did much of the necessary day-to-day labor. These women also could be used as concubines or wives of free men, thus adding to the growth of community members and future laborers. The Atlantic trade itself commoditized the slave, however, ignoring the human element beyond the physical body's worth, and the worth of the offspring who sometimes inherited their slave status, in traded goods and currency. Not surprisingly, the short- and long-term impacts of the Atlantic slave trade on western and western central Africa, despite the profits that some African traders and leaders reaped, were devastating. As historian Gwendolyn Midlo Hall aptly concludes: "Chaos, warfare, and empire building connected with the slave trade had an incalculably destructive, disruptive and demoralizing effect."[26]

Narratives of enslaved persons from the height of the slave trade in the eighteenth century are instructive. Ukawsaw Gronniosaw, the kidnapped grandson of a king, was born in Bornu in northeastern Nigeria and sold to the Gold Coast before being handed over to British traders headed for Barbados and then New York. His cost at the Gold Coast, he recalled, was "two yards of check" cloth.[27] Ottobah Cugoano recalled of his Fanti childhood that he was raised as the companion to a king's son. He was kidnapped by some of his "own complexion" along with 18–20 other "boys and girls," "decoyed and drove along" until they were "conducted to a factory" on the Gold Coast. His captor was paid "a gun, a piece of cloth, and some lead" for him. Cugoano "cried bitterly" when he realized his fate.[28]

Joseph Wright, of the Egba (Yoruba), recalled how devastatingly violent his capture was, an experience that did not become less brutal as he was moved to the coast. "Many were killed," Wright noted of the wars that came to enslave him and his people. "They killed our Captain, Jurgoonor by the riverside, and they killed Barlah in his gate. He was second to the king. He was a very high man in the city. Nothing could be decided without his presence." And they

2.3 The inspection and sale of a negro, c. 1854
Source: Cones Collection

did not only kill men, but sexually assaulted women, adolescent boys, and male and female children as well for, as Wright noted: "The enemies satisfied themselves with little children, little girls, young men, and young women; and so they did not care about the aged and old people. They killed them without mercy." It was, as far as Wright could understand, a complete unraveling of their social fabric:

> Father knew not the son, and the son knew not the father. Pity had departed from the face of mothers. Abundant heaps of dead bodies were in the streets, and there were none to bury them. Suckling babies were crying at the point of death, and there were none to pick them up. Mothers looked upon them with contempt – a lamentable day![29]

Enslaved Africans, therefore, entered the Atlantic trade through numerous avenues: as sold war captives, kidnap victims, social outcasts, criminals, as tribute payment, or drawn from the pool of bonded laborers traditionally found in many western and central African societies. Some were sold from one locale in Africa to another, and then eventually sold to Europeans bound for the market in the Americas. The trips that they took from their earlier places of residence or servitude to the coast for embarkment to the Caribbean or beyond could be hundreds of miles. Often, they were sold and resold along the way to the coast. They marched in single or double file, chained to each other with only the clothing they had on when taken, eating and drinking only what their captors provided. Exhausted, undernourished, physically, psychologically, and sexually abused, and often dehydrated as well, some became ill; others perished en route. It was only the beginning of their travails and their travels. Once the bonded reached the coast, they were placed in holding stations, baracoons, or castle basements with tens or hundreds of others and kept until time to board the ships to America. Wright recalled how a fire began in the town where he was being held and at least fifty in the holding pen where he was being kept died as a result.[30]

Ottobah Cugoano described in vivid detail his march to the coast. He had already traveled two days with the hope that he would be returned to his family when he realized that those who had promised to help him were just part of a devious plot to keep him from running away during the three-day trip overland to a trading fort. "I saw," he noted, "many of my miserable countrymen chained two and two, some handcuffed, and some with their hands tied behind." At the castle, Ottobah "was conducted to a prison" where he "heard the groans and cries of many." After three more days, traders placed him aboard a ship that would take him to Cape Castle. It was then, at the point of departure from his first prison, that the emotional trauma became even more intense as Ottobah and his fellow captives began to understand that they had lost all hope of returning home. "It was a most horrible scene," he explained. "There was nothing to be heard but rattling of chains, smacking of whips, and the groans and cries of our fellow men." Those who refused to move were "lashed and beat in the most horrible manner."[31]

Olaudah Equiano, who identifies himself in his narrative as an Igbo from Nigeria, and the son of a well-to-do member of the community who owned slaves in his own right, was kidnapped, along with his sister, and sold multiple times in West Africa before being sent to the British colonies. Equiano, about eleven years old at the time of capture, recalled vividly the moment he and his sister were seized by two men and a woman who climbed over his family's compound walls, grabbed them, "stopped their mouths," and ran off with them "to the nearest wood," where they tied their hands. The next day, the kidnappers separated Equiano and his sister, selling them to different persons. "It was in vain that we besought them not to part us," he noted. "She was torn from me, and immediately carried away, while I was left in a state of distraction not to be described. I cried and grieved continually; and for several days I did not eat any thing [sic] but what they forced into my mouth," he explained. He remained a slave in West Africa before traveling to the Americas.

Olaudah's first African master was a goldsmith, whom he assisted in the day, working with the female domestic slaves in the evening. Sold again for 172 cowrie shells, he then became the companion of a wealthy boy about his age. Equiano had hoped that he would be adopted into the family as was sometimes the custom in some western African slave societies, but instead he was sold again. "Thus I continued to travel, sometimes by land, sometimes by water, through different countries, and various nations, till at the end of six or seven months after I had been kidnapped," he noted, "I arrived at the sea coast."[32] Equiano soon found himself on a slaving vessel, bound across the Atlantic for the Caribbean.

Middle Passage/Maafa

This trip – termed by some as Maafa, or the African holocaust[33] – could take up to two or three months in the sixteenth century, but was reduced to about a month by the nineteenth. The travel time, of course, depended on the sailing technology in use, the points of departure and arrival, the nationality of the carrier, and natural forces including wind speed and direction and the ocean currents. While the British were not the swiftest carriers, they did carry the most slaves on their ships.[34] Moreover, enslaved persons often spent more time in oceanic transit than that necessary to actually cross the Atlantic to the Americas. Some enslaved persons were boarded on ocean carriers soon after they were sold but were then compelled to move up and down the African coastline until the ship they were on was filled to capacity before they began their oceanic voyage. Anyone placed on the ship early might have spent seven months in this prolonged "middle passage."[35] This extended trip would especially be the experience of those seventeenth- and early eighteenth-century slaves arriving in North America because most were trans-shipped after arriving first in the Caribbean.

Maafa has come to symbolize the violence, abuse, and horror of the Atlantic trade and, indeed, slavery itself. It is for good reason. Enslaved Africans, already traumatized in multiple ways by the time they boarded, were subject to even more barbaric treatment as they crossed the Atlantic. The devastating conditions were beyond description for some and most simply were not comparable to other oceanic travel experiences of the day. As slave-trade historian James Walvin notes: "Even when we examine the worst experience of convict or military transportation in the age of sail, the data of human misery come nowhere near the levels of suffering endured by the slaves."[36] Crowding was always an issue. The British ships typically carried 390 Africans by the end of the eighteenth century; the French and Portuguese 340. Death rates were between 10 and 20 percent. Placed naked into a dark, hot, and dank hold, chained together, fed only enough to sustain life, given on average only one pint of water a day, it was only a matter of time before people became physically and mentally ill. Joseph Wright of the Egba recalled of his middle passage trip after being purchased by the Portuguese that: "We were very poor for water. We were only allowed one glass of water a day and we were allowed only breakfast, no dinner. Many of the slaves had died for want of water, and many men died for crowdedness."[37]

The feared sickness – dysentery or "bloody flux" – and other stomach ailments filled the urine-soaked holds with feces, blood, mucus, and vomit. Other diseases and ailments included smallpox, yellow fever, hookworm, flea and other forms of insect infestation, and malaria.[38] With the dying and living all chained together, was it any wonder that illnesses spread quickly? That "horror" as descriptive of the experience is an understatement? Most of these slaves at the height of the Atlantic trade were compelled to travel (actually live for several weeks) in narrow strips that had only two feet of headroom and 5–7 square feet of space. Many only could lie in spoonlike fashion against one another. "Sleep being denied us from the confined position of our bodies," Mahommad Baquaqua noted of his trip as a slave to Brazil, "…we became desperate through suffering and fatigue."[39] Few middle passage experiences were comparable to that of the Liverpool slave ship *Zong* in which crew members in 1781 killed at least 142 African bondsmen, women, and children by throwing them, chained together, overboard in order to collect insurance payments for their loss.[40] Nonetheless, the example of the *Zong* is useful as an accurate indicator of the relationship of the slave trader to his slave cargo – the slave was only cargo, valuable dead or alive.

From the size and make of the ship, to the orders of the crew, the food and water rations, the numbers of enslaved persons packed into close quarters, the rampant sexual abuse of women, children, and young men, and the lack of medical expertise, the voyage of enslaved Africans to America was brutal in obvious as well as nuanced and layered ways. Ottobah Cugoano and some of his fellow slaves believed that death was preferable to enslavement and plotted a shipboard revolt. "Betrayed," he believed, by one of his "country-women," the sexual slave of some of the "head men" of the ship, the plot failed, leading to a "cruel, bloody scene."[41]

Olaudah Equiano was completely terrified from the moment he arrived on board. Like Ottobah, he was afraid of the European traders and sailors because he assumed he was going to be cannibalized by the white men. Equiano's fear, and no doubt his exhaustion from the long trip to the African coast, led him to faint. His African captors tried to assuage his anxieties while British crew members gave him liquor to drink to calm him, but Olaudah was not to be consoled. He longed to return home or even to his former enslavement. Equiano's dread increased exponentially after being forced into the ship's hold. "There," he added, "I received such a salutation in my nostrils...so that with the loathsomeness of the stench, and crying together, I became so sick and low that I was not able to eat." He wanted to commit suicide. This desire only increased when, after refusing to eat food that the crew offered him, they tied his hands and feet before brutally whipping the adolescent.[42] Once the ship was actually under way to Barbados, conditions worsened below deck. "Loathsome smells," intense heat and a lack of fresh air to the point of near suffocation, crowded conditions by which "each scarcely had room to turn himself," the want of food, the filth of the filled "necessary tubs," in which some of the children fell trying to use them, led to sickness and several deaths. "The shrieks of the women, and the groans of the dying," he added, "rendered the whole a scene of horror almost inconceivable."[43] So too did the numerous suicides and the severe floggings that were the answer to every infraction.

And there were "infractions." Many Africans resisted their enslavement and the brutal, dehumanizing treatment they received at every turn. From the point of capture to the point of arrival in the Americas, they ran away, refused to eat, committed suicide, murdered, fought, argued, plotted, and executed revolt. According to historian Eric Taylor, for example, Africans aboard these ships instituted 493 known slave revolts during the long slave trade era, many during the peak eighteenth century.[44] Records indicate that, on average, there was at least one form of violent resistance by enslaved persons in the middle passage each month of the trade. These attempts, and successes, at gaining their freedom, David Eltis notes, reduced the numbers of persons who were enslaved by 10 percent! It also is estimated that 33 percent of slaving crews were hired specifically as additional security. The resistance came not just as an attempt to gain freedom or, in the very least, to return to some form of life from the places from where they were sold, but also to resist the life-threatening conditions aboard these ships destined for the Americas. The Reverend Pascoe Grenfell Hill, chaplain on the *Cleopatra* on its way to Rio de Janeiro in 1842 with 400 slaves, for example, recalled one violent scene of Africans trying to escape the suffocating heat of the hold after being forced below during a storm. Fifty-four were crushed and mangled in the attempt to get air, their bodies thrown overboard the next day. A total of 163 of the slave cargo died during the fifty-day voyage.[45]

Once enslaved Africans arrived in the Americas, they were cleaned, fed, and prepared for sale. This process could take another one to several months as traders trans-shipped their human cargo all over the Americas, often across national lines, from island to mainland or vice versa. Even then, buyers purchased them principally at centralized market locations and then took their slave property, either by land or boat, sometimes both alternately, across lengthy territories to their final destinations. Those arriving on the Atlantic coast of South America, for example, but meant for a Pacific coast colony, such as Peru, walked across the continent's rainforests and tall mountain ranges. One does not need to employ a great deal of imagination to understand how physically and emotionally agonizing the transport from western/central Africa to Cuzco would have been. Most of the 11 million or so transported to the Americas did not endure these additional thousands of miles of travel, but the trip was devastating nonetheless. Those arriving at places in a "boom," either agricultural (especially sugar in Brazil and the Caribbean) or metal (gold and silver, for example in Mexico and Peru), usually were bought quickly since the need for labor, and the profitable return on the investment in slave labor under these extreme economic bounties, was very high.

Further Reading

Bennett, Herman. *Africans in Colonial Mexico: Absolutism, Christianity and Afro-Creole Consciousness, 1570–1640*. Bloomington, IN: Indiana University Press, 2003.

Berry, Daina Ramey (ed.) *Enslaved Women in America: An Encyclopedia*. Greenwood, CT: Greenwood Press, 2012.

Davis, David Brion. *Inhuman Bondage: The Rise and Fall of Slavery in the New World*. New York: Oxford University Press, 2006.

Eltis, David. *The Rise of African Slavery in the Americas*. Cambridge: Cambridge University Press, 2000.

Gallay, Alan. *The Indian Slave Trade: The Rise of the English Empire in the American South, 1670–1717*. New Haven, CT: Yale University Press, 2002.

Landers, Jane G. *Atlantic Creoles in the Age of Revolutions*. Cambridge, MA: Harvard University Press, 2010.

Lovejoy, Paul. *Transformations in Slavery: A History of Slavery in Africa*. 3rd edn. Cambridge: Cambridge University Press, 2011.

Miller, Joseph. *Way of Death: Merchant Capitalism and the Angolan Slave Trade, 1730–1830*. Madison, WI: University of Wisconsin Press, 1996.

Smallwood, Stephanie. *Saltwater Slavery: A Middle Passage from Africa to American Diaspora*. Cambridge: Harvard University Press, 2007.

Walvin, James. *The Zong: A Massacre, the Law and the End of Slavery*. New Haven, CT: Yale University Press, 2011.

3

African People in the Colonial World of North America

"My name is Omar ibn Seid.... there came to our place a large army, who killed many men, and took me, and brought me to the great sea, and sold me into the hands of the Christians, who bound me and sent me on board a great ship and we sailed upon the great sea a month and a half, when we came to a place called Charleston in the Christian language. There they sold me to a small, weak, and wicked man called Johnson, a complete infidel, who had no fear of God at all."

Omar ibn Said[1]

Early Spanish, French, Dutch Settlements and Slavery in North America

The British were not the first Europeans to explore, or settle, North America during the Atlantic slave-trade era, nor the first to bring Africans to that mainland. The French and the Spanish made several forays into the southern, gulf, and western regions, African slaves in tow, before the British. Spain had claimed all of the east coast of North America in the early sixteenth century, and the Spanish Crown was eager to create settlements to protect their claim. In 1526, for example, Spaniard Lucas Vazquez de Ayllón founded the colony of San Miguel de Guadalupe on the Peedee River in an area thought to have been the current location of South Carolina or Georgia.

He possessed a number of black slaves who, in 1526, revolted. Some escaped to surrounding Native American territory.[2] Hernando de Soto, who had been, as a teen, with Pedro Arias Dávila in Panama, Honduras, and Guatemala, and with Francisco Pizarro in 1530 during his "discovery" expedition to Peru, commanded his own three-year expeditionary force, beginning in 1540, to the Gulf Coast region. He was the first European to reference the Mississippi River, and traveled through what are now Florida, Georgia, Louisiana, Arkansas, and Alabama. De Soto also brought with him African slaves, male and female; and throughout his travels in the Southeast and the Gulf, he fought with, and enslaved, many indigenous peoples. Father Juan Baptista de Seguera began a settlement in southeastern Virginia in 1560. Other Jesuit priests established a short-lived colony in the Chesapeake Bay, near present-day Yorktown, in 1570.[3]

Further down the Atlantic coast, Admiral Pedro Menéndez de Aviles, the first governor of Spanish Florida, created a fort at St Augustine in 1565. It was to become the first permanent European city on the mainland, and the first of sixteen presidios or forts that the Spanish would establish in East Florida (from the Atlantic to the Apalachicola River) and West Florida (from the Apalachicola to the Perdido River). Aviles, like those who would follow him, erected this first fort to protect Spanish territorial claims on the east coast and Gulf of Mexico. Jean Ribauld, Aviles's French antagonist, had founded Charlefort (present-day Charleston) in 1562, but the settlement proved to be quite temporary. The French then succeeded in creating a fort (Caroline) near Jacksonville, Florida on the St John's River in 1564 that was supposed to be settled by Huguenots. King Philip II of Spain, who wanted to make a definitive statement to the French, ordered Aviles to destroy the Protestant village and fort. Aviles succeeded, burning the fort and slaughtering almost everyone there. The following year, he created a fort, Santa Elena, on what is now Parrish Island, South Carolina, close to the abandoned French Charlefort. Santa Elena served as the capital of Spanish Florida until 1577. From there, the Spanish launched two attempts to create forts northward and to convert the indigenous population to Catholicism. They succeeded in constructing a series of small fortifications in present-day Tennessee and North Carolina.

Eventually, local native peoples in these areas struck back, destroying all of their fortifications. Santa Elena, too, faced indigenous peoples' retaliations. It was burned and several colonists killed in 1587. The surviving residents removed to St Augustine, which would continue to serve as Spanish Florida's capital until 1821.[4] There, peninsulares, criollos, obliging native peoples, convict laborers, Catholic priests, Africans, and their descendants created a community at the northern edge of the Spanish-American Empire.[5] Given the importance of the African slave trade and African labor to the Spanish in their New World settlements and to the importance of their service in Spanish military and expeditionary forces, there is no doubt that Africans were with them in Virginia, North Carolina, and Tennessee. They certainly played an important role in St Augustine and in the nearby town of Fort Mosé.

Fort Mosé, or Gracia Real de Santa Teresa de Mosé, located two miles north of St Augustine, was the first permanent settlement of free people of color in what became the United States. It was a farming community, but its significance to the Spanish government lay in Fort Mosé's free black militia, accompanied by slave forces, which provided protection for St Augustine and was also used throughout the Spanish Caribbean in a defensive capacity. While the fort was only erected in 1739, the militia, which had operated out of St Augustine for more than a century, proved to be important to the defense of Spanish Florida against both regional indigenous peoples and the British, who had settled in South Carolina in the 1660s and in Georgia in 1733, and also as defense against British pirates who had targeted Spanish mainland colonies since the mid-sixteenth century. The cause, and numbers, of Spain's colonial black militia in Florida had been aided by King Charles II of Spain who, in 1693, offered religious sanctuary to escaped male and female slaves from the British Carolinas in Florida as free people. While proof of conversion to Catholicism became a requirement for freedom in 1733 for those runaway slaves from British colonies who managed to escape, the numbers of black militiamen in Spanish Florida grew as these fugitives, both African and creole, continued to arrive. They created a vibrant, multiracial, multicultural community that interacted with residents in St Augustine as well as with those local indigenous peoples who were not hostile to the resident Spaniards. There were 38 free black families in Fort Mosé in 1739, with a population of approximately a hundred persons for the next twenty years. And while James Oglethorpe of Georgia and his troops destroyed the original town in 1740, the community had rebuilt and reinhabited Fort Mosé by 1752.[6]

Indeed, during the era of the American Revolution (the Spanish had ceded Florida to Britain in 1763 in the Treaty of Paris at the conclusion of the Seven Years War so that Britain would return Cuba to the Spanish), when the British colonists in St Augustine remained loyal to the Crown, it is estimated that hundreds, or even thousands, of slaves escaping from South Carolina and Georgia arrived in St Augustine to claim their freedom. But it was not just the Spanish who offered black fugitives their freedom if they took their side against the British or helped to defend the colony against indigenous attacks. The converse was true as well – enslaved blacks also fled their Spanish masters in Florida, seeking freedom from the British and indigenous peoples in exchange for military information and/or services to them. The British and Spanish contest for the Southeast was so intense that the astute slave found possibilities for his freedom sometimes more than once, even if it meant sometimes trading sides to gain it. Thómas de la Torre, for example, was a resourceful mulatto slave who elected to travel with Spanish forces in their attempt to destroy the English colony of South Carolina in 1686. While in Charleston, however, de la Torre offered to assist the British in their efforts to destroy St Augustine. Eventually returning to St Augustine, ostensibly to continue to pursue his quest for freedom, de la Torre continued to attempt to take advantage of the legal possibility of emancipation through purchase, special services (especially military), and/or support from an important free person who could act as godparent or patron for his cause.[7]

Not all those who escaped from mainland British territory to St Augustine, however, found freedom, especially before Fort Mosé was established. In 1729, for example, Governor Antonio de Benvanides sold ten fugitives from South Carolina, including Mandinga-born Francisco Menendez, former commander of a militia, to local elites and to planters in

Cuba. Benvanides used the funds garnered by the public auction to reimburse their Carolina masters.[8] As a potent indicator of the legal fluidity of blacks in Spanish Florida society, some of these re-enslaved persons eventually regained their freedom and actually became important members of their communities. Francisco Menendez, for example, regained his free status, went on to "govern" Fort Mosé and led a militia for the next forty years. Others attempted to reach Florida, as had been the plan of some of those who executed the Stono Rebellion in South Carolina in 1739, but never made it. Some created their own maroon societies in the everglades or the remote marshland, but did not join with the Spanish. Still others found refuge in the villages of some indigenous peoples, although Cherokee and other Native Americans in the region also enslaved blacks.

The first of the Cherokee to own large numbers of black slaves typically were full-bloods of the warrior class who received African slaves as part of the "spoils" from victoriously fought battles with other slave-owning tribes and southern frontier settlers. Legend among the Cherokee indicates, for example, that the first of their tribe to own a black slave was a woman, Nancy Ward, also known as Ghi-gu-u, or "Beloved Woman." Supposedly she accompanied her husband, Kingfisher of the Deer Clan, to a battle with the Muskogee Indians. Kingfisher was killed during the battle, and his wife, "who had been lying behind a log chewing the bullets so that they would lacerate the more," picked up his weapon and fought "as a warrior" for the remainder of the battle. As a result of her skill, the Muskogee were defeated and Nancy Ward received, as her portion of the "spoils," a black slave.[9] Although some of these slaves were treated as the traditional *atsi nahsai*, more than a few of these warriors eventually expanded their agricultural productions and employed black slaves as surrounding whites did. So too did the Choctaw, Chickasaw, and Creek. The Seminoles in Florida were less likely to enslave blacks but were known instead to provide refuge for fugitive blacks escaping from whites and native groups alike.

By the turn of the nineteenth century, the possibility of a "free" Spanish Florida for enslaved runaways had ended completely. As part of the second Treaty of Paris in 1783, which concluded the hostilities of the American Revolution, Britain returned Florida to Spain. In 1790, however, Spain ended its policy of allowing slaves escaping from the new United States of America to gain "freedom" in their Florida Territory.[10] Spain maintained its Florida colonies, designated as East Florida and West Florida, until the Adams–Onis Treaty of 1819. Spanish Florida's white residents, and many of the colony's free people of color, finally evacuated in 1821, taking their slaves with them. They largely chose to settle in the nearby Spanish slave society of Cuba. Among those who left for Cuba, for example, were Andreas Bacas, his two adult sons Isaac and Justo, and their families. All three men had been enslaved in Georgia before they escaped and received religious sanctuary in Spanish Florida where they served in the free black militia.[11]

Spanish Florida, therefore, operated a system of slavery in North America a century before slavery was recognized in Britain's permanent colony of Virginia. But the Spanish not only settled in what became Florida, but also in land that would become Texas during the sixteenth and seventeenth centuries.

In 1528, the Moroccan slave Estevanico arrived with his master Andrés Dorantes de Carranza near Galveston. Estevanico was among the first Atlantic world explorers and slaves to travel in what is today the American Southwest, but what was then the northwest frontier of the Spanish-American Empire. Sold as a child without parents or kin in 1513 by Portuguese slave traders to Carranza, Estevanico eventually journeyed to, and was enslaved in, Florida, Texas, Mexico City, and the Gulf of California, before being killed by the Zunis in 1539.[12]

For the next three hundred years, Texas, first as a part of the Spanish Empire, and then in 1821 within the new Republic of Mexico, was the site of black slavery.[13] Under Spanish control, the institution largely was centered in and around the towns of San Antonio, Nacogdoches, and Goliad (Bahia).[14] Colonial Texas slavery, however, was extremely marginalized – numerically and in terms of economic impact – when compared to the African presence and influence in other parts of the Spanish Empire, particularly Hispaniola (later Santo Domingo), Venezuela, Peru, Puerto Rico, and

Cuba, and even when compared to other areas of New Spain such as Mexico City, Veracruz, Guerrero, Oaxaca, Morelos, Michoacán, and the Yucatan.[15] Historian L. B. Rout Jr calculates that, overall, 1.5 million Africans arrived in Spanish America during the entire colonial era (1500–1810)[16]; while Herman Bennett estimates that almost 680,000 blacks (slave and free) resided in all of Mexico in 1796.[17] In 1790, however, only 37 slaves lived in what would become Texas.[18] Documents from these eras indicate that black slaves had a variety of places in the colonial economies of New Spain – working in gold and silver mines, on agricultural estates and livestock ranches, as pearl divers, in textile factories, at Catholic missions, in cities as domestics of all sorts, and as skilled artisans, sex laborers, teamsters, and even as members of the local militias.[19]

Prices for African and African-descended slaves in New Spain could be steep.[20] A receipt from 1554 indicates that the widow Velez Rascon, of the Mexican city of Puebla, for example, was willing to pay 1,110 pesos of "pure gold" for six slaves – two men, two women, and two children – a rather inflated price since most adults typically cost about 150 gold pesos at the time.[21] Although the Catholic Church expected slaves in the Spanish Empire to convert to Christianity and counseled their owners to allow them to take on the sacrament of marriage, most slaveholders acted out of beliefs that blacks, even Catholic blacks, were morally and intellectually inferior – good only for work and the production of future workers.

French efforts to colonize North America in the Gulf region and beyond were not far behind those of the Spanish. By 1682, their "New France" also included La Louisiane, named for King Louis XIV. This was a vast territory that included the present-day states of Louisiana, Mississippi, Arkansas, Oklahoma, Missouri, Kansas, Nebraska, Iowa, Illinois, Indiana, Michigan, Wisconsin, Minnesota, North and South Dakota. While the French never settled much of this land, they did create mercantile and agricultural settlements in and around the lower Mississippi River that included indigenous and African slaves. The first such settlement was the rather temporary Fort Maurepas (near Biloxi) in 1699. The first permanent settlement was at Natchitoches in 1714.

Evidence of the first shipment of Africans to Gulf French colonials places the date as 1719, when two ships carrying slaves arrived in the port of New Orleans. Thousands more landed in the next several decades, many from Africa's Senegambia region, the Ivory Coast, the Bight of Benin, and Angola.[22]

Like all of the French territories in the Americas, slavery was determined, in part, by the Code Noir, first established by Louis XVI in 1685 and instituted in Louisiana in 1724. It was meant to be a guide to master–slave relationships; a clarification of the economic, social, and legal status and behavior of blacks, free and slave; a determination of the status, behavior, and privileges of whites in the French colonial empire; a legal expulsion mandate for Jews; and a determination that Catholicism would be the only religion legally practiced. Indeed, the Code Noir also stipulated that only Catholics could supervise slaves. It provided, therefore, the most extensive blueprint in the Americas for legislation of slave life, while also delineating a master's obligations to his/her human property's physical and moral upkeep. Slaveholders, for example, were obliged to baptize their slaves and not to force them to work on Sundays or religious holidays. Slaves also could only marry, and priests officiate at their weddings, with their owners' consent. The Code Noir forbade miscegenation, providing the disincentive that the children of slave women fathered by masters were to be reared by these masters/fathers. Typically, however, children inherited their status from their mothers. This early body of legislation also permitted masters to sell pre-adolescent children away from their slave parents, if the parents and children had the same owner. Slaves who physically harmed their masters, the Code further stipulated, could be executed; fugitive slaves could have their ears slit, hamstrings cut, suffer branding, and, upon the third attempt at escape, be executed. Otherwise, masters were not to kill or dismember their human chattel. Slaves of different masters, however, were forbidden to meet together, were not allowed to have weapons, except with the consent of their owners for hunting purposes, and were prevented from testifying in court except to gather contextual evidence, and could not sue or bring criminal charges. They also could not sell anything without their masters' permission, or sell sugar, even with their owners' consent. Masters were compelled to provide minimum amounts of food and clothing for their slaves, even the old and infirm. Adult masters could free their slaves. Freed slaves were considered French citizens with equal rights to other citizens, *but* they were to maintain a "notable respect" for their former owners, thus retaining some obligatory ties.[23]

Even though the Code Noir might have indicated some "leniency" toward bondsmen and women, there is ample evidence that slaves were just as brutalized, and sometimes even more so as in the case of Saint-Domingue, by French owners as by others in the Atlantic world. Fugitive slaves in French Louisiana, for example, were routinely bound to the ground by stakes and received 100–200 lashes of a whip.[24] And so it was with slave codes throughout the Atlantic world. These laws were a guidebook to treatment and control, but not necessarily an effective one. They were codes that colonists could choose to follow or that local authorities might act to enforce, but not necessarily, given the rural isolation of most slaves, the socioeconomic and political power of their masters, and the inability of slaves to testify against them in court.

Large plantations in French Louisiana generally were not the norm during the early decades of settlement. A census from 1727, for example, indicates that 78 percent of slaveholdings between the port city of New Orleans and the parish of Point Coupee had fewer than 20 slaves; and 23 percent for the entire region had fewer than five.[25]

Although Louisiana became known for its sugar production, it was not until 1751 that the slaves of Jesuit missionaries planted the first successful crop. It took until the end of the eighteenth century for sugar to become the region's most important export crop. Sugar produced before that time was distilled into crude rum that was consumed locally.[26] The most important crop to the Louisiana economy until the blossoming of sugar was indigo. Outside of the numerous unskilled and skilled work slaves performed on indigo and sugar plantations, rural slaves in French Louisiana labored on cotton and tobacco farms and plantations, handled livestock (sheep, cattle, pigs, horses, and poultry), cleared forests, drained swamps, and built houses, outhouses, and fences.

The French, however, lost Louisiana at the end of the Seven Years War. The 1763 Treaty of Paris gave Spain, until

1800, control over all of French Louisiana, with the exception of New Orleans, adjacent lands, and the area around Lake Pontchartrain. The Spanish placed a governor on the ground in New Orleans but largely administered the colony from Cuba. Spanish migrants from nearby West Florida and immigrants from the Canary Islands soon began to settle. Still, French immigrants and their African slaves continued to arrive too. By 1726, there were 1,385 slaves. That number had grown to 4730 by 1750. The largest French contingent eventually came from Nova Scotia and Saint-Domingue – especially during the 1790s when much of the colony was in the throes of a slave revolution. Saint-Domingue planters, as well as mixed-race *gens de couleur*, brought their slaves with them. Indeed, slaves outnumbered whites by the end of the eighteenth century, comprising 52 percent of Louisiana's population.[27] An 1800 census, that also included the Spanish territory of West Florida, indicated that there were more than 24,000 slaves compared to approximately 20,000 free people (white and nonwhite).

The French, but especially the Spanish, provided significant competition to the British in early colonial settlement of North America. The Dutch, as well, claimed portions of the northern mainland as part of their "New World" empire, establishing "New Netherlands" in 1624. Africans, many pirated from Spanish ships, arrived in the first or second year of settlement. Dutch settlements – New Amsterdam (New York City); Fort Casimir; Fort Orange (present-day Albany), Swaunendael (Fort Nassau), and Esopus (Kingston) – took up the territory that would become most of the "middle colonies" – Pennsylvania, New Jersey, and New York. A Swedish settlement, Fort Christina on the Delaware Bay, was formed in 1638 in defiance of the Dutch attempt to secure the region. Eventually, New Sweden was comprised of several settlements along the Delaware Bay. Swedish and Finnish colonists had begun to import Africans in 1639, but the numbers of blacks did not increase substantially until the Dutch gained control of these settlements in 1655.[28]

In 1630, the Dutch West India Company, New Netherlands' settlements founding force, decided to grant large landed estates, or patroons, that would be worked by slaves.[29] The Company hoped that New Netherlands would supply food for their markets in Brazil – grains such as rye, wheat, and barley, as well as beef. They expected to exchange these goods in Brazil for African slaves. Those granted patroonships, therefore, were told that the "West India Company shall allot to each patron twelve men and women out of the prize in which Negroes shall be found, for the advancement of the colonies of New Netherlands." Later, the number of slaves was expanded to "as many as possible." [30] Not many settlers, however, purchased slaves in these first years, leaving the Dutch West India (DWI) Company itself as New Netherlands' largest slaveholder. It was not a complete economic loss for them. The DWI gained profits from this unique position by renting out, instead of selling outright, enslaved black men and women. In the rural areas, slave males worked principally as agricultural workers; but in towns like New Amsterdam, they took up numerous skilled and unskilled occupations, including fort maintenance and repairs. They also served in military positions in the Company's effort to protect settlements from potential attacks by indigenous peoples. Many slave women labored as domestics. Urban life, coupled with the lease system, afforded many enslaved persons a kind of "freedom" of movement and congregation for social, political, and economic endeavors that few rural slaves could hope to attain. [31]

Evidence points to a growing, albeit small, community of blacks – slave, free, and "half slaves" (Africans and creoles who had gained their freedom, but who still had labor and monetary obligations to their masters) – by the 1640s. What was this path to freedom? Slaves petitioned for emancipation in a manner that suggested that, like the blacks of Spanish Florida and, to some extent, those in the French Gulf, the need that the sparsely populated Dutch colonies had to protect themselves from defensive native peoples could prove to be a window of opportunity for individual manumissions. In New Netherlands, therefore, black "slave" status was not a "given." Indeed, "slavery" had not been legislated in the North American mainland Dutch colonies at the time, so there were no legal guidelines to determine who was, and who was not, a slave. A manumission act of 1644, for example, determined that eleven company "slaves" who had been "freed" – Paul Angola, Big Manuel, Garcia, Simon

Congo, Jan Fort Orange, Little Anthony, Anthony Portugis, Peter Santome, Little Manuel, Manuel de Gerrit de Reus, and Jan Francisco – still owed obligations to their previous owners. Indeed, they could gain their freedom, and a plot of land where they could support themselves through farming "on condition that they...shall be bound to pay for the freedom they receive each man for himself annually, as long as he lives, to the West India Company" – their former owners. Each of these males was to provide a certain amount of corn or wheat, beans or peas, and a hog annually and work for the Company for "fair wages." The land that they received legally became theirs in twenty years; but their children had to remain Company slaves "forever," unless their parents were able to purchase them outright.[32]

Dutch rule of New Netherlands ended in 1664 when the British ousted them. But many Dutch colonists remained, as did their Dutch-speaking slaves. This was in spite of the British commander-general's 1665 order allowing him to confiscate all of the property of the Dutch West India Company in the former New Netherlands – lands, houses, goods, cattle, slaves, debts, "and all other revenue of what sort soever."[33] The middle colonies under the British, as they had been under the Dutch, were intimately tied to the economic agenda of a trading company, in this instance the Royal African Company that, after 1672, held a monopoly on the slaves traded in the British colonies, at least until the end of the century.

Europeans in seventeenth-century North America, therefore, were a curious mix of people from the British Isles, the Netherlands, France, Sweden and Spain – men, women, and children who had come to far-flung colonial outposts for specific economic, political, spiritual, and cultural reasons. There, they negotiated with native populations of many different cultures who numbered over ten million, and who answered with an array of responses to these interlopers.[34] Into this cauldron of cultural clash and physical aggression came African slaves. What was this volatile and oftentimes devastating emotional and physical experience for the enslaved as they transitioned from being native-born Africans of diverse language and cultural groups to enslaved immigrants in America?

British North American Colonization and the Evolution of African Slavery

One thing is for certain, Africans and their descendants were not the first, or only, bonded laborers of the British settlers. The British, as had the Dutch, French, and Spanish, used white immigrants (indentured and convict) as laborers along with Africans from the earliest period of settlement. Enslavement of indigenous peoples usually came as a result of hostile relations between the two, some time after initial European settlement. The British in Virginia, for example, did not legally enslave native peoples until 1667, and then with some important exceptions.[35] Keep in mind, moreover, that the Dutch had no clear designation of the legal status of Africans and creole blacks in New Amsterdam – some Dutch West Indian slaves were treated as persons maintaining a status somewhere between slave and indentured servant. Likewise, the windows of opportunity available to gain freedom for some slaves who demonstrated a clear conversion to Catholicism, as in Spanish Florida and to some extent in the French Gulf, also muddied the waters of an African's legal status in the northern frontiers of these European colonial empires in the Americas. The British were no different. The first Africans who arrived in Virginia were not enslaved there, at least not for the first few decades.

It is still not certain when the first Africans came to work in Virginia, the first permanent British mainland colony in North America and the first to have black residents. In 1619, a divided parcel of contraband enslaved Africans arrived in Point Comfort near present-day Hampton, but there already were 32 blacks living in the colony.[36] Those who came that summer, however, were probably from the kingdom of Ndongo who had been aboard the *Sao Joao Bautista* from Luanda. The slaver was on its way to Vera Cruz when it was pirated by a Dutch man-of-war and the British ship *Treasurer*. The Dutch ship docked in August, with 20 of the original 100 Angolans taken aboard. Their names bore the marks of their Catholic baptismal.[37] The *Treasurer* landed only one of its contraband in the colony, a female named Angela.

Evidence strongly suggests that these Angolans actually were Ambundu, taken during a series of violent raids mounted by Portuguese forces between 1618 and 1620. They would have come from matrilineal societies in the "royal district" of Ndongo. Fifteen of those 1619 arrivals went to live and work as indentured servants for the most powerful Englishman in the colony – Royal Governor George Yeardley – on his frontier estate at Flowerdew Hundred. The rural nature of early colonial Virginia, with its very thin white and black populations, would have been a decided change from their Angolan homeland. Flowerdew Hundred had only 60 residents in 1624. The Ambundu, however, were mostly an urbanized people in Angola, living in and around a group of cities of about 20,000–30,000 residents each.[38]

Since they came from the royal district, Angela, Isabel (another early import), and their male peers probably represented a variety of classes and occupations, including farmers, skilled artisans, royal servants, and royal persons. Unless they were of a particularly high class, however, they would have known much about the agricultural work that was required of their Virginia indentureship. In Ndongo, many urban dwellers still grew grains like millet and sorghum. In the more rural areas, they also raised cattle, goats, chickens, and other livestock. The women were responsible for domestic labor and farming, as well as participation in the market. In Virginia, they helped to grow tobacco – in 1624, Yeardley's laborers produced a tobacco crop valued at 10,000 pounds. Most of the Ambundu servants had been introduced to Catholicism before they arrived in Virginia and, therefore, would not have found the religious beliefs and practices of the Anglican colonists, relatively speaking, unfamiliar. As historian John Thornton notes: "By 1619, a Kimbundu-speaking Christian community existed in Angola" which "quite possibly" included those who arrived in Virginia in 1619.[39]

The Ambundu had an ethnic identity, based in part on their shared language, political affiliations, and perceptions of themselves as "people of the court" that probably was the basis for the beginning of their own cultural community in Virginia. Given that most of those who arrived in 1619 came from the same region of Angola, spoke the same language, and shared other cultural attributes, it is not surprising that there remains evidence of community life among them in the British colony. Isabel married Anthony, a fellow member of the 1619 cargo. By 1624, they had a son whom they had baptized at Jamestown. Years later, their grandson, John Jr, named his farm at Somerset, Maryland, "Angola."[40]

These early black Virginia residents were indentured servants. There is evidence that most adults served a traditional term of seven to ten years, based on the price their masters paid for the contract that temporarily bound them, and then gained their freedom at the end of it. Of course, there were some contractual stipulations that could lengthen their terms. Women were the most likely to suffer from these provisions. Those who had children while indentured, for example, had their terms extended and their children were indentured until adulthood. More than a few, however, like the Johnsons, came to own land. Anthony even came to have a black indentured servant, whom he tried to claim was his "slave."

The indentured servitude of seventeenth-century British America was not an easy load to bear. It was not slavery as slavery came to be defined in American law and practice in the next several decades, but neither was it freedom. An indentured person "belonged," for all intents and purposes, to his or her "master." Their contracts and, thereby, they themselves could be sold by one master to another. Their children were bound to their masters even after the parents were freed. Hard work, obedience, and few material necessities in the way of food, clothing, shelter, and medical attention were the order of the day – servants usually were allowed only the barest minimum. Masters had a right to physically chastise servants they deemed lazy, disobedient, or "troublesome." They often sexually harassed and abused them. The labor that servants performed was hard. Black men and women worked in the fields alongside white indentured men; but indentured white women tended to be exempt from this kind of agricultural labor. For those who were confined to the tobacco fields, there was much work to be done. Many were responsible for as many as 10,000 tobacco plants per year, tending to them from seedling to harvest.

The Ambundu would have arrived at just about the time that the first agricultural boom in North America was taking off. Their work hours and conditions would have reflected the harsh realities of cash-crop labor on a forested frontier surrounded by an indigenous population that was growing more wary of, and hostile to, the English by the day. Moreover, these Africans had to acclimatize quickly to a new physical environment rife with wild animals, mosquitoes, questionable (at best) drinking water, cold winters, and European diseases. Culturally, they had to learn a new language, or at least enough of English to take orders and do their work effectively. The population, black and white, was sparse, but there were many more whites of similar language, religion, and other cultural designs and beliefs than Ambundu in those first few decades after 1619. No matter how fiercely Anthony, Isabel, and the others clung to their language and culture, they had to learn the language and culture of their masters if they were to survive long enough to gain the freedom that their indentured labor eventually bought.

This access to freedom, however, did not last long for Africans forced to Virginia. By the 1640s, the colony's court records and laws indicate that questions regarding the longevity of the "indentures" of Africans, along with other conditions of their residence, were being raised. In 1640, for example, blacks in the colony were excluded from the requirement to possess arms. Two years later, black women were categorized as "tithable," or taxable, a distinction from white women. By 1662, colonial law began to reflect a decided change in black status that would not be altered for another two hundred years. In that year, legislation mandated that the children of a black woman took on the social location of their mothers. This law was meant to answer the query regarding the legal status of a biracial child. Previously, English law had determined that a child's status would be the same as that of his or her father. Once the inheritance of legal status children was tied to the black mother, of course, slave masters could increase their slave holdings by forcing slave women to bear children, black or biracial. In 1663, the possibility of life servitude for black "servants" was created in law. Four years later, baptism no longer meant free status for blacks. By the late 1660s, criminal/justice sectors of the law began to treat black slaves differently, and as inferiors. According to legislation passed that year, masters (or their representatives, including mistresses and overseers) who killed slaves who were resisting "correction" were not to be punished. There was indeed a separate legal system being created for blacks with distinct trial processes and more severe punishments for crimes than whites. And in 1670, "servant for life" was deemed the "normal" condition of blacks who, along with indigenous peoples, were outlawed from owning "Christian servants."

Virginia colonial law from 1667 forward distinctly categorized blacks as slaves and, as such, differentiated them from others under the law. This certainly was not surprising given that British colonial legislators in Barbados determined in their slave code of 1661 that blacks would not be treated equally under the law. The Barbadian Code influenced, as well, Jamaica's first slave laws of the 1660s and Jamaica's later 1684 slave code that, in turn, was largely adopted by South Carolinian seventeenth-century legislators. Slaves in British southern colonies and the Caribbean, therefore, were legally linked to a growing body of repressive and discriminatory legislation.[41]

African slavery spread swiftly in the British mainland colonies, as it did in the British Caribbean. By 1680, Virginia had 3,000 slaves, but that number had grown more than five times by 1700 to over 16,000. By 1750, the slave population in Virginia, the most populous mainland British colony, had increased to 46 percent of the total number of residents, amounting to 107,000. Their numbers would expand by

3.1 "Slaves working in seventeenth-century Virginia," by an unknown artist, 1670
Source: Wikimedia Commons

more than three and a half times over the next sixty years.[42] Of course, Virginia's black slave population's representation in the overall population of the colony was small when compared to the sugar colonies of the era, when places like Barbados could boast that, by 1685, slaves were well in the majority, reaching to almost 80 percent of the island's population by the 1780s.[43]

Where Virginia went, other British mainland colonies followed, at least in the importation of Africans and seasoned and creole blacks from the Caribbean and in the creation, as well, of a native-born (or creole) black slave population. This tremendous growth, and its importance to colonial economies and security, meant a flourishing of slave legislation, north and south.

Massachusetts promulgated the first law in the thirteen colonies that validated black slavery in 1641. It might seem ironic that the first British mainland colony to legalize the institution was in the North, since notions of US slavery, even in the colonial period, still lives in the popular imagination as a southern institution. Slavery, however, was a factor in all the thirteen colonies and the institution of slavery had some economic, political and cultural impact on all of them. Slave labor clearly had tremendous economic importance in southern colonies, as well as significance in northern colonies through the building and outfitting of the slave ships, the provisioning of supplies for the Atlantic voyages and, of course, the actual shipping of Africans to the South and the Caribbean. Connecticut legalized slavery in 1650, Rhode Island in 1652, New York and New Jersey in 1663, and Pennsylvania in 1700. New Hampshire (which was considered part of Massachusetts until 1691) had black slaves as early as 1645; and Vermont also had slaves, but because France, as well as other British colonies, including Massachusetts, New Hampshire and New York, claimed the land that became Vermont, it is difficult to say precisely when slavery began there. Yet certainly it came with early settlement. Maine remained part of Massachusetts until 1820 and, thus, shared in its slavery heritage. In the southern colonies, Maryland sanctioned the institution in law in 1663, North and South Carolina around 1670, and Georgia in 1735.

Slave Legislation and Economy in British North America's Middle and Northern Colonies

Massachusetts initially led the way in the northern British mainland colonies in slave ownership and investment in the slave trade, but not for long. It is believed that Samuel Maverick was the first resident of that colony to own slaves in the 1620s. Seventeenth-century Massachusetts's colonists not only imported Africans, some from as far away as Madagascar on the African Indian Ocean coast, but also seized Native American captives, especially the Pequot, to trade for black slaves in the British Caribbean, particularly Barbados. By the end of the century, Massachusetts slave traders were providing slaves to British colonies along the mainland coast from North Carolina and Virginia northward to Connecticut. The black Massachusetts population was small, only slightly more than 2 percent of the total number of residents by the mid-eighteenth century, with the majority located in Boston. Massachusetts only had 170 slaves in 1680, but there were 1,250 by 1720, and 4,100 in 1750. Connecticut eventually had more slaves by 1770, but its slave population remained smaller than that of Massachusetts until then, with only 3,000 in 1750. By 1770, Massachusetts had 4,750, Connecticut 5,700, and Rhode Island 3,800. New Hampshire had 550 slaves in 1750, and 650 in 1770. Vermont had so few that only 25 were recorded in 1770.[44]

Massachusetts's legislators attended to their black presence in a growing body of legal mandates that was meant to control their social and economic activities. Between 1720 and the 1750s, for example, Massachusetts Bay Colony passed legislation that forbade blacks from trading in markets; from raising or selling hogs; from sailing on ships; from having weapons; and from being on city streets after nightfall without permission from their owners. Interracial marriage was strictly prohibited, as was sexual contact across racial lines. The trends of social and economic control apparent in the laws of Massachusetts were found throughout the colonies. Not surprisingly, the laws were most comprehensive, and strictest, in those colonies with the largest slave populations.

Massachusetts was the first non-southern British colony to have black slaves, but British New York had the largest slave population north of Maryland. Most were located in the city of New York (previously New Amsterdam). When the British gained control of the city, there were approximately 300 enslaved blacks and 75 free, out of a total population of 1,500.[45] The colony's black population, like its white one, grew quickly. There were 1,200 slaves in 1680, 5,700 forty years later, and twice that many by the middle of the eighteenth century. New Jersey had smaller numbers, but still more than the northern colonies. There were 200 in 1680; 2,400 in 1720; 11,000 by 1750; and 19,000 in 1770. Although many households had enslaved blacks in Pennsylvania, including that of William Penn, overall the numbers were comparatively small for the middle colonies, with only 2,800 in 1750 and reaching a peak of 5,500 in 1770. Delaware was part of New Amsterdam in 1680 when it was recorded that 55 slaves lived there. By 1682, the Duke of York had ceded Delaware to William Penn and it was termed the "Lower Counties" of Pennsylvania. Even though some Upper South slaveholders came to reside there, the number of slaves in Delaware still grew slowly to 700 by 1720 and just 1,800 in 1770 – only 5 percent of the colony's overall population.[46]

New York passed a number of laws regarding slavery that were both similar to, but more expansive than, those one could find in Massachusetts and most of the other northern and middle colonies. In 1702, the Act for Regulating of Slaves allowed owners to punish their slaves as they saw fit with the exclusion of death and dismemberment; did not permit three or more slaves to meet together without the consent of their owners; forbade free people to trade with slaves without their owners' permission; and restricted slave testimony in court except against another slave.[47] Security, internal and external, was always an issue. Masters were determined to keep their slave property and themselves safe; while many slaves were determined to gain their freedom by whatever means available. It was a constant tug of war that characterized master–slave relations and black physical and spatial repression and regulation seen throughout the Atlantic world. The British mainland colonies were no exception.

New York law in 1705 stipulated that slaves found guilty of trying to escape to French Canada could be executed. The next major attempt at providing more substantial slave legislation in colonial New York occurred as the result of a slave revolt on April 6, 1712 that involved both black and indigenous slaves.

On that day, approximately twenty-three armed slaves purportedly set fire to a centrally located building in New York City and then attacked white colonists as they rushed to put it out. Nine whites were killed and six wounded. But once they regained control of the city, they implemented all legal and extralegal powers they could muster to strike back. Twenty-seven slaves were captured, twenty-one of whom were executed and six purportedly committed suicide rather than face their fates. As a result of this rebellion, which only underscored the constant fear whites had of black rebellion, the New York colonial legislature passed an Act for the Suppressing and Punishing the Conspiracy and Insurrection of Negroes and Other Slaves that allowed slaves found guilty of rape, arson, murder, or assault to be punished by death. The act also reaffirmed that, for other criminal offenses, slave owners had the right to punish their slaves, excluding dismemberment and death. Since there typically was fear that local free people of color undermined the institution of slavery either through example or by giving clandestine aid to enslaved friends and relations, it is not surprising that this post-rebellion legislation also provided that a strict financial penalty be placed on those who freed their slaves – £200 sterling at the time of emancipation for each, and an additional £20 to be paid annually to each freed. Eighteen years later, additional security measures were encoded in law to provide protection from the lingering threat of black revolution. New York's Montgomerie Act forbade slaves to own potential weapons; limited the numbers meeting to two at a time; instilled a curfew at dark without an owner's written permission; and disallowed any public disorderly behavior. In 1740, additional legislation forbade slaves from selling fruits and vegetables on public streets.[48]

Late eighteenth-century Pennsylvania came to be known as a center for early abolitionist thought among whites living in North America due to the large numbers of Quaker

residents with abolitionist tendencies and the colony's significant population of German farmers and artisans who did not
embrace the institution. During the first century of Pennsylvania's development, however, the colony hardly would have
been characterized in that way. The colony's laws, like those
of others, validated the status of enslaved black persons.
During the seventeenth century, slaves and indentured servants were treated similarly in law, with two profound exceptions: slaves held their condition for life, and their children
inherited this position. Indentured servants, however, were
held only for a very specific term that typically did not extend
for one's entire life and the children born to an indentured
mother remained indentured only until adulthood. In 1700,
the status of blacks, slave and free, in Pennsylvania, like those
in Virginia, the Carolinas, and the British Caribbean, was
distinctly captured in their inferior status before the law. The
colony established separate courts for blacks without juries
and different penalties for convictions of crimes than those
that whites received. Moreover, slaves, as in New York and
other places in the Americas where there was a healthy fear
of slave revolt, were forbidden from having firearms without
their masters' permission. By 1700, one-tenth of Philadelphia
household heads, most of whom were Quaker in faith, owned
at least one slave.[49]

In 1725, the Pennsylvania colonial legislature issued a
more comprehensive law regulating the black presence in
their society. An Act for the Better Regulating of Negroes in
this Province forbade miscegenation and biracial marriage,
banned slaves from drinking in public and from leaving their
master's residence or being away from this residence after 9
pm without written permission. More than four slaves could
not meet together outside of work-related activities and slave
owners were not allowed to permit their slaves to seek work
on their own, an ordinance related to the popular practice of
slave rental. Masters who wished to free their slaves had to
leave a bond of £30 sterling. The 1725 Act also provided for
compensation to masters for slaves sentenced to death for a
crime and it fined those persons found guilty of harboring
fugitive slaves. While punishment of slaves for smaller crimes
was left to their masters, owners were forbidden from mur-
dering, torturing, "overworking," or starving their slaves.

Later colonial legislation detailed specific, and different, punishments for slaves (versus whites) for such crimes as participating in horse racing, shooting matches, the use of fireworks, and hunting on forbidden lands or on a Sunday.[50]

The attention to detail of these slave codes indicates the importance of slave property, the trade, and the institution to colonial northern societies. As historian Lorenzo Greene indicates, slavery, particularly the slave trade, was essential to New England colonial economies, noting that: "The effects of the New England slave trade were momentous. It was one of the foundations of New England's economic structure; it created a wealthy class of slave-trading merchants, while the profits derived from this commerce stimulated cultural development and philanthropy."[51] Greene's conclusions could have extended to the middle colonies as well. Indeed, slave trading was the foundation for economies of most seaport towns, including New York, Newport, Boston, Salem, Charlestown, and New Kittery, Massachusetts; Providence, Jamestown, and New Bristol, Rhode Island; Middletown and New London, Connecticut; and Portsmouth, New Hampshire. In Rhode Island alone, two-thirds of merchant ships and mariners were involved in the African slave trade. This business was the bread and butter of regional shipbuilders, lawyers, agents, scriveners, clerks, insurers, the actual traders and insurers, as well as coopers, rope makers, tanners, and sailmakers. Goods packed on slave trips for long-distance commerce to the Caribbean portion of the slave trade came from New England loggers, fishermen, and farmers. Local distillers and industrialists sold traders millions of gallons of rum and countless numbers of trinkets and iron bars that were used to exchange for slaves on the African coast. Rhode Island, for example, had thirty distilleries and Massachusetts had sixty-three. Consider, for example, part of this correspondence from Boston slave trader Timothy Fitch to Captain William Ellery of the *Snow Caesar* on January 14, 1759. Fitch was the trader who brought Phillis Wheatley from West Africa to Boston in 1761 on his slave ship the *Phillis*. He wrote to Ellery two years earlier:

My Orders are to you that you embrace the first favourable Opportunity of Wind and Weather and proceed to the Coast of

Affrica, touching first if you think proper at Sinagall, where if you find Encouragement, You may part with such part of your Cargo, as you can sell to your liking. Otherwise I hope you won't Tarry twelve Hours, and then proceed down the Coast to such Ports or Places as you judge best to Dispose of your Cargo to Advantage So as to purchase a Cargo of Slaves with which you are to proceed to South Carolina, unless a Peace should happen, or a good Opportunity of coming off with a Man of Warr, or some Vessell of Force for ye West Indies in that case I would recommend the Island of St. Christophers, being Handy to St. Eustatia for the Sail of your Slaves – Wherever you may sell your Slaves, wither in the West Indies or So.-Carolina, you may Load your Vessel with the Produce of the Place, such as you are acquainted with the Value, which may be of some help to the Sale of your Slaves and for the Remainder take not but undoubted Bills of Exchange, Otherwise Cash.[52]

Indeed, slave merchants were some of the great patriarchs of these colonies – the Eastons of Connecticut; Willing & Morris of Philadelphia; the Cabots, Fanueils, and Royalls of Massachusetts; the Wantons, Champlins, and Browns of Rhode Island; and the Whipples of New Hampshire. Six slave traders were mayor of Philadelphia. Nicholas, John, Joseph, and Moses Brown, for whom Brown University was named, were active in the trade and employed slaves to build part of the university.[53]

But it was not just individuals and private companies that became rich from the trade. Colonial governments in Rhode Island, New York, New Jersey, and Massachusetts all gained some tax revenue from the trade. Likewise, newspapers in every colony received revenues from selling advertisements of slave rentals, sales, and rewards for fugitives. The *Pennsylvania Gazette* on September 4, 1740, for example, advertised "A PARCEL of Likely Negro Boys and Girls just arrived in the Sloop Charming Sally – to be sold – for Ready Money, Flour or Wheat."[54] Typical as well were notices of runaways, such as this one from Philadelphia's first newspaper, the *American Weekly Mercury*, on November 14, 1722, for a "Negroe Man named Fransh Manuel of a pretty tall stature, and speaks indifferent english" who "wears a dark coloured homespun coat, an Ozenbrig Jacket, old Leather breeches, Sheep-russet Stockings, new Shoes and an old Beveret hat" and pretends "to be a Freeman." "Whoever takes up the said Negroe," the ad notes, "shall have forty shillings reward." The *New York Gazette* printed a similar notice on August 31, 1730 for "two Negro men, both branded RN on their shoulders; one remarkedly scarrified over the forehead, clothed with trousers, the other with a coat and trousers."[55]

Slave Labor in the Northern and Middle Colonies of the British Mainland

Clearly, the slave trade was important in numerous ways to the economies of northern and middle colonies. But what about slave labor? What did the slaves do, and how essential was their labor to colonial life north of the cash-crop seaboard colonies of Maryland, Virginia, and the Carolinas?

In the earliest years of settlement for all of these colonies, slaves, like indentured servants and wage laborers, were particularly needed to clear the land and to build houses, fences, barns, outhouses, roads, and other edifices. Most of the northern and middle colonies, beyond the diverse businesses centered on the sea coast, had early economies based on subsistence agriculture where slave labor was very important, particularly if white indentured servants were not to be had. As the seventeenth century passed and fewer white contract servants were available, the necessity for slave labor increased. In the countryside, slaves were farmhands and domestics.[56] Enslaved farm workers, male and female, not only cleared the land, but planted, weeded, and tended crops, built and repaired structures, and tended to tools, as well as herding work animals. Massachusetts's most important subsistence crops were corn, pumpkins, squash, wheat, barley, and potatoes. Exported farm and manufactured items produced with the help of slave labor included wheat flour, rum, fish, fur, cattle, whale products, and lumber.[57]

Narragansett "planters" in southern Rhode Island created an early eighteenth-century society that, in some ways, probably came closest to New World plantation society with regard to land and slave ownership, although the region certainly could not rival the large tobacco estates of the colonial Chesapeake, the rice plantations of South Carolina, and certainly not the sugar manors of the Caribbean or Brazil. On large tracts of land, some several thousands of acres in size, the slaves of Narragansett masters cultivated wheat, hay, and oats, produced milk and cheese, and herded and butchered sheep and beef for export. Rowland Robinson, for example, owned 28 slaves and more than a thousand acres of land. During the 1760s, he sold thousands of pounds of cheese and hundreds of sheep, as well as hay, horses, and milk, to a local agent who shipped them through Newport to the Caribbean. While Robinson clearly was one of the most successful of his cohort, others too had similar success with slave labor.[58]

With the help of slaves, middle-colony farmers produced similar crops to those found in the North, particularly wheat, corn, barley, and potatoes, as well as buckwheat, peaches, nectarines, melons, and apples. As in the northern colonies, masters used slaves as fishermen, livestock handlers, whalers, and oystermen. They traded grains locally and long distance. Other exports, to the Caribbean principally, included fish, apples, cider, beer, and cattle.[59] Delaware, more similar to Virginia and Maryland than the other middle colonies, used slaves to produce tobacco as well as grains, livestock, iron, and lumber.[60] Those slaves who worked in the house not only tended to cooking, cleaning, child care, spinning, weaving, sewing, and washing, but also planted and tended kitchen gardens, cared for, slaughtered, smoked, preserved, dried, and salted livestock, typically poultry, cows, pigs, sheep, and goats. The work regime, although different from that of the colonial South, was a rigorous one. Moreover, the smaller numbers of slaves held in the North (compared to the larger holdings in the South or other places in the Americas) did not translate into bondswomen and men being treated better than those in the South or even the Caribbean. They all shared a fate of overwork, malnourishment, and violence. John Jea, who came from Old Calabar (a major site of Igbo slave export) as a child with his parents and siblings to New York in the mid-1770s, for example, was purchased in New York, he recalled, by a man who was "very cruel" and "used…in a manner, almost too shocking to relate." Oliver and Angelika Triehuen, his owners, were grain farmers but also grew fruit and raised cattle for export. According to Jea, the slaves received a very small food allowance, were worked almost twenty hours per day in the summer and were brutally whipped if any resistance was offered. "We dared not murmur," he noted, "for if we did we were corrected with a weapon an inch-and-a-half thick, and that without mercy, striking us in the most tender parts." Any complaint led only to a more torturous form of punishment, and physical resistance from the slaves resulted in "shooting them with some gun, or beating their brains out with some weapon."[61]

Life differed substantially, however, for most of those who lived in urban environments. Rural slaves almost certainly lived with their owners and had very limited mobility. Urban slaves often lived outside their masters' homes and were known to congregate with other blacks, slave and free, as well as white indentured servants in both social and economic ventures, prompting the legislation noted above regarding miscegenation, restriction of gatherings, movement without owners' permission, and slave entrepreneurship. In Philadelphia, most colonial slaves were domestics and were owned by wealthy masters; but there were a substantial number of middling-class owners as well, some of whom apprenticed their slaves in specific skilled trades. Many slaves, therefore, were employed outside their owners' homes, performing skilled work as bricklayers, blacksmiths, goldsmiths, bakers, brush makers, carpenters, coopers, refiners, sailmakers, distillers, printers, shoemakers, sailors, tailors, and tanners. Some also worked in iron furnaces. Urban slave women allowed to work outside their masters' residences typically labored as washerwomen, cooks, seamstresses, and midwives.[62]

Seacoast towns and cities like Philadelphia, Boston, New York, Providence, and New Haven certainly used male slave laborers not only as rope makers, sailmakers, coopers, and carpenters, but also in shipbuilding and repair, and as stevedores to both load and unload goods, much of which related to the slave trade.[63] Slaves in New England and the middle colonies, therefore, could be found in almost every category of non-professional economic endeavor. The labor that slave men and women provided in agricultural, industrial, domestic, and mercantile moneymaking endeavors of the colonies north of Maryland not only helped to sustain the local and regional economies but also to develop and expand them.

Colonial Southern Slave Culture, Labor, and Family

Delaware produced a profitable tobacco crop at the turn of the eighteenth century, but nothing compared to the wealth, and the numbers of slaves purchased to produce it, that this crop was responsible for in Virginia, Maryland and the upper regions of Carolina. Slavery mattered – economically, legally, and culturally – in the northern and middle colonies of British North America that would become part of the United States – that is a certainty. Still, there is much to the public perception that the true slave societies of early British American were located from Maryland south, in the Chesapeake and Lowcountry. Maryland, Virginia, Carolina, and later Georgia in the British colonies (as well as French Louisiana) were especially important as destinations for the majority of Africans who were to arrive before the American Revolution. Like the vast Atlantic slave trade, those who arrived in these colonies came from many parts of western and western/central Africa. There were, however, some specifics of these southern imports that were determined, in part, by the economic designs of the traders and the expressed needs and preferences of their customers. Slave-ship manifests, newspaper advertisements, and the records of shipping companies and individual traders indicate that various combinations of ethnic concentrations likely occurred in the regions that imported large numbers of slaves, particularly the southern colonies of Virginia/Maryland, the Carolinas/Georgia, and Louisiana. One must be keenly aware, however, that African ethnic designations during the period of the slave trade are, at best, vague labels that should be thought of as "umbrellas" under which numerous groups of people, who might have boarded a slaving ship together, or left for the Americas together, were counted.

Table 3.1 Slave population in French/Spanish Louisiana

Colony	1720	1750	1770	1790
Louisiana[64]	1,385	7,430	5,600	18,700

Table 3.2 Black population in Spanish Florida

Colony	1740	1770	1790
Florida	100[65]	1,500[66]	1,653[67]

Table 3.3 British North American colonies, slave population[68]

British Colonies	1680	1700	1720	1750	1770
New Hampshire	75	130	170	550	654
Vermont				25	
Massachusetts	170	800	2,150	4,075	4,754
Connecticut	50	450	1,093	3,010	5,698
Rhode Island	175	300	543	3,347	3,761
New York	1,200	2,256	5,740	11,014	19,062
New Jersey	200	840	2,385	5,354	8,220
Pennsylvania	25	430	2,000	2,822	5,561
Delaware	55	135	700	1,496	1,836
Maryland	1,611	3,227	12,499	43,450	63,818
Virginia	3,000	16,390	26,550	107,100	187,600
N/S Carolina	210/ 200	1,000/ 3,000	3,000/ 11,828	19,800/ 39,000	69,600/ 75,178
Georgia				600	15,000

Slaves coming to Virginia/Maryland, often designated as the geocultural locale "Chesapeake" or the tidewater regions of the Upper South, found the black landscape dominated by peoples from the Bight of Biafra, particularly the Igbo.[69] It was a trend that had begun during the last decades of the 1600s. Overall for the 1700s, 40 percent of Igbo imported to the southern colonies came to the Chesapeake, rendering them an overwhelming majority (up to 60 percent in the 1710s and 1720s) in that region.[70] Most came from rural areas where much of the work was agricultural – sowing, weeding, and harvesting yams, cocoyams, bananas, maize, African breadfruit, cowpeas, and beans.[71] Other enslaved Biafrans, such as the Mokos and Efkins, were present, but in much smaller numbers. The second-largest group of Africans imported to the Upper South, representing about 20 percent of imports, were from Angola. Those persons primarily were Kongo, but also included Nsundi, Yombe, Mbala, and Yaka.[72] Western central Africans were important among the first imports to the region, but their numbers were overwhelmed by Igbo, and, to a lesser extent, Senegambians, by the end of the 1600s. By the middle of the eighteenth century, however, enslaved people from Central Africa were again among the majority of imports. Senegambians, primarily Bamana and Wolof, made up approximately 7 percent of those imported to the Chesapeake – similar in number to Africans from Sierra Leone/Windward Coast. Yet, in the decades between 1680 and 1720, Senegambians came close to rivaling the dominance of the Igbo among those enslaved people imported to this region.[73] People from the Gold Coast – the Akan and Ga, but often referred to in the eighteenth-century South as Coromantees – brought to the Upper South were just slightly more significant in number, but much less consistently imported across the decades. For example, only about 3.5 percent of Africans arriving in the Chesapeake came from the Gold Coast between 1730 and 1745, but they represented fully one-third of imported Africans from 1760 to 1775. Indeed, by the time of the American Revolution, enslaved African imports from Senegambia, the Gold Coast, and Angola were the majority in the Chesapeake region.[74]

The Africans who arrived in Virginia and Maryland during the colonial era, particularly the seventeenth century, found there white masters, but also indentured white servants and indigenous peoples, some of whom were enslaved. White servants especially were prevalent. As historian James Horn notes, "Servitude was a defining characteristic of settler society in the Chesapeake."[75] Indeed, two-thirds of the 75,000 white immigrants to the Chesapeake from 1630 to 1680 were indentured servants. Their significance was especially great from 1650 to 1680 when an estimated 16,000–20,000 arrived per decade.[76] It was these white servants, most of whom were men, who would dominate Chesapeake labor markets during the great tobacco boom of the seventeenth century.[77] Indigenous peoples, as enslaved and indentured workers for the British, were much smaller in number than either European servants or Africans. "By 1700," Philip Morgan notes, "blacks were numerous and Indians scarce in Virginia (the ratio was three to one)."[78]

Still, during the early decades of British settlement, indigenous Americans in Virginia, and throughout the South as well as further north, served both as slaves and as slave traders. Indeed, many Amerindian groups felt slave-trading was a necessary means to acquire European goods and allegiance, as well as an opportunity to gain wealth and to lessen the threat from enemy native groups. British slave owners and traders benefited from these trade relations, sending many bonded Indian slaves to the British Caribbean, particularly Barbados and Jamaica, where they often exchanged them for African slaves. Africans, after all, did not have nearly the same opportunity to escape or to mount a revolt in North America as Indian slaves did who, therefore, were more valuable in the Caribbean and less desired in the mainland colonies. Alan Gallay estimates that the British and Native Americans captured between 30,000 and 50,000 Amerindians before 1715 for sale as slaves to settlers in the British mainland and the Caribbean. Most were women and children.[79] French colonists in Louisiana and Canada likewise sold Indian slaves to the French Caribbean. Nonetheless, European and creole settlers in the mainland colonies did enslave Native Americans alongside blacks. In 1708, for example, there were approximately 2,900 black slaves in South Carolina, but also 1,400 Indian slaves.[80] By later in the eighteenth century, however, the pendulum definitely had swung toward the black slave market as the dominant source of agrarian labor in the British South, even though Amerindian slaves remained an important source of labor in South Carolina at least until 1730.[81]

If the Igbo were the majority of enslaved Africans in eighteenth-century Virginia and Maryland, they were not the most populous in South Carolina. The colony was chartered in 1663 and the first English settlement there, the Province of Carolina, was founded in 1670 when three ships of settlers from Barbados and Bermuda arrived. The colony was a proprietorship given to John Colleton, a Barbadian planter, and seven others who received the land grant as reward for their loyalty to King Charles II.[82] Carolina was unique in its personal, cultural, and business association with the British Caribbean island of Barbados, where many persons viewed the fledgling mainland colony as having significant financial promise for those wanting to leave the tiny sugar island. The philosopher John Locke, who was secretary for the proprietors, penned Carolina's Fundamental Constitution, which noted that "Every freeman of Carolina shall have absolute power and authority over his negro slaves, of what opinion or religion soever."[83] Most of the settlers who arrived brought slaves with them, so that early on blacks constituted approximately 25–33 percent of the residents and black men were the decided majority of those slaves.[84] Slaves in Barbados that might have been taken to Carolina were derived from numerous locales in western Africa including the Asante, Ewe, Fon, and Fante peoples from the Gold Coast, as well as Yoruba, Efik, Igbo, and Ibibio from the Bights of Benin and Biafra, and some from western central Africa.[85]

Those early slaves, along with enslaved native peoples and white indentured servants and convicts (their terms of service typically were twice as long as that of the indentured servant), were busy in numerous productive and economic arenas meant to provide maintenance for residents and to produce wealth for white landholders and proprietors. The latter were anxious to achieve financial success and believed that the colony could produce profit through agrarian endeavors – grapes, tobacco, cotton, olives, ginger, and indigo. Cattle, however, proved to be initially most important and many of the Africans brought to the colony, and other southern colonies as well, were skilled in the open-grazing method used in Carolina.[86] It was rice, however, that would prove to be the cash crop that was hoped for by white Carolina settlers and investors. It was rice as well that led to the rapid increase of the colony's slave population. By 1708, the colony had a black majority – the only one on the British mainland of North America to do so.

The growing number of slaves was accompanied by the development of slave laws to guide the institution's function and the treatment of slave property. South Carolina's slave laws were similar to those found in Barbados and Jamaica. Barbados had established in 1661, in "An Act for the Better Ordering and Governing of Negroes," that slaves were property; that there would be no tolerance of a slave's physical aggression toward "any Christian"; that no master would be held "liable" if a slave was killed while his or her master was attempting to mete out punishment; and that, unlike Englishmen, slaves being "brutish" had no right to trial by a jury "of twelve men of their peers." In no manner, therefore, were slaves to be equal to Englishmen, or women, before the law.[87] The Jamaican Act of 1684 was perhaps even more influential in South Carolina, leading one historian to conclude that the South Carolina Assembly, in comprising their slave code in 1691, "copied" it "almost word for word."[88] This act, among other things, reiterated the property element of slaves, instituted guidelines for fugitive slaves and, perhaps most importantly, substituted the word "Christian" for "white."[89] South Carolina's 1691 slave code, and later ones established through the early eighteenth century, included all of these elements of institutional design, control of slave property, and the rights that whites, and masters in particular, had with regard to their black bondswomen and men as they tried to manage their expanding slave population and reliance on black labor.

Congo/Angolan men and women were dominant among the imports to South Carolina/Georgia (the "Lowcountry") during the colonial era. Forty percent of the Africans from the western central region arriving in North America were enslaved in South Carolina. Indeed, before 1739, 70 percent of South Carolina's African labor force was from this area.[90] Unlike Virginia, South Carolinians imported few Igbo, only about 5 percent.[91] South Carolina masters, in particular, seemed to fear what they believed was the prevalence of suicide among Igbo. They did, however, import quite impressive numbers from Sierra Leone (Mende, Temme, Kissi) and Senegambia (Bamana and Wolof). Senegambians, in fact, eventually represented about 20 percent of those enslaved. Sierra Leoneans were important as well. Combined with enslaved people from Senegambia, they comprised approximately 12 percent of South Carolina's Africans arriving in the 1730s, 54 percent in the middle decades, and an impressive 64 percent by the time of the American Revolution.[92] Like masters in the Chesapeake, as well as in Louisiana and Florida, Lowcountry planters advised their agents that they wanted tall, healthy males between the ages of 14 and 18, with very dark skin and blemish-free bodies. For these "ideal" physical types, eighteenth-century planters paid, on average, between £100 and £200 sterling, which in today's money would be between US$11,630 and US$23,200.

Senegambians and the Congolese-Angolans also dominated the African immigrant population in French Louisiana, comprising 30 and 35.4 percent respectively of those enslaved in the region. Other significant numbers of Louisiana-bound Africans came from the Bight of Benin, principally from among the Fon-Ewe-Yoruba peoples. The estimated 26.2 percent who arrived during the latter half of the eighteenth century clearly distinguished the ethnic makeup of Louisiana's enslaved population from those in the Chesapeake and the Lowcountry. Slaves from Sierra Leone comprised 5.3 percent of the African population in Louisiana; those from the Gold Coast only about 1.1 percent; and the Igbo about 8.6 percent.[93]

It is important to consider the development of cultural and communal patterns among the slaves. Culture is defined broadly here as a panorama of responses of a community and its members to the various forces within their society, and the multiple and complex attributes of that society itself. It also touches on the related concerns of how to identify, understand, and, most importantly, control that culture. Scholars have debated issues regarding slave culture and cultural retention for decades. Perhaps the most famous episode in this discourse was ignited by Melville J. Herskovits's classic monograph, *The Myth of the Negro Past*, published in 1941.[94] It appeared at a time when most American social scientists, black and white, did not believe that Africans, as US slaves, had retained any significant attributes of their African cultures. Herskovits argued otherwise. As such, much of the discussion of early black culture revolves around the debate on African retention. Atlantic-world anthropologists Sidney Mintz and Richard Price, for example, argued in 1972 that: "No group, no matter how well-equipped or how free to choose, can transfer its way of life and the accompanying beliefs and values intact from one locale to another. The conditions of transfer, as well as the characteristics of the host setting, both human and material, will inevitably limit the variety and strength of effective transfers."[95]

Allen Kulikoff, in his 1984 classic study of the colonial Chesapeake, *Tobacco and Slaves*, outlined three stages of cultural change and development for Africans: assimilation due to small numbers spread over large distances; cultural conflict during the period of concentrated importation of large numbers of Africans to much more focused locales; and cultural creation – the development of a new black creole culture that was widely inclusive. A host of Chesapeake scholars of Kulikoff's and later generations, including Lorena Walsh, Russell Menard, Darrett and Anita Rutman, as well as Philip Morgan and Ira Berlin, whose expertise expands much beyond the Chesapeake, have largely adhered to this pattern.[96]

Mechal Sobel, Peter Wood, Gwendolyn Midlo Hall, Daniel Littlefield, Charles Joyner, Margaret Washington, Michael Gomez, Douglas Chambers, Albert Raboteau, John Thornton, Joseph Holloway, Sterling Stuckey, and other historians – to say nothing of at least three generations of sociocultural anthropologists, folklorists, ethnomusicologists, archeologists, material culture scholars, and African historians and art historians – have contributed mightily to this discussion.[97] Gomez notes, for example, that "The African American represents an amalgam of the ethnic matrix; that is, the African American identity is in fact a composite of identities. In certain areas and periods of time, the composite approached a uniform whole.... But for other times and locations, the composite was fragmented and incomplete."[98] The end result was a "polycultural" phenomenon of which "the African antecedent would inform every aspect."[99]

Slaveholders, whether in the American South, Latin America, or the Caribbean, understood that enslaved blacks, African and creole, had cultural attributes and attitudes that were distinct and Africa-derived. Some traits masters viewed as oppositional to their New World social, cultural, and economic priorities. Other African cultural traits, knowledge, and work experience, however, American masters believed worthwhile, even necessary, to their economic success. Slaveholder recognition of these African-derived cultures not only informed their "preferences" for bondspeople from distinct African "ethnicities" or western/central African locales, but also influenced colonial legal codes and customs meant to control and/or destroy African cultural attributes that they regarded as threatening. Slave masters, for example, were particularly concerned with cultural expressions that they believed might unite the enslaved against the slave regime – physically, psychologically, spiritually, and, therefore, politically. These cultural attributes included ritualized group meetings for the expression of slave religious beliefs, funerals, masquerades, and political elections. Masters were similarly opposed to the slaves' use of coded forms of African-derived communications, such as languages, secular stories and jokes, religious tales, and drumming, fearing – rightfully so – that they hid or, at the very least, encouraged resistance plots.[100]

Other evidence of slaveholder recognition of African-based cultural traits is suggested by their exploitation of enslaved people's productive skills, particularly in the realms of agriculture, fishing, textile, domestic object production, medicine, and carpentry. African women's labor experiences and skills were as important as, if not more so than, those of men in the predominantly agrarian economies of the Americas. Indeed, studies of African women residing in areas drawn on by the Atlantic slave trade have emphasized their productive capacities in their indigenous communities. Claire Robertson and Martin Klein assert, for example, that "there is no reason to suspect that in pre-colonial time [African] women did not perform most of the agricultural work ... [and] the more labor-intensive work. Thus slave women weeded, or spun thread for male weavers' use."[101] Slave masters in the Lowcountry rice-producing areas of South Carolina and Georgia were particularly interested in acquiring women, and men, from the "grain" coast of West Africa (Liberia and Sierra Leone). Colonial masters soon realized that Africans not only brought with them the capacity to do a great deal of physical labor, but also valuable experience as agriculturalists, hunters, fishermen, miners, carpenters, spinners, midwives, healers, cooks, and childcare providers. Masters privileged that which they could exploit to their own advantage and suppressed that which seemed threatening, consistently imposing external pressures on enslaved people, their cultural development and community formation. In so doing, they left behind for historians a dense description of traditional African ideals, beliefs, and practices that they witnessed enslaved people embracing and perpetuating in one form or another.[102]

The debate regarding the culture of African slaves and their descendants regularly moves back and forth from the particular – the feasibility of single or even collective (that is, cultural complex) indicators of west and central African cultures that blacks actively employed or that were at least recognized by them – to the more general and philosophical – the "cultural" identities of enslaved people and how, when, why, and for whom that identity changed over time.[103] While scholars have not agreed on an effective manner in which to identify and "measure" cultural retention or the rate and directions of change, the process by which culture, within the context of slavery – and resistance to it – evolved over time, or even if the discussion of cultural retention should have taken up as much historiographical energy as it has, they have agreed on certain methodological steps essential to this fraught discourse.

Scholars recognize, for example, the importance of slaveholder and enslaved demography, cultural histories, and various planes and structures of interaction. One needs to know details of African provenance, the locales, language groups, or identifiable ethnicities from which enslaved people came. One also needs to have command of the actual numbers and the percentages of African ethnic groups living and working within localized slave societies; the size, cultures, and managerial styles of the interactive and/or adjacent

European and European American populations; and compre-
hend interactions as well with indigenous New World populations. Then one must understand the cultures of the various
African groups from which the enslaved were derived and
be able to identify – philosophically, structurally, and stylisti-
cally at least – these cultural traits and attitudes as they
reemerged in individual African American behavior, households, and/or communities. Likewise, one must have some
knowledge of the manner in which "culture," in the contributing African groups, was "traditionally" transmitted verti-
cally and horizontally; be able to elucidate in particular the
kinds of forces, external and internal, that had impact; and
understand when, how, and to what extent this impact was
operative and when it was resisted. Gender and one's generation, of course, certainly must also be considered.

Much of the discussion of African cultural retention in the
mainland British colonies that proposes a lengthy tradition
of west/central African lingering cultural influence has centered on the black majority of slaves in South Carolina,
particularly those who were located along the rice-producing
coastline and small islands that actually extended from what
is now Fayetteville, North Carolina, to northern Florida and
parts of the Everglades. Scholars such as John Blassingame,
Michael Gomez, Douglas Chambers, Walter Rucker, and
Gwendolyn Midlo Hall, among others, however, have also
argued for extensive influence in other areas.[104]

The Gullah, also known as the Geechee, derived from an
intense period of importation during the eighteenth century
of large numbers of Africans (more than 50,000) from specific, culturally linked, ethnic groups from Senegambia, Sierra
Leone, and Liberia, among whom were the Djolas, Wolof,
Serer, Mandinga, Mende, Temme, and Vai. These slaves,
lowcountry coastal region, derived a unique culture that
included a language, religious rituals, artistic forms (pottery,
basket weaving, and carving, for example), naming practices,
textiles, fishing nets and techniques, food preparation, work
tools like the mortar and pestles used to remove the hull off
rice, musical styles, and age-grade initiations linked to their
African cultural antecedents. They were able to do so not
only because of their large numbers, physical isolation, and

indigenous cultural characteristics, but also because there were few whites in residence to force them to assimilate European ways and words, or at least to give up their African ones. Because whites believed that this malaria-infested, hot and humid region was unhealthy for them, large numbers did not reside in the region and masters were often absent for several months at a time, hoping to avoid the oppressively hot spring, summer, and fall seasons. They believed that their slaves were "immune" to malaria – an assumption that was only partially correct. Many slaves imported from the Windward (Rice/Grain) Coast of Sierra Leone and Liberia actually carried the sickle-cell trait that partially protected them from malaria. Those inflicted with the debilitating and painful disease of sickle cell, however, undoubtedly suffered mightily from the harsh work routine that owners maintained on these plantations. Even today, part of the language that they spoke in the eighteenth and nineteenth centuries is retained and, with it, words from original African languages as well as Sierra Leone Krio. Some words still used by the Gullah include: *joso*, which means "witchcraft," from the Mende *njoso*, or forest spirit; *gafa*, or "evil spirit," from the Mende *ngafa*, or masked "devil"; *wanga*, defined as "charm," from the Temne word *an-wanka* that translates as fetish or "swear"; *bento*, "coffin," from the Temne word *an-bento*, signifying bier; *defu* or "rice flour," from the Vai word *defu*, which also means rice flour; *do* or "child," from the Mende *ndo*, which also denotes child; and *kome*, "to gather," from the Mende word *kome*, which is a meeting.[105]

The culture(s) of those enslaved in the South, as in the middle and northern colonies, of course, evolved, or was retained or lost, against the backdrop of a life filled with work, resistance, and the continual struggle to maintain a meaningful social existence, particularly kin relations. Export markets, for the most part, drove slave labor.

In the Chesapeake, tobacco production occupied most of the time and efforts of enslaved agricultural workers, although a minority labored in grain production and domestic and skilled service that was similar in regimen and responsibility to slaves in the middle and northern colonies. Tobacco exports increased from 65,000 pounds annually in the 1620s to 20 million pounds annually by the end of the 1670s.[106] Tobacco cultivation was especially essential to the colonial economies of Virginia and Maryland, but was also important in Carolina, especially in the northern and piedmont regions. This crop, while certainly not nearly as important as sugar in the Caribbean, also was grown in seventeenth-century Barbados and Jamaica, as well as in Brazil and other sites in the Americas.

Tobacco farms and plantations could differ in size tremendously, given the land and labor resources of the owner, the quality or "grade" of the tobacco produced and how welcoming the fickle English market proved to be. While the average farmer had only a few hundred acres, landholdings could be much smaller or a good deal larger. Both the size of one's labor force and of one's family affected the size of one's farm since most seventeenth-century landholders received land grants as a reward for importation of persons through the headright system, typically 50 acres per imported person – free, servant, or slave.

Whatever the size of the tobacco field, farm, or plantation, the labor needed to bring a crop to harvest and then to sale was intensive. In order to produce tobacco, as other crops, land had first to be cleared of dense forest. Slaves cleared fields and created new ones in the early winter. Workers girded trees to kill them, burned the smaller trees and bushes, and planted the seed in the rich topsoil that was produced when it was mixed with the ash. They then made this soil into planting beds. Slaves planted seeds in winter and transplanted the individual seedlings to individual hills in the early spring. They spent the rest of the spring and most of the summer tending to the maturing plants, weeding, pulling off the lower growing leaves and suckers, and killing pests, such as the hated hornworm. Along the many rivers and waterways of the Chesapeake where the largest tobacco plantations were located, late summer harvest came with temperatures in the high nineties with correspondingly high humidity. At harvest, pickers hand-cut each leaf, then hung, dried, and cured it, before they sorted, prized, and packed it into barrels for shipment. Adult, or prime, workers could be responsible for six to ten thousand tobacco plants (one to two acres) per growing season; child workers tended to work half that amount.[107] Many tobacco farm slaves worked in small groups or "gangs," but only if their master's workforce was comprised of enough workers to divide the labor in this way. When they were not tending to tobacco, there were the corn, potatoes, berries, and fruit trees to mind, livestock to tend to, fences, roads, shipping barrels, outhouses and barns to build and mend, woodcutting, blacksmithing, sewing, spinning, and weaving, soap and candle making, dairying, cooking and cleaning, and other routine chores to perform.

While tobacco dominated the work routines of many Chesapeake-area slaves, wheat and other grain production became increasingly important in this locale during the eighteenth century. Many farmers and planters grew both since wheat was sown and grown during the down season of tobacco. It was sown in the fall (after the tobacco harvest) and cut in July, after the labor-intensive moving of tobacco seedlings had been completed. Wheat harvest, comprised of cutting, stacking, and threshing, which was the most labor-intensive aspect of the crop, lasted only two weeks. However, wheat production did not translate into less work for slaves. Planters and farmers were determined that their black workers not remain idle. George Washington, who began to transition from tobacco to wheat production before the American Revolution, for example, demanded that his slaves be "at their work as soon as it is light – work 'till it is dark – and be diligent while they are at it..." so that "every Labourer does as much in the 24 hours as their strength, without endangering their health, or constitution, will allow of."[108]

The most important crop produced south of the tobacco fields of the Chesapeake was rice, followed by indigo. While tobacco required only two to three workers if the farm, resources, and ambitions of its owner were small, rice production required large numbers of workers for a successful operation. The average farming slaveholder in the Chesapeake colonies of Virginia and Maryland, for example, owned between 8.5 and 13 slaves.[109] The largest colonial tobacco plantations, like that of George Washington's Mount Vernon estate in Fairfax County, Virginia, for example, were actually divided into a number of separate farms with ten to fifteen prime workers per tract.[110] On the largest rice plantations, where the land was divided into small tracts to facilitate the task system of labor, many more slaves resided. The average slaveholder in the rice-growing Lowcountry at the end of the colonial period held thirty-three slaves. The largest slaveholders, such as three members of the Horry family in the like-named county who owned 779 in total, were responsible for a workforce that produced an overall population much more like the slave-dominated Caribbean than found elsewhere in most of the mainland. While Virginia continued to have the largest numbers of enslaved persons by a wide margin, South Carolina's population remained more black than white throughout the era (see Table 3.3).

Rice production was centered along the coasts and islands of South Carolina and Georgia. It was a long and laborious process, usually lasting twelve to fourteen months from start to a harvest processed for sale. Slaves cleared marsh lands in January and February by cutting trees and burning brush and then built embankments of about 6 feet tall and 15 feet wide, a tremendous movement of earth. Enslaved workers then built canals around the embankments and hanging "trunks" that controlled the flow of tidal waters into the fields. Once fields, embankments, and canals were built (they also had to be routinely repaired), slaves had to plant, hoe, and weed the rice crop, about three acres each – working much of the time in ankle-deep water filled with mosquitoes, snakes, and sometimes alligators. Planting took place from April to June. Hoeing and weeding occupied their time from June to August. Rice slaves worked on the task system, where each prime worker usually was assigned from a quarter to a half acre of rice to work daily.[111] Harvest began in September and meant cutting, drying, tying, and carrying the bundles of wheat stalks to the stackyard. After further drying, slaves threshed and milled. The milling process, which slaves performed between November and mid-winter, was a labor-intensive mortar and pestle process, followed by winnowing, sifting, and polishing the rice. By the time of the American Revolution, some planters were using both wind fans and pounding machines, both livestock- and water-powered, to help with rice processing, thus relieving some of the backbreaking labor of slaves employed in post-rice harvest processing during the colonial era.[112]

When it was not necessary to tend the rice fields closely, many of the same Lowcountry planters, as well as those residing in East Florida, turned their slaves to indigo production since, given their complementary growing and harvesting schedules, both could be produced on the same plantation by the same workforce. Indigo production was particularly important in the second half of the eighteenth century, when the number of pounds exported increased tenfold to one million in 1775.[113]

Sowing began in April, and the indigo harvest occurred in July and August. Each slave was responsible for growing approximately four acres. Slaves planted and weeded the crop, then cut its leaves at harvest. Preparation of the popular dye then moved to large vats: one for fermentation; one for stirring; and one for creating limewater to be mixed in during the last stage of preparation.[114] In order to remove the dark blue color, slaves first soaked the leaves in water and beat the liquid while it fermented. The fermentation period required 24-hour surveillance so that the necessary limewater could be added at precisely the right moment. The solution was allowed to settle, and slaves then scooped out the solid matter, strained, shaped it and cut it into squares. Processing typically ended before November.[115]

Sometimes slaves, either in gangs or on the task system, were able to work alongside their family members. As the enslaved population grew in the eighteenth century, both north and south, and especially with the increase in the number of enslaved women, marriages and families began to develop. Enslaved persons, of course, did not arrive in the "New World" without their own distinct notions of family and community, some of which they recorded in their autobiographical accounts and which certainly influenced the kinds of family structures, relations, and ideals they sought, even as slaves. Before arriving in the early 1730s' Maryland, Ayuba Suleiman Diallo (also known as Job Ben Solomon), for example, left a Malinke family that was elite, patriarchal, extended, and polygamous. Fathers were responsible for passing on skill and knowledge to their sons, as did Diallo's – teaching him Arabic and lessons of the Qur'an. Adult sons, in turn, helped their fathers with their work. Both males and females married early. Job was fifteen when he married his

3.2 A Virginia tobacco field
Source: Wikimedia Commons

3.3 A South Carolina rice field
Source: Wikimedia Commons

first wife, who was eleven. Fathers arranged marriages, and the groom's father had to provide a hefty dowry for the bride. Once married, women remained veiled for three years and were expected to be pious and modest. Polygamous husbands divided their time equally between their wives' households. Job's first marriage produced three sons; his second wife had a daughter. Communities celebrated the important occasion of a child's birth with naming ceremonies. Husbands and wives could separate, but only with substantial reason and sometimes with serious consequence for the wife if she initiated the separation.[116]

James Albert Ukawsaw Gronniosaw, who too was born a Muslim, and probably Hausa, in northeastern Nigeria but was enslaved in Dutch American households in mid-eighteenth-century New York City. He described his West African family and community as tight-knit with highly structured, stratified social and cultural institutions in which an individual knew his or her station and how to behave in it. In Ukawsaw's family, for example, the pinnacle of power was located in kingship and his grandfather was the king. Power then flowed downward through this royal family to his father, mother, older siblings, and finally servants. It was a rich social world where children were to obey their elders and, in turn, parents and older kin supported their children materially and emotionally. Family members were expected to be emotionally close and, while children were not to question their parents, mothers and fathers were not tyrants. The values and behaviors of Ukawsaw's larger Bornu community mirrored those of his family. Friends were supposed to be kind and loyal, while community members demonstrated public respect for operative political and social hierarchies and worshipped and marked other important communal events together.[117]

Diallo and Gronniosaw, like most of those men, women, and children enslaved in British North America, came from complete and complex social networks with clearly defined familial and communal roles determined by age, gender, and station. What they encountered in the colonies clearly was different, diverse, and anything but stable. Small numbers of enslaved persons in the colonial period combined with a scarcity of females of marriageable age (65 percent of the imports were males); significant cultural differences (among them: Muslim vs Catholic vs indigenous religions; matrilineal vs. patrilineal; polygamous vs monogamous; agrarian vs nomadic vs urban and linguistic differences, for example); and suffering from high mortality and low fertility. These conditions certainly limited the ability of enslaved people to recreate the communal and familial structures, relations, rituals, and obligations they experienced in central and western Africa. In the Chesapeake, the relatively small size of slave holdings added to the difficulty, and few owners wanted their slaves to move beyond the boundaries of their farms and plantations to establish marriages or communities abroad. As Allen Kulikoff notes, "as late as the 1730s, plantations were not conducive places in which to create a settled social life" because of the small numbers of slaves located on them.[118]

What one found during the late seventeenth and early eighteenth centuries then were growing numbers of long-term emotionally and physically connected relationships and some instances of children having been born to couples, but there was no significant pattern of domestic alliance. There were, for example, instances of nuclear and extended households, fictive kin residences and residential buildings with single male adults. The continual influx of Africans via the very active eighteenth-century slave trade contributed to the difficulty of creating slave families since the new arrivals, throughout the British mainland colonies, had to acclimatize to their new social, legal, linguistic, work, and health environments before it was possible for most to establish marital, blood, or even fictive relations. South Carolina continued to import large numbers of Africans after mid-century compared to other colonies, even Virginia, and this had, relatively speaking, a significant impact on social and cultural life.[119] Charley Barber of South Carolina, for example, recalled that both his grandparents had been born in Africa, could speak to one another, and had other similar cultural traits, but found it difficult to communicate with or culturally connect with others.[120] There is evidence as well that some creole women preferred creole men and that some African men preferred African women and friends. Even in the antebellum era, after the legal slave trade had ended (1808), for example, Charles Ball of Calvert, Maryland made note of his African grandfather's preferences – he had contempt for "African Americans" because of the elevated "rank" he had held "in his native land."[121] Ball's grandfather did, however, welcome relations with his son and grandson, often taking the young Charles to stay with him in his cabin.[122]

Many of the newly arrived enslaved escaped as soon as they could, hoping to find a way back to their families in Africa. Most searched for linguistic and cultural compatriots with whom they could commune. In 1745, for example, the *Virginia Gazette* ran an advertisement for "Sambo" who "speaks English so as to be understood; who absconded with Aaron and Berwick, neither of whom knew English. According to their master, They are all new Negros and went together; they have not been above 8 months in the Country." That same year, two skilled artisans who originally were from "Madagascar" also ran away together, taking with them a "country-born" domestic by the name of Spark. Although the two men from Madagascar had been in Virginia for some time, they undoubtedly still retained a connection to their cultural past and, therefore, to each other. Spark, a domestic whom they probably worked near and lived with (many single men lived in the same quarters), clearly had become part of this fictive kin network. Roger, an Angola-born slave, on the other hand, ran away with his country-born slave wife who, at the time, was "very big with child," perhaps wanting to start their family together as free rather than enslaved.[123] The dangers to family remaining a physically tied unit were clear enough to inspire flight.

Colonial slave owners certainly did not hesitate to divide kin groups through sale, inheritance, or gifts for the benefit of their own families. Slaves were valuable property and, while slave marriages produced children who enhanced the wealth of masters, owners often exercised the right to destroy slave families if it proved financially prudent to do so. The death of a master, in particular, meant loss and dispersal for slave families and slave communities since owners typically divided their slave property among their heirs, regardless of the impact on slave family ties. The result was the retention of bits and pieces of family units only. At his death in 1745, for example, John Andrew of Charleston County in South Carolina left to "his beloved Daughter Ann and to her heirs

forever my Negro Judith and her Child Peg with my two
Negro Children Bob and Maria."[124] Upon his death in 1761,
Barnaby McKinny of Halifax County, North Carolina
decided that his

> [B]eloved wife Ann during her natural life [should have] a negro
> woman called Moll and three negro children to wit Chesser, Gibb
> and Juno and after my wife's decease I will that my wife's son Isaac
> Ricks have the afs[d] negro named Gibb to negro Woman Moll afs[d]
> to my sister Patience McKinnie...the negro called Juno afs[d] to my
> wife's daughter Mary Ricks...the negro called Chesser afs[d] to my
> sister Martha McKinnie.[125]

In 1764, Thomas Potts, a wealthy planter in Craven County,
South Carolina, divided his thirteen slaves (and the future
increase of his female slaves) among his children and grand-
children with no regard to slave family ties. He also left
instructions to purchase future slaves out of his estate.[126]

These escape records and last wills and testaments clearly
affirm that there were some African men and women who
married and had children before the middle of the eighteenth
century. The large influx of slaves during the eighteenth
century, before and after the American Revolution, might
have, as Kulikoff and others suggest, stirred the cultural and
communal pots of slave communities, but it also eventually
meant greater availability for couples to form, marriages to
take place, and children to be born. Groups of family units in
the quarters led to the development of communities and
fictive kin possibilities for single adults, orphaned children,
and the elderly. A denser slave population in general also
meant greater interaction between plantations and farms,
leading to area-wide slave social networks. Social gatherings,
many clandestine but some approved of by masters, particularly during harvest and holiday seasons, meant dances, court-
ship rituals, religious meetings, storytelling, and funerals.

While creolized ideals of enslaved black family life are
difficult to discern, given the lack of firsthand accounts from
the pre-Revolutionary era, some examples are available.
David George, who eventually fought in the American Revolution, for one, lived with his parents and siblings in Essex
County, Virginia before the war. His memories were filled
with painful scars of the physical torture of his kin – his sister

whipped, his brother's back whipped raw and rubbed in salt. "The greatest grief I then had," David explained, "was to see them whip my mother, and to hear her, on her knees, begging for mercy." David escaped, but eventually was re-enslaved in South Carolina, where he married. He wrote lovingly of his wife and children, and his desire, as a father and husband, to safeguard and provide for them. He also spoke of his community – a diverse social network that at times included Creeks and Nautchees native peoples, as well as persons from local free black and slave communities. According to his narrative, they all provided him some material relief, emotional comfort, and advice in times of crisis.[127]

Much of the narrative information regarding colonial black family life is embedded in documents that speak to acts of slave resistance. This is not surprising, given that slave resistance was an everyday occurrence in colonial life. Indeed, family, community, culture, and working conditions all situated the presence, and persistence, of numerous forms of resistance among slaves. Enslaved persons took the opportunity to resist their status, ill-treatment, and displacement in every way possible, including armed struggle and individual acts of physical, cultural, and psychological resistance. The Americas, along with the Caribbean, were rife with slave resistance, marronage, sabotage, rebellion, and revolution, and the mainland colonies were no exception. Some of this resistance represented multiple racial-group participation as witnessed, for example, in escapes of persons of varied African ethnicity, along with indigenous American slaves and white indentured servants. The plot to burn New York in 1741–2 implicated slaves, free blacks, and whites, as did Bacon's Rebellion in Virginia in 1676. Still, most of the resistance associated with slaves was fundamentally an attempt to gain black relief from white oppression. Although there were rumors of dozens of slave revolt plots in the British North American colonies, two actual events of armed resistance have been documented: the New York Slave Revolt of 1712 (discussed earlier); and the Stono, South Carolina Rebellion of September 1739.

In the early morning of September 9, 1739, a group of slaves, one of whom was named Cato and many whose African provenance has been determined as Angolan, attacked two white shopkeepers and robbed Hutchenson's warehouse at Stono Bridge, about 20 miles from Charleston. Scholars assert that these slaves intended to try to gain their freedom by escaping to Spanish Florida, a real possibility given the sanctuary that Spain provided fugitives from the British colonies. At the warehouse, the slaves armed themselves with weapons and took other supplies, leaving the two shopkeepers to die. As word of the attack spread, blacks joined the resistance effort and whites armed themselves to put down the rebellion. Ultimately, approximately twenty-one whites and forty-four blacks were killed, and the white community prevailed. Those blacks who were captured, tried, and found guilty were killed, and their heads placed on poles as a warning to others who might consider open rebellion. As in New York, the long-term effect of the revolt at Stono River was the implementation of a harsher slave code.[128]

Armed revolt, while capturing the imagination of many of the enslaved and free, was far from the typical form of colonial, or for that matter antebellum, slave resistance. On a daily basis, many slaves decided not to work and to undermine the authority of white masters, mistresses, managers, and overseers. Men and women feigned illness, broke work tools, implemented work slowdowns and stoppages, destroyed crops, burnt food, stole goods and livestock, refused orders, talked back, fought back with slaps, kicks and punches, and attacked with any available object that could inflict bodily harm. Retribution for disorderly or rebellious slaves was swift and harsh, even deadly at times, as codified in custom and law. Massachusetts authorities executed a slave woman in 1681, for example, for arson; Virginia did so in 1705; and North Carolina in 1766. Indeed, more than 35 slave women were executed for some form of resistance, typically murder, in the British mainland colonies. Women controlled their reproductive powers and took advantage of their physical intimacy with whites through gendered labor, as child-rearers of their masters' offspring and cooks, with maddening forms of resistance – refusing to have children themselves, harming those of their masters for whom they were given charge, and poisoning all whites who ate the food they prepared.[129] Short-term escape was particularly prevalent among these "troublesome" people, but the colonial newspapers were largely funded by paid notices for the capture and return of long-term fugitives. The numbers indicate a gendered pattern – decidedly more men (two-thirds of the total) than women escaped. This is not surprising, given that women were reluctant either to run away with children or to leave them behind. In addition, it was much more common for a man than a woman to be on the road running some errand for his master or being sent out to work, which could be used as a cover for escape. The "typical" creole runaway was young, male, sometimes skilled, and lived close to an urban center or seaport where he could pass for free and gain some employment, or could escape by sea to a destination where fewer questions regarding his status would be raised. The "typical" African escapee was also male, but he usually sought a place of marronage, that is, a geospatially isolated locale (mountains, dense forests, swamps) to join with other like-minded "outlandish" slaves in order to create a free society of their own. The most successful and long-term maroons were established outside of British North America in Jamaica, Brazil, Suriname, French Guiana, Veracruz, and Peru. Still, maroon societies of escaped slaves existed both north and south in the mainland colonies, but perhaps were most "notorious" in the Great Dismal Swamp, which extended from Virginia south to Florida, the Appalachian Mountains, and the Florida Everglades.[130]

Slavery in the Age of the American Revolution and the Early Republic

One of the most significant opportunities that enslaved men and women had to escape bondage presented itself during the era of the American Revolution. The ideals of the Revolution – "freedom from tyranny" – appealed to enslaved blacks throughout the thirteen mainland colonies. But their political consciousness, centered on their desire for freedom and equality, was demonstrated in their resistance initiatives long before, and after, the heated speeches of the white revolutionaries reached their ears. Nonetheless, African Americans listened carefully to the revolutionary rhetoric of the patriots, hoping that they could benefit from this discourse on the natural rights of mankind.

In the southern colonies, many enslaved persons believed that the additional British militia forces were there not only to police the patriots but to liberate them as well. Others sided with white patriots who they hoped would extend their ideals of liberty to black bondsmen and women. Slaves in Charleston, for example, held their own protest in 1765 after whites held a parade to oppose the Stamp Act. Ten years later, Thomas Jeremiah, a wealthy free black Charlestonian who owned land and slaves, became the target of suspicion that he was aligning himself with loyalists and trying to incite slaves to rebel against their masters in support of the British. The fear that the majority slave population in South Carolina would rise up against their masters as they had in the Stono Rebellion led, in part, to Thomas Jeremiah's defeat in court and a death sentence. Hanged and then burned on August 18, 1775, Jeremiah became one of the first southern "loyalists" to be publicly executed. Five years earlier in Massachusetts, Crispus Attucks, a fugitive slave who had lived for years clandestinely as a free man, was the first to die in the early skirmishes between patriots and the British militia. He and four others were killed during the multiracial Boston massacre of March 5, 1770.[131] Attucks and the others who fell with him became instant martyrs to the cause, their names often invoked as evidence of British brutality and disregard for colonists.

Enslaved black males, who had been called on to militarily defend their masters and other whites in times of violent crises, knew that their ability to fight was a valuable asset, perhaps valuable enough to wrest them, and their families, from slavery. They served as soldiers, scouts, wagoners, and workers for British forces during the Seven Years War, receiving honors for their service at Forts Duquesne, Cumberland, and the Plains of Abraham near Quebec.[132] In the American Revolution, both slave and free blacks fought in the first ground and naval skirmishes between the British and colonists, primarily on the side of the patriots. Peter Salem and Salem Poor, for example, both fought at Bunker Hill. Freedom and equality were their ultimate political goals, but there was no certainty that they would receive it. Still, there was a brooding controversy, on both sides of the struggle, over the inclusion of blacks in the war effort and what would be their reward as a result of bearing arms.

General George Washington was a Virginia slaveholder who was acutely aware that large slaveholding colonists in Virginia and South Carolina, in particular but not exclusively, were opposed to arming their slaves or free blacks for fear that these efforts would lead to widespread slave insurrection. Indeed, many of the leading patriots, or founding fathers, were slaveholders – large slaveholders. George Washington and his wife Martha collectively owned more than 200 slaves at the time of the Revolution and 316 at the time of the nation's first president's death in 1799. Washington's slave property ownership began at the age of ten when he inherited eleven slaves from his father. By the time he was twenty-two, his slave property had increased to thirty-six.[133] George Mason, Washington's neighbor whose Declaration of Rights for Virginia became the blueprint for the nation's Bill of Rights, held scores of slaves at his Gunston Hall Plantation. Thomas Jefferson, the principal author of the Declaration of Independence, owned more than 100 slaves at the time of the Revolution and more than 200 at his death in 1826, most of whom were sold to pay his debts. Although Jefferson went on to draft bills that would have ended slavery in Virginia had they been approved by that state's legislature, his famous 1781 essay, *Notes on the State of Virginia* (first published anonymously in 1785), clearly documents that his distaste for the institution centered on his fear of its negative impact on whites and white society, not on the enslaved.[134] Charles Carroll of Maryland, the only Catholic signer of the Declaration of Independence, was one of the largest slaveholders in North America, with more than 400 bonded blacks at the time of the Revolution. Richard Henry Lee of Virginia, who chaired the Continental Congress committee that assigned the writing of the Declaration of Independence, owned more than fifty slaves.[135] Henry Laurens, a slave trader and rice planter from South Carolina and president of the Second Continental Congress, had one of the largest slaveholdings in the Lowcountry.[136] And the list goes on and on. While some of the patriots, most famously Jefferson and Mason, were ambivalent about the institution of slavery, all agreed that blacks were fundamentally different, and inferior, to whites. They had no vision of a new nation where the two races lived equally, despite their idealist phrasing regarding the natural rights of mankind in the Declaration of Independence, the Bill of Rights, or the Constitution. Most resisted the enlistment of blacks in their military efforts that might mean freedom for slaves or expanded rights for free blacks. British officials initially refused black military recruits as well.

At the beginning of 1775, blacks in southeastern Virginia appealed to Royal Governor John Murray Dunmore in Williamsburg, saying that they would fight on his behalf if he would guarantee their freedom. Dunmore rejected the idea outright, threatening to have them whipped if they returned with a similar request. By the summer of that year, however, Dunmore was in dire straits. In July 1775, Joseph Harris, a black waterman from Hampton who knew the tidewater waterways well, again offered assistance, and Dunmore did not turn him down. Harris helped in the Battle of Hampton in October, the first southern military event of the Revolution. Surrounded by patriots, Dunmore had already fled the governor's palace in Williamsburg for the ship *William* out in the Norfolk Harbor. On November 7, he issued his soon to be infamous Proclamation which read in part: "I do...hereby declare free all indentured servants, Negroes or others...free that are able and willing to bear arms, they joining his MAJESTY's troops." The result was immediate – throes of able-bodied slave men, their wives, and children began to leave farms and plantations to attempt to get to Dunmore. Men fought while their wives and other female family members worked as laundresses, seamstresses, nurses, and cooks. A week later, Dunmore's largely black force defeated the patriots at the Battle of Kemp's Landing.[137]

Virginia's whites, including George Washington, were outraged. They promised death to any slave who fought for Dunmore unless he immediately returned to his master. Despite their threats, however, many enslaved believed freedom was worth the risk of death. As a result of the black response to Dunmore's Proclamation, General Washington had to reverse his exclusion of blacks from the patriot military forces, promising those who fought freedom as well. Four years later, British General Henry Clinton issued another emancipatory decree – the Philipsburg Proclamation – which not only freed all those who served in the British military, but also all of those slaves owned by American patriots, promising land and protection to all who left their masters.[138] Almost 10,000 enslaved persons, many from Virginia and South Carolina in particular – no surprise given the large numbers of bondspeople in those colonies – fought for the British. Thousands more absconded, not to fight necessarily, but to try to gain freedom on their own terms, in Spanish Florida or elsewhere. Many of them were women, who refused to be left out of the bid for freedom, and their children. British General Clinton eventually ordered some slaves to be returned to their owners and put others to work growing food for his troops. Five thousand blacks also eventually fought for the continental army and naval forces. Maryland was the only southern colony to allow black enlistment, although slaves could take the place of their white masters in other southern states.[139]

The decision about which side to join was not an easy one to make. Most slaves decided according to the opportunity for freedom and whether or not they could trust former slaveholders to abide by the promise to free them. Thousands more used the distraction of war to escape, particularly from South Carolina and Georgia, to freedom in Spanish Florida. Dunmore's Royal Ethiopian Regiment, which had "Liberty to Slaves" embroidered on the chest of their uniforms, and the Black Brigade, recruits from New Jersey and remnants of the Ethiopian Regiment, primarily were black, but also included some immigrant whites. Others were part of the Black Pioneers.[140] Boston King, from South Carolina, recalled that he ran away from his master and joined the loyalists at Charleston in large measure because of the brutality of his owner. In King's words: To escape his cruelty, I determined to go CharlesTown, and throw myself into the hands of the English. They received me readily, and I began to feel the happiness, liberty, of which I knew nothing before, altho' I was grieved at first, to be obliged to leave my friends, and reside among strangers."[141] James Armistead, on the other hand, was a slave who provided the patriots at Yorktown with necessary information about the movements and plans of British General Cornwallis. In October 1784, the Marquis de Lafayette wrote that James Armistead performed "Essential Service" in providing "Intelligence from the Enemy's

Camp" and was "Entitled to Every Reward His Situation Can Admit of."[142]

Both Armistead, a patriot, and King, a loyalist, received their freedom as a result of their efforts in the Revolutionary War. Many did not. Although ten thousand purportedly fought for the Crown, only three thousand were able to leave with the British. While some who remained eventually gained freedom and others were able to escape to Florida, some were re-enslaved in the United States and others in the British Caribbean. Those black loyalists who actually went with the British came to reside in Canada, London, and later Sierra Leone. It was not an easy road for them. Most were immediately settled in small all-black settlements in Nova Scotia that were characterized by economic blight and external discrimination by white loyalists who had also moved to the area. The largest community was Birchtown, where approximately half of the black loyalists resided. Land for farms – they typically received 40 acres, less than whites – was notoriously of poor soil quality; unemployment rates were disproportionately high; and wages for day labor were only about 25 percent of that paid to whites for comparable work. The results were not surprising – Shelbourne's "Black Town" was the location of the first black/white race riot in North America. In the summer of 1784, as a result of white loyalist soldiers who violently chased blacks from their homes to exclude them from the local labor market, many black homes were destroyed and people dislocated. Local white resident Benjamin Marston, who had been educated at Harvard, but emigrated to Nova Scotia when the patriots turned against England, recorded the events of the riot in his diary, noting that on Monday, the 26th, there was a "great riot." The following day, Marston added: "Riot continues. The soldiers force the free negroes to quit the Town – pulled down about 20 of their houses." Many blacks had to work as indentured servants for whites or face starvation.[143]

Some black loyalists eventually decided to seek a life, livelihood, and freedom away from North America. In 1792, blacks from Nova Scotia, including Boston King and his wife Violet, sailed to Sierra Leone under the auspices of the Sierra Leone Company. They were not the first to arrive in the colony. The initial pioneers of the "back to Africa" movement, or colonization, were comprised largely of black loyalist naval forces who had been taken to England after the Revolutionary War. There, most fared as badly, socially and financially, as those in Lower Canada. Slavery was abolished in England (not its colonies) in 1772,[144] but the country did not welcome black emigrants from the United States or Canada. Many of England's staunchest supporters of abolition, including Granville Sharpe, advocated free black removal to a West African colony – Sierra Leone.

As with black colonization societies that were to be developed in the United States during the second decade of the nineteenth century, the motives of the English supporters of the Sierra Leone Company varied. Some hoped that the colony would give great economic opportunities to the impoverished black loyalists and would, as well, help the indigenous Africans (many were Temne and Mende) to embrace Christianity and other attributes of western European life and culture. Other colony backers clearly viewed the new colony as a dumping ground for undesirables, including former slaves and white prostitutes from England, some of whom were probably kidnapped and others certainly duped into going. The first attempts at settlement were not successful. There were periods of starvation for these English free blacks, unrest, epidemics; some were sold into slavery, others became part of slaving organizations, and there was destructive war with the local Temne. Still, some colony supporters sent another group of free people of color, this time from Nova Scotia, to Sierra Leone. John Clarkson was overwhelmed by the number of black loyalists who wanted the opportunity for a better life outside of North America. He had initially planned to take 500, but 1,190 sailed on January 15, 1792. It was in this group that Boston King, who had become a highly regarded minister in Nova Scotia, went to convert the indigenous peoples to Christianity. King opened a church and school, even traveling back to England to receive a more formal education to assist in achieving his goals.[145] Other freed slaves taken off illegal slave-trading vessels after 1807 by the British and returned to Africa were relocated in Sierra Leone. Those former slaves who won their freedom as a result of fighting on the side of the patriots in the Revolution, however, joined a growing number of free blacks in the new nation.[146]

Indeed, the American Revolution was quite the momentous event in the lives of enslaved blacks and for the institution of slavery in the former British mainland colonies. Free black efforts practically ended slavery in the northeast and northern plains, destabilized the institution, albeit not permanently, in the Upper South, and helped to ignite a moral debate that only ended in 1865 with the Thirteenth Amendment. The first formal anti-slavery societies emerged during the Revolutionary era: the Pennsylvania Society for Promoting the Abolition of Slavery in 1775; the New York Manumission Society in 1785; the Maryland Society for Promoting the Abolition of Slavery and for Relief of Poor Negroes and Others Unlawfully Held in Bondage in 1789; the Virginia Abolition Society in 1790; the New Jersey Society for Promoting the Abolition of Slavery in 1793; the Dover and Wilmington, Delaware abolition societies in 1788 and 1789 respectively; the Providence (Rhode Island) Abolition Society of 1790, and many other local groups, as well as the first national "umbrella" organization, the American Convention for Promoting the Abolition of Slavery, which was created in 1794.[147]

Equally, if not more importantly, most of the newly formed states in the new United States of America abolished the African and international slave trades (the Continental Congress actually banned it in 1776, and subsequent federal laws addressed the trade more thoroughly), even though evidence proves that illegal importations were rampant in the southern states during the first two decades after the Revolution and continued throughout the antebellum era. Rhode Island and Connecticut legally forbade slave importation in 1774; Delaware in 1776; Virginia in 1778; Maryland in 1783; New York in 1785; New Jersey the following year; and North Carolina imposed a crippling tax on importation and then banned it in 1794. South Carolina legally ended it in 1793 and Georgia in 1798.[148]

Revolutionary-era blacks, slave and free, hardly relinquished the legal fight to end the trade or the institution of slavery to whites. As early as the first years of the 1770s, they began, individually, and in small groups, to petition legislatures and sue in court for their freedom. Most of their efforts were, however, undergirded by religious, philosophical (Enlightenment), and legal arguments that aligned with the ideals of the American Revolution. Their efforts, therefore, were supported, in part, by nascent, but growing, anti-slavery sentiment held by whites. The lack of economic incentive for slaveholding in many of the northern states also contributed to these complementary efforts. The results of the combination of advocacy from blacks and whites were tremendous, leading to the gradual regional isolation of the institution. Vermont ended slavery in 1777 through its state constitution. Enslaved blacks in Massachusetts petitioned the Massachusetts legislature for freedom on January 13, 1777, noting in their plea that: "Thay [They] have in Common with all other men a Natural and Unaliable [inalienable] Right to that freedom which the Grat Parent of the Unavers [universe] hath Bestowed equalley on all menkind and which they have Never forfuted [forfeited] by any Compact or agreement whatever..."[149]

Massachusetts's 1780 Bill of Rights stated that "all men are born free and equal, and have...the right of enjoying and defending their lives and liberty." Testing the implications of these universal rights, Elizabeth Freeman sued for her freedom in 1781 and won. That same year, Quok Walker sued in court for his freedom and back wages. The Massachusetts court agreed that, like Freeman, Walker's enslavement violated the terms of the state's 1780 constitution. New Hampshire's state constitution also forbade slavery. Many states went on to pass gradual emancipation laws in the last two decades of the eighteenth century: Pennsylvania in 1780 (Quakers in the state forbade their members from owning slaves in 1775); Connecticut in 1784 and 1797; Rhode Island in 1784; New York in 1799; and New Jersey in 1804.[150] Native American slaves also benefited. Virginia, which first forbade Native American slavery in 1705, for example, reestablished its illegality in 1777.[151] This law, however, did not guarantee that native peoples who were enslaved would immediately gain freedom – some had to sue in court to do so. It also did not prevent native peoples from enslaving blacks – a growing trend among the southern "civilized" Cherokee, Chickasaw, Creek, Choctaw, and even some Seminoles who, after being enslaved alongside blacks and influenced by European and creole traders and farmers, implemented institutions of black slavery similar to their white neighbors during the late eighteenth century.[152]

Indeed, the new United States government formulated policies regarding these five groups east of the Mississippi that promoted Native American "civilization" – that is, assimilation of white, southern lifestyles that they hoped would stimulate the growth of a sense of commonality and end the history of itinerant violence, In 1791, the federal government noted in Article Fourteen of the Halston Treaty, for example, that the United States would provide the Cherokee Nation with "useful implements of husbandry" so that they may "become herdsmen and cultivators instead of remaining in a state of hunters." This attempt by the Cherokee to assimilate white southern ideology and culture, coupled with the growing influence of white traders and settlers on the Cherokee economy, ideals, and institutions, gradually led to the adoption by significant numbers of Cherokees of the farm and plantation system of agriculture worked by black slaves under many of the same conditions and restrictions as white masters imposed. Ironically, while gradual emancipation efforts in the early Republic liberated northern enslaved blacks and many east coast Native Americans who had white owners, federal government policies and southern agrarian culture conspired to institute the exact opposite condition for southern blacks who would continue to be enslaved in the South by anyone who could purchase them, including members of the "civilized" southern tribes of native peoples.[153]

Gradual emancipation not only occurred in the northern and middle states during the Revolutionary War era, but also led to Upper South legislation that made it less difficult for slaves to acquire their freedom. Virginia and Maryland passed laws that allowed owners to free their slaves more easily than before the era. So, too, did South Carolina and Georgia, but the Chesapeake region was most affected. In 1782, for example, Virginia enacted a law that allowed owners to manumit their slaves by deed or will – before that, the law stipulated that manumissions had to be approved by the colonial legislature and only in cases of extreme merit. In order to make certain that unscrupulous owners did not free only those incapable of caring for themselves because of age or infirmity, there was a stipulation in the 1782 law that mandated owners continue to financially support such persons if freed.[154] In 1796, Maryland passed a similar law allowing masters to free slaves through will or deed, if the slaves were less than 45 years old and could continue to work to support themselves.[155] As a result, Virginia and Maryland continuously had the largest numbers of residential free blacks and Baltimore, Maryland's capital, the largest number of free blacks of any US city (see Table 3.4).

In Fairfax, Virginia, George Washington took advantage of this opportunity and emancipated all of his three hundred-plus slaves upon the death of himself and his wife Martha, who brought the bulk of Washington's slave property into their marriage as part of her dowry. Washington's last will and testament is an example of adherence to the legal stipulations that owners wishing to free their slaves had to provide for their financial futures. The nation's first president, and one of the few founding fathers who actually freed his slaves, bound his heirs to "comfortably" clothe and feed those who were either too old or too young to care for themselves. Washington also provided that those of his enslaved youths who did not have parents to care for them should receive their freedom when they were 25 years old and, thereby, able to maintain themselves. He further stipulated that those youths who were to be retained in slavery until age 25 were to be taught to read and write and should have a lucrative skill. Mindful of those of his neighbors and acquaintances, who had left similar bequests in their will only to have them foiled by unwilling benefactors, Washington demanded in his will that "every part thereof be religiously fulfilled at the Epoch at which it is directed to take place; without evasion, neglect or delay, after the Crops which may then be on the ground are harvested." He was especially determined that his elderly former slaves be cared for, instructing his executors to create a fund to provide for them "so long as there are subjects requiring it." He also expressly forbade "the Sale, or transportation out of the said Commonwealth, of any Slave I may die possessed of, under any pretence [sic] whatsoever."[156]

The legislative and customary changes that led to widespread emancipations in more than half of the new nation were direct responses to black advocacy and the political and moral evolution of many who lived during the era of revolution, aided by the influence of Quakers, Mennonites, and some

Germans, particularly in the middle states and Upper South, who were increasingly opposed to enslavement.[157] It was also a result of the belief that the economic necessity of slaves was lessened by a gradual, but decided, shift in the agrarian economy in the Upper South, principally from tobacco production to the less labor-intensive grain industry.[158]

Table 3.4 Slave and free black state populations in the early Republic[159]

State	1790 Slave/Free Black Population	1800 Slave/Free Black Population	1810 Slave/Free Black Population
Massachusetts	0/ 5,463	0/ 6,452	0/ 6,737
New Hampshire	158/ 630	0/ 818	0/ 970
Vermont*	0/ (255)	0/ (557)	N/A
Maine*	0/ (538)	0/ (818)	N/A
Connecticut	2,764/ 2,808	951/ 5,330	310/ 6,453
Rhode Island	948/ 3,407	380/ 3,304	108/ 3,609
New York	21,324/ 4,644	20,903/ 10,417	15,017/ 25,333
Pennsylvania	3,737/ 6,537	1,706/ 14,564	795/ 22,492
New Jersey	11,423/ 2,762	12,422/ 4,402	10,851/ 7,843
Delaware	8,887/ 3,899	6,153/ 8,268	4,177/ 13,136
Maryland	103,036/ 8,043	105,635/ 19,587	111,502/ 33,927
Virginia	287,959/ 12,254	339,796/ 19,981	383,521/ 30,269
North Carolina	100,572/ 4,975	133,296/ 7,043	168,884/ 10,268
South Carolina	107,094/ 1,801	146,151/ 3,185	196,365/ 4,554
Georgia	29264/ 398	59,406/ 1,019	105,158/ 1,799

*Note: It is not certain exactly how many free blacks lived in Vermont or Maine since the census only designates a category of "All Other Free Persons." These numbers in parentheses seem to be a substantial overcount. Information for the 1810 census was not available.

The ambiguity of the new nation toward the institution of slavery, and the place of blacks more generally in this society, was reflected in the US Constitution. The Articles of Confederation, adopted in July 1788, does not mention slaves or slavery. It does allude to the rights of "free inhabitants of each state," which suggests that all free persons had some basic rights, regardless of race. A later statement in the Articles, however, specifies only the "number of white inhabitants in each state" in the determination of the number of state volunteers for the "land" (versus naval) forces of the new nation, a statement which indicates that free blacks and free whites were not to be regarded as the same in all matters regarding obligations to the nation and vice versa.[160]

The US Constitution, which went into effect in 1789, like the Articles of Confederation, did not directly speak to the issue of slavery. Still, this document makes three important concessions to slave interests. Article 1, section 2, noted that, for the purposes of enumeration of residents to determine representation and taxation, "three fifths of all other Persons," who are not free or non-taxed Indians, should be counted. Enslaved blacks would not be considered whole persons. Article 1, section 9, stipulated that there can be no federal prohibition of the international slave trade before 1808, allowing the "Migration or Importation of such Persons as any of the States now existing shall think proper to admit" and permitting taxes to be levied on each such person imported. Lastly, Article 4, section 2 of the Constitution created the nation's first federal fugitive slave law indicating that "No Person held [legally] to Service or Labour in one State" who manages to escape to another shall be "discharged for such Service or Labour," but must be returned to the person to whom he or she owes that service or labor.[161] The nation's Bill of Rights, which constituted the first ten amendments to the Constitution, was ratified in 1791 but also did not mention slavery, slaves, or free blacks.

Early sessions of Congress did, however, enact other legislation that was aimed directly at the institution of slavery and the slave trade. While these early laws protected the property rights of slaveholders, they also curtailed activity associated with the Atlantic slave trade. The Second Continental Congress, for example, enacted in 1787 "An

Ordinance for the Government of the Territory of the United States North-West of the River Ohio" that, in part, forbade slavery in states (eventually Wisconsin, Michigan, Illinois, Indiana, Minnesota, and Ohio) to be created out of this region.[162] In 1793, Congress further dictated the procedures for returning runaway slaves in "An Act respecting Fugitives from Justice, and Persons Escaping from the Service of Their Masters." This law allowed anyone who claimed a fugitive slave to present evidence of ownership to a local magistrate by "affidavit" or "oral testimony" so that the slave could be returned. This act also levied sanctions on those found helping a fugitive slave.[163] The following year, Congress approved "An Act to prohibit the carrying on the Slave Trade from the United States to any foreign place or country" that forbade US shipbuilders from constructing vessels to be used in the international slave trade. Likewise, it further criminalized participation in the trade, banning citizens from using ships as merchants or conveyors of slave laborers. In 1800, restrictive federal measures regarding the Atlantic trade also excluded the right of US citizens to work on slave ships, even those of foreign origin. Three years later, persons were fined for bringing "new" slaves into states and territories that had outlawed the foreign slave trade. Finally, in 1807, Congress voted to put a complete end to the international slave trade to the United States, effective January 1, 1808.[164]

The immediate impact of the Constitution on the institution of slavery was felt particularly in the surge in the numbers of imported Africans. While the trade had almost disappeared during the war years and many new states had decided to outlaw the international trade in their state constitutions, the largest numbers of Africans imported to North America, per decade, occurred after the ratification of the Constitution with its indication that the trade would be federally outlawed after 1807. Tens of thousands arrived, many of them brought by New England shipping and merchant interests. Some 156,000 slaves were brought to the United States in the period 1801–8, almost all of them on ships that originated from New England ports that had recently outlawed slavery. Rhode Island slavers alone imported an average of 6,400 Africans annually into the United States in the years 1805 and 1806. South Carolina, which legally reopened its slave trade in 1803, imported 39,000 slaves in the next five years and 90,000 between 1782 and 1810![165]

While 1808 marked the legal end to the international African slave trade, tens of thousands, perhaps as many as 50,000 arrived in the United States after that date. The federal government did make some attempt to stem the tide of the illegal importations, many of them arriving at the Lower South ports of Charleston, and particularly those of New Orleans, Mobile, and Galveston. In 1819, Congress enacted a law that established the "African squadron," naval patrols off the coasts of western central and western Africa and the United States in order to intercept slave traders. Another federal law in 1820 declared all those persons found guilty of trading slaves to the nation would be tried for piracy and face the death penalty (hanged).[166] Still, the trade continued. The story of the *Clotilda* provides one telling narrative regarding the extension of the African slave trade to the United States beyond 1808. On July 7, 1860, 110 enslaved persons from Ouidah in the Bight of Benin landed in Mobile Bay, Alabama and were brought to their owners, Timothy Burns Meaher and John Dabney.[167] While neither owner was hanged (enough evidence did not seem to be available to convict since at the time of the court hearing, none of the slaves could be found!), the ship's captain, William Foster, was fined US$1,000.[168]

The legal "end" of the African slave trade to the United States came at a time of competing influences on the contours of the institution of slavery and its future in the Americas. In the Caribbean, for example, a momentous revolution (1791– 1804) in Saint-Domingue, the region's richest colony, ended France's dominance of the global sugar market; freed hundreds of thousands of slaves; scattered wealthy planters and privileged free people of color to, among other Atlantic destinations, Louisiana, South Carolina, Virginia, and other slavery "sanctuaries" in the United States; created the second republic in the Americas – this time a black one; and sent shivers throughout the slaveholding New World that their bondsmen and women too would succeed in a bloody revolution. Indeed, Gabriel Prosser's failed black rebellion in Henrico County, Virginia in 1800 has been directly linked to the currents of black revolution set sail by Toussaint

L'Ouverture's momentous overthrow of French colonial power in the Caribbean.[169]

Gabriel Prosser, whom many considered a deeply religious man, planned a massive slave rebellion in what was the center of the slave world in North America – Richmond, the capitol of the nation's largest slaveholding state. Prosser, who purportedly enlisted more than a thousand slaves to form his army, planned to attack on August 30, 1800. The literate blacksmith, slave of tobacco farmer Thomas Prosser, intended to raid the city's armory and equip his followers as they fanned out across the state and beyond. The day before the planned assault, however, a violent summer downpour washed out bridges and roads leading to the city. Prosser was betrayed to local authorities, and his "revolution" was foiled. Gabriel and many of his men, including his two brothers, were hanged.[170]

The future of black slavery in the United States at the turn of the nineteenth century was, therefore, an uncertain one. The institution was dying both in the northeast and northern plains due to gradual emancipation acts and the Northwest Ordinance of 1787. Still, the institution was hardly dead, at least not for the next several decades. Eli Whitney's patent of the short staple cotton gin, in 1794, combined with a westward movement of farmers from Virginia to West Virginia, Tennessee, and Kentucky, and migration of persons from the Upper to the Lower South in search of affordable, fertile farm/plantation lands that would provide raw cotton to feed the developing industrial revolution in England and the northern states, signaled not an end, but rather a rebirth. Indeed, the acquisition, from France, of the more than 828,000 square miles of southern and southwestern lands that made up the Louisiana Territory in 1803 doubled the size of the nation and increased slave territory with inclusion of land that would become the slaveholding states of Arkansas and Missouri and parts of Texas and Louisiana. The settlement and eventual statehoods of Mississippi in 1817 and Alabama in 1819 added to the growing endorsement of slavery in the Deep South and the reign of cotton as king of an economy wedded to slave labor. Between 1790 and 1820, for example, cotton production increased 300-fold from just over 3,100 bales to more than 334,000 annually. The increase in the slave population also was impressive, from 694,000 to 1.5 million, and even more so when one considers that the vast majority of this population gain was through natural increase, not African imports.[171] Moreover, this growing slave population was shifting from the Upper to the Lower South to accommodate white slaveholding migration to new cotton territories. By the second decade of the nineteenth century, the domestic slave trade was rapidly replacing the international trade and making certain that slavery would not die out from a lack of bonded labor in the newly developing plantation economies of the Deep South and Southwest.

This upsurge in the institution meant that African-descended people, enslaved and free, faced devastating challenges. The nation's enslaved population, while finally able to form families and communities because of the increased numbers of creoles among them and an equal adult sex ratio, faced new threats to social stability with the developing domestic slave trade that, typically, did not recognize slave communities, marriages, or parental ties. Few could expect never to be sold, or to stay with their husbands, wives, or all of their children during the span of their lifetimes. If the domestic slave trade did not sever marriage and family ties, then the death of a master and the distribution of his or her property, including slave property, meant slave family dispersal.

The growing free black population likewise faced many obstacles to creating lives of social and economic stability. North, south, and west, free people of color met walls of discrimination that kept them on the margins of an unwelcoming society. The federal government had not been clear about the citizenship status or rights of free blacks. It was clear, however, about some of the restrictions they would face. It restricted their ability to work in federal agencies such as the postal service, to become elected officials in the federal capital, to participate in militias and, as immigrants, to become naturalized citizens. Despite their ban from militias, however, the US government did allow blacks to fight in the army, Marine Corps, and navy during times of warfare with both France and Britain.[172]

Those aspects of free black life in "free" and "slave" states and territories that the federal government did not clearly define in law were taken up vigorously by white males as part of growing bodies of restrictive local, state, and territorial legislation. Where no laws were erected, discriminatory practices became customary. Even in those few states where black males were not outright denied the franchise, tradition often prevented men from voting. As such, by 1840, 93 percent of free males of color in the North were largely restricted from voting; and no southern state allowed the black franchise. By that date, free men of color could still vote in Maine, Massachusetts, New Hampshire, and Vermont, but New York insisted on property requirements of US$250; and New Jersey, Pennsylvania, and Connecticut, which once allowed free black men to vote, withdrew that right entirely.[173] Solomon Northup, for one, noted of his father, a freed black in New York, that he "acquired, by his diligence and economy, a sufficient property qualification to entitle him to the right of suffrage."[174] Few others could proffer such a boast.

Earlier in the period, Massachusetts led the way in restricting the citizenship rights of its black residents. The state forbade, for example, marriage across racial lines and limited the entrance of free people of color from other states or nations.[175] A few other examples are clear indications that the "North" was no haven of racial equality for those blacks who were "free." Rhode Island prevented blacks from marrying whites. Connecticut would not let African-descended people enter the state for educational purposes unless the local governments agreed. New Hampshire disqualified blacks from joining their state militia.[176]

The Northwest Territory, where slavery mostly had been barred (those who had slaves in the Territory before the passage of the Northwest Ordinance were able to keep them), was no better. Most of the states that were created from this area, such as Illinois and Indiana, forbade blacks from relocating there unless they could prove their freedom *and* post hefty bonds of US$500–US$1,000 – a fortune in the early nineteenth century. Ohio was one of the first in the Territory to create a legislative slate of black laws. In 1804 and 1807, for example, white male residents passed legislation that: excluded black immigration without a substantial bond; barred interracial marriage; disallowed gun ownership; and outlawed free blacks from testifying against whites in court.[177]

Disfranchisement, barred admission, exclusion from the body politic, and restrictions on marriage partners were only part of the marginalization of free people of color. As in Ohio, the right to testify in court (against whites) was denied in most areas of the nation. Many states outside of the South, including Indiana, Illinois, Iowa, and California, once it entered the Union in 1850, for example, forbade black testimony against whites or black-jury participation; and blacks certainly could not serve as judges.[178] In the northeast, only Massachusetts allowed blacks to sit on juries. As historian Leon Litwack notes, "Where courts refused to admit Negro testimony, legal protection obviously had its limits. A white man could assault, rob, or even murder a Negro in the midst of a number of Negro witnesses and escape prosecution unless another white man had been present and had agreed to testify."[179] The result of this exclusion from participation in the judicial system led, not surprisingly, to particularly high incarceration rates and disproportionately long sentences for convicted free black men and women.[180]

Custom replaced law in creating segregated public spaces that foreshadowed the Jim Crow era in the South of later decades. Public transportation, public entertainment venues, hotels, and restaurants all either forbade black customers or greatly limited their presence. This system of apartheid included churches as well as schools, hospitals, prisons, and cemeteries.[181] Likewise, black children and teens who actually could attend schools mostly studied in segregated, physically inferior facilities with teachers who were paid only a fraction of what white instructors could expect to receive. Pennsylvania, New York, Rhode Island, and Ohio, for example, only provided segregated schools for free black children, a trend that was popular in other northern, midwestern, and western states.[182] Even when Massachusetts and Connecticut allowed some integrated schools, the outcry against them from white residents was loud and incessant.

Prudence Crandall, for example, tried to service the educational needs of both white and black girls in Canterbury, Connecticut in 1831. The response was immediate. White parents frantically withdrew their children; townspeople organized a ban on providing the school with necessities, such as food; residents destroyed the school's well-water with horse manure; and then stoned and tried to burn down the school building. The Connecticut legislature hurriedly passed a law that forbade any school from admitting black pupils from out of state, or those who did not have the approval of local authorities to be in the state. In one of several trials of Crandall, who was arrested for being in violation of this new state law, a judge declared that blacks were not citizens. Prudence Crandall finally gave up her efforts to educate black girls in Canterbury in 1834.[183]

This partial ban on black education included not only grammar schools, but colleges and professional schools as well. Still, a few free people of color managed to graduate from college. John Russwurm graduated from Bowdoin in 1826; and Dartmouth allowed black students after 1824, as did Oberlin and Western Reserve in the 1830s.[184] The vast majority of free blacks, however, received only the bare rudiments of a formal education, if that. Very few indeed could hope to attend college.

The lack of educational opportunity was only one of the deterrents to free black economic success. Most free men of color in urban areas worked as day laborers and the majority of women were domestics and washerwomen. Those in rural locales provided farm help for very small compensation, often working beside servants and a dwindling numbers of slaves in northern states. Skilled male labor consisted of work as blacksmiths, carpenters, painters, barbers, coopers, cooks, and bakers. Some black men owned small shops, while many who lived in sea-coast towns found work as seamen or as manual laborers on wharves. More than a few women in towns and cities sold baked and cooked goods on the street, along with fruits and vegetables. Unlike men, females had very limited skilled work options, serving mostly as midwives and seamstresses.[185] The large majority of whites in the North, East, and West simply believed that blacks were inferior – intellectually, physically, and morally – and, therefore, should not have equal access to the same educational, cultural, occupational, political, legal, or social resources as white residents of locales, states, or the nation.[186]

As such, they did not hesitate to impose "controls" on free people of color whom they believed were moving outside their designated places. Anti-black race riots were not

3.4 Virginia minstrels advertisement, 1843
Source: Wikimedia Commons

unusual in the early to mid-nineteenth century. There were, for example, at least five in Philadelphia between 1832 and 1849 and others in Cincinnati, New York, Boston, and the nation's capital.[187] Physical violence and forced removal were not the only tactics employed. The use of racial epithets, such as the hated term "nigger," was common as a way to diminish free blacks who dared suggest they lived beyond the margins of society. Characterization of blacks as buffoons through minstrelsy became a popular form of entertainment, and stereotypical images of blacks in political cartoons published in newspapers, broadsides, and on posters were grist for the mill.[188]

In the Upper South, the location of the largest numbers of free people of color, state legislation in both the early national period and the antebellum era was extremely constricting. Virginia serves as a good model. There, free people of color could not migrate into the state, vote, marry across the racial line, hold elected office, testify against whites, be part of the militia, own weapons, or, after 1806, legally remain in the state if freed after that date.[189] As in all slave states and territories, free blacks in Virginia had to prove that they were, indeed, "free" by carrying with them formal documentation of their free status. "Free papers" and registration in county-wide free black ledgers were necessary if one hoped not to be imprisoned or even sold into slavery. Legislation that restricted the social and economic location of free people of color in Virginia only grew as the decades passed. The heyday occurred, not surprisingly, after the Nat Turner slave rebellion of August 1831 in Southampton County, Virginia that left approximately sixty whites dead. This event was only one that occurred in the new nation which whites took as indicative that greater restrictions should be placed on the slave and free black presence.

On the night of January 8, 1811, for example, Charles Deslondes, a mulatto probably from Haiti, but perhaps from Jamaica, along with approximately 500 other armed slaves, some of whom had fought in the Haitian Revolution, marched toward New Orleans. They turned their working tools into weapons and carried handmade flags and beat drums. Raiding and killing while advancing toward the port city, they soon faced a local militia. A battle ensued and that left the rebels defeated. The revolt lasted three days, but lingered for decades in the minds of white slaveholders.[190] So, too, did the thwarted Denmark Vesey slave revolt of June 1822 in Charleston, South Carolina and the 1829 publication of David Walker's *Appeal in Four Articles; Together with a Preamble, to the Coloured Citizens of the World, but in Particular and Very Expressly to Those of the United States of America*, in which the free black man from North Carolina sanctioned violence to end slavery. These events in the South, and the growing northern abolitionist movement, symbolized by the forming of the American Anti-Slavery Society in 1833, were all influential in the growing legislative and customary restrictions on free black southern life.

Virginia legislation forbade free people of color from learning to read or write, and prohibited them from preaching or holding church services unless they had written permission from white officials.[191] Likewise, an 1839 Virginia law granted local white patrols the right to search slave and free black homes without prior notice or permission. Moreover, free people of color could only sell agricultural goods if they were certified by elite whites; and free black men and women, who worked as herbalists, midwives, and folk doctors, could no longer perform any medical treatments or prepare any medications after 1843. Later legislation barred free people of color from selling liquor; and in 1860, state law allowed the courts to place free people of color in "absolute slavery" if convicted of a felony.[192]

The place of free people of color in the Lower South certainly was no better. One significant difference, however, was the familial affiliation that many free people of color in this region had with their former owners as the mulatto (or lighter) offspring of sexual relations between white masters and enslaved black women. It was that affiliation, and the elite white sponsorship that these fathers sometimes afforded their "colored" offspring, particularly in urban centers like Charleston, New Orleans, and Mobile, that led to an increase in regional emancipations during the early national period. It was also this sponsorship that meant many more of these free people of color were literate and/or skilled. Most free people of color in this region lived in the cities; and many were artisans, rather than day laborers. Historians Michael Johnson and James Roark indicate that in Charleston, South Carolina, for example, the majority of free black men were carpenters, tailors, painters, barbers, butchers, bricklayers, and pliers of other trades. The women also were especially skilled, and worked as dressmakers, seamstresses, and in other types of needle trades. "A similar pattern," Johnson and Roark noted, "prevailed in New Orleans, but it contrasted sharply with the occupations of free Afro-Americans in Northern cities, where about three-quarters of them worked as common laborers."[193] In Savannah, Georgia, which held the largest numbers of free people of color in the state, most were day laborers or had menial jobs, although there were also a significant number who were skilled or small-scale entrepreneurs. In 1823, for example, the majority of employed free women of color were washerwomen, seamstresses, street hawkers of fruits and cakes, and domestics.[194] Three years earlier, property tax records indicated that 36 free people of color owned homes with a value that exceeded

US$200, despite an increasingly enforced law of 1818 that forbade them from owning real estate.[195]

Like the Upper South, free black status within the economy, criminal justice system, and political structure of the Lower South deteriorated with time. By 1860, for example, the number of black property owners in Savannah, and the amount of property they possessed, had declined.[196] Likewise, each Lower South state eventually passed anti-migration laws that prevented free people of color from entering them. South Carolina legislated, in 1820, a ban on slave emancipations.[197] Georgia decided in 1815 that free people of color had to be tried in the same manner as slaves; and that masters could no longer free their slave property by last will and testament. Four years later, that state's lawmakers agreed that free people of color had to annually register with their county courts or risk being sold into slavery. In 1827, black seamen, except from South Carolina, were barred from leaving their vessels while in a Georgia harbor unless their captain posted a bond of US$100 for each. In 1829, the year that David Walker's *Appeal* was found in the possession of black seamen in southern ports, Georgia blacks were banned from education; from circulation of printed material "for the purposes of exciting to insurrection, conspiracy or resistance among the slaves, negroes, or free persons of colour, of this state, against their owners or the citizens of this state"; and from communicating with black seamen. Other eventual laws mandated exclusion of Georgia's free people of color from using a printing press (1833); from working as druggists or in the medical trades (1835); from performing work as mechanics or masons in building construction or repair (1845); and required that all males and females beyond the age of 21 pay a US$5 annual tax (1851) when only adult white males, not females, were taxed, and only 25 cents each annually.[198]

Some southern free people of color, however, did thrive. None were more successful than the few who held slaves themselves. Historian Larry Koger indicates that, according to the 1830 census, free people of color in Virginia, Maryland, South Carolina, and Louisiana collectively owned more than 10,000 slaves.[199] Although most slaves in the households of free people of color were family members who were in the process of being legally freed by a household head who had purchased them, there were some free people-of-color masters who, like their white neighbors, held black slaves for economic gain and the convenience of their very poorly rewarded labor. Many were the descendants of white masters (89 percent) who had been freed and skilled or propertied in the process.[200]

Acquiring slaves of their own through purchase, and sometimes through inheritance, they employed their black male and female laborers in tasks with similar material support and punishments as other southern masters. The mulatto John Stanley of North Carolina, for example, owned 163 slaves and 2,600 acres of land in 1830. That same year, mulatto William Ellison of South Carolina owned 900 acres and 63 slaves. Andrew Durnford of Louisiana, also a mulatto, had 77 slaves to work his sugar plantation; while mother and son Ciprien and Pierre Ricard, also of Louisiana and members of the *gens de couleur* community, owned 168 slaves who labored on their sugar estate.[201] These wealthy free people of color, however, were a tiny minority of the expanding southern free black population forced to live on the very margins of US society.

Given the growing animosity toward free people of color across the developing nation, it is little wonder that the notion of colonization of locales outside of the United States seemed to some to be a viable, if not exclusive, solution to remedy free black oppression. The idea, not surprisingly, was more popular among whites, many of them influential political figures such as Andrew Jackson, Henry Clay, James Madison, Bushrod Washington, and Daniel Webster, than among free blacks who largely believed that it was a blatant attempt to get rid of them, rather than to offer them equal rights in the land of their birth.

The movement began, however, as part of efforts by early black and white abolitionists who believed that African-descended people, regardless of their status as "free," would never be accepted as equals in American society. Some colonization supporters even believed that the movement could lead to a gradual end to slavery. Others hoped that blacks who returned to Africa would help to Christianize and westernize indigenous Africans. Many white supporters, however, clearly had ulterior motives that derived from racist-held notions of black inferiority and their desire to rid the nation of a black presence that was not enslaved. Colonizationists from the South, for example, typically were slaveholders; others heartily supported slavery and viewed free blacks as a continual threat to the institution, as well as to white security and civilization. Charles Fenton Mercer, of Virginia, spoke for many when he described free people of color in his state as an ever-increasing population that was "every day polluting and corrupting public morals" because "more than half the females are prostitutes and [half] of the males rogues."[202]

The American Colonization Society formed in 1816, when delegates from several states met in Washington, DC for the purpose of aiding "voluntary" emigration of free people of color to Africa. Those states with colonization organizations, along with the federal government, pledged to financially support the effort. While some free and recently freed blacks went voluntarily, others were given a stark choice – either remain enslaved, or gain freedom and emigrate. In 1821, the national organization chose the present-day site of Liberia, on the west coast of Africa, to create its black colony.[203]

Initially, certain statewide organizations supported different settlements along the Liberian coast. The Commonwealth of Liberia eventually was formed in 1838 by the joint efforts of the Virginia Colonization Society, the Quaker Young Men's Colonization Society of Pennsylvania, and the American Colonization Society. A group from Mississippi joined the others in 1842. Liberia claimed sovereignty from the United States in 1848, with a Declaration of Independence whose wording was similar to that of their "mother country's" founding document. Nine years later, the Maryland colony, for which Bowdoin graduate John Russwurm served as governor, also became part of Liberia.[204]

The free black colonization project that became Liberia was formed in the face of vehement opposition from many of the nation's free people of color, regardless of their social class affiliation. Indeed, Paul Cuffee, the wealthy African American Quaker shipbuilder and merchant from Massachusetts, was in quite the minority when he began to promote the idea of black colonization to Africa in 1812. Cuffee was interested in removing his own family and others to Sierra Leone, where English abolitionists such as Granville Sharpe, Thomas Clarkson, and William Wilberforce had established a free black colony of former loyalist blacks from Nova Scotia in 1787. Cuffee, at his own personal expense, eventually did remove approximately thirty-eight US blacks to Sierra Leone in 1816.[205]

Paul Cuffee's enthusiasm and experiment prompted others to join the colonization movement, but he never could convince large numbers of free blacks to do so. In that same year, for example, more than 3,000 free people of color met at Philadelphia's black Bethel Church to protest colonization on several grounds: that white colonizationists were supporters of slavery and that their efforts were derived from a racist ideology and view of American society; that there were early reports of rampant illness and high mortality rates among settlers in nearby Sierra Leone; and that there was a general lack of desire to return to an unknown Africa for which they felt no cultural or genealogical affinity.[206] James Forten, a wealthy Philadelphia free black sailmaker and abolitionist who helped to organize the Bethel Church meeting, later reported to Paul Cuffee that "there was not one sole [sic] that was in favor of going to Africa."[207] "This is our home and this is our country," those who protested colonization asserted. "Beneath its sod lie the bones of our fathers; for it, some of them fought, bled, and died. Here we were born, and here we will die."[208] The American Convention of Abolitionist Societies concurred with the black protestors, voting, in 1817, to denounce colonization.[209]

The war of 1812 between the United States and Britain might have temporarily delayed colonization pioneer Paul Cuffee from beginning his "experiment" in Sierra Leone, but it did provide slaves, as during the American revolutionary war, some opportunity to gain their freedom. The first war of the new nation fought on US soil was a two-and-a-half-year series of battles up and down the east coast and in the Gulf of Mexico. Blacks, slave and free, fought on both sides. As with the Revolution, British forces in the South were able to attract large numbers of slaves by offering freedom if they fought against the United States. They sweetened the enticement by extending freedom as well to the family members of able-bodied soldiers and sailors. While some blacks fought for the United States – approximately 15 percent of US naval forces, for example, were people of color – enslaved blacks could not resist the temptation to acquire freedom if they could reach British warships and seized territories. It is estimated that 4,000 joined the British. When the war ended in 1814, many of these freed men, members of the Corps of Colonial Mariners, along with their wives and children, settled in the British Caribbean, principally Trinidad.[210] There, they pursued a life away from the United States and its growing angst regarding the destiny of the institution of slavery and its bound black workers that would, in merely two generations, divide the nation in civil war.

Further Reading

Berlin, Ira. *Many Thousands Gone: The First Two Centuries of Slavery in North America*. Cambridge, MA: Belknap Press of Harvard University Press, 1998.

Blassingame, John W. (ed.) *Slave Testimony: Two Centuries of Letters, Speeches, Interviews and Autobiographies*. Baton Rouge: Louisiana State University Press, 1977.

Carney, Judith A. *Black Rice: The African Origins of Rice Cultivation in the Americas*. Cambridge, MA: Harvard University Press, 2001.

Foote, Thelma Willis. *Black and White Manhattan: The History of Racial Formation in Colonial New York City*. New York: Oxford University Press, 2004.

Gilbert, Alan. *Black Patriots and Loyalists: Fighting for Emancipation in the War for Independence*. Chicago, IL: University of Chicago Press, 2012.

Gomez, Michael A. *Exchanging Our Country Marks: The Transformations of African Identities in the Colonial and Antebellum South*. Chapel Hill, NC: University of North Carolina Press, 1998.

Hall, Gwendolyn Hall. *Slavery and African Ethnicities in the Americas: Restoring the Links*. Chapel Hill, NC: The University of North Carolina Press, 2005.

Klein, Herbert, and Vidal Luna, Francisco. *Slavery in Brazil*. Cambridge, UK: Cambridge University Press, 2009.

Litwack, Leon F. *North of Slavery: The Negro in the Free States, 1790–1860*. Chicago, IL: University of Chicago Press, 1965.

Schwartz, Philip J. *Slave Laws in Virginia*. Athens, GA: University of Georgia Press, 1996.
Taylor, Alan. *The Internal Enemy: Slavery and War in Virginia, 1772–1832*. New York: W. W. Norton, 2013.
Washington, Margaret. *Sojourner Truth's America*. Urbana-Champaign, IL: University of Illinois Press, 2009.

4
Slavery and Anti-slavery in Antebellum America

"De first thing dat I 'member hearing about de War was one day when Marse George come in de house and tell Miss Emmaline dat dey's gwin have a bloody war. He say he feared all de slaves would be took away....from dat minute I started payin' for freedom. All de rest o' de women done de same."

Dora Franks[1]

If you asked anyone in the rapidly growing United States in 1820 whether or not they believed that black chattel slavery in the nation would come to a screeching halt forty-five years later with the passage of the Thirteenth Amendment to the Constitution, probably no one would have answered affirmatively. Even in the northern and midwestern states and territories that had "ended" slavery during the eras of the American Revolution and the early Republic, black emancipation typically was a gradual process. Indeed, by 1820, there were still slaves in Connecticut, Indiana, Illinois, New York, New Jersey, Pennsylvania, and Rhode Island. While the large slave population certainly had shifted below the Mason Dixon line by that date, New York still had 10,000 slaves and New Jersey 7,500. Moreover, the fledgling anti-slavery movement was still just that – fledgling. It would be another thirteen years before the American Anti-Slavery Society was founded. There were some weak, moral-driven indicators. Abolition, for example, was never a dead issue – the creation of the American Colonization

4.1 George Carter's Oatlands Plantation, Loudoun County, Virginia, c. 1803
Source: Cones Collection; Photo credit, Beverly and Carla Harris

Society and active abolitionist societies in much of the North and in the Upper South, along with indications of a simmering resistance to a nation purportedly based on ideals of freedom becoming the largest slave society in its hemisphere, pointed to a possibility of perhaps gradual national emancipation, or at least a shrinking physical space where slavery might be contained. Still, market forces that rewarded slave production of raw cotton, and other crops, seemed to rule the day and the social consciousness of the "typical" nonblack American.

The invention of the cotton gin undoubtedly contributed greatly to the development of the antebellum South as the largest slave society in the Americas. Cotton especially, which equaled more than half of US exports between 1820 and 1860, but also sugar, rice, tobacco, and corn dominated the local and export markets of the Lower South and Southwest.[2] In South Carolina alone in 1860, for example, black workers helped to produce 15 million bushels of corn, 119 million pounds of rice, 490,000 pounds of tobacco, and 353 thousand bales of ginned cotton.[3]

Slave Population Growth and Relocation

Enslaved black workers made each of these crops profitable choices for their masters who, in turn, craved more and more land and slaves to insure their ongoing financial wellbeing. Indeed, one of the truly differentiating attributes of slavery in the antebellum South, in relation to slavery in most of the other locales of the Americas during this period, was that the US slave population doubled in size from two million in 1820 to four million in 1860, almost completely by natural growth. At the same time that the southern slave population was doubling in size, much of this population was being shifted to the Lower South and West. The end of the antebellum era told much of the story for the earlier decades. There was an overall increase in the slave population of the Lower South of 34 percent in the decade 1850–60 alone, while the Upper South only registered a 9.7 percent increase during those ten years. During this decade before the initiation of the Civil War, the cotton states documented an enormous rise in the numbers of resident slaves: Mississippi, 40.9 percent; Texas, 213.9 percent; Alabama, 27.2 percent; Arkansas, 135.9 percent; Georgia, 21.1 percent; and Louisiana, 35.5 percent. The domestic slave trade was the profitable vehicle for the forced migration of a minimum of 875,000 black laborers with an estimated value of US 430 million dollars.[4] One in every four enslaved persons left Virginia in the 1830s; and more than 250,000 relocated from the Upper to the Lower South between the 1830s and the 1850s.[5] The majority of these slaves – historian Steven Deyle estimates one-half million – were moved alone, without kin or friends.[6]

Ironically, the slaves' hope of having a family was never more physically realistic, given their expanding numbers and their equal sex ratio in the antebellum era. But the possibility of slaves losing family or community was also never greater. Whenever the loss occurred, devastation prevailed. "When a child was sold it nearly grieved the mothers and brothers and sisters to death. It was bad as deaths in the families," Mattie Fannen from Arkansas noted.[7] This scene was played out repeatedly, particularly in the Upper South and increasingly in the Lower. Families were often torn apart, leaving significant and generations-deep trauma. Movement of slave property, therefore, might have been a lucrative enterprise for owners, but it was a physically and emotionally brutal experience for the enslaved. Mariah Robinson was given away as a wedding gift. She traveled by steamship and stagecoach to Waco.[8] Others came in wagons, and many walked. Henrietta Ralls, for one, walked as a child from Mississippi to Arkansas and then to Texas.[9] Hezekiah Steel also walked. So too did Ben Simpson of Georgia, along with his mother and sister. Simpson's sadistic master killed Ben's mother because she could not keep up with his pace.[10]

Antebellum Slave Labor

The kinds of labor that enslaved southern workers performed in the antebellum era, as in the colonial and early Republic periods, helped to define their status among other slaves, and certainly among their owners. It was a hierarchy imposed by whites, but one which bondswomen and men still found opportunity to refine. This was particularly so in those slaveholdings that boasted enough slaves to allow some true occupational differentiation. Interviewed decades after emancipation, ex-slaves still held tightly to the status they derived from their slave labor. "Cook? No, ma'am! I never cooked until after I was married, and I never washed... All I washed was the babies and maybe my mistress's feet. I was a lady's maid."[11] Former slave Rosa Starke only recognized two classes of whites: "buckra slave owners and poor white folks dat didn't own no slaves." In her estimation, "dere was more classes 'mongst de slaves." Starke went on to delineate five: first, house servants; second, domestics who worked outside the owner's home such as carriage drivers, gardeners, barbers, and stable men; third were skilled slaves – wheelwrights, wagoners, blacksmiths, foremen and those who cared for livestock and hunting dogs. "All dese," she informed her interviewer, "have good houses and never have to work hard or git a beatin'." The fourth class of slaves, she asserted, were the skilled agricultural workers – "cradlers of de wheat, de threshers, and de millers of corn and de wheat, and de feeders of de cotton gin." Last, came the "common field niggers."[12] They not only produced subsistence and cash crops and reared livestock, but also helped to manufacture raw materials for home consumption and the marketplace. Most slaves were of this last "class." The vast majority of antebellum bondswomen, men, and teens were agricultural workers on farms – cotton farms.

Planters experimented with cotton production for years before Eli Whitney's patent of a cotton gin in 1794 provided them with the means to a worthwhile profit margin. Other technological innovations that positively affected the cotton textile industry included improvements in spinning, weaving, and usage of steam power.[13] Advanced technologies also increased the average acreage that cotton hands were responsible for cultivating. In 1820, for example, slaveholders believed a "prime hand" could successfully work six acres of cotton and eight acres of corn. Some years later, they began to expect their slaves to cultivate an average of ten acres of cotton and ten acres of corn. Field slaves confined to cotton plantations began the annual routine in the winter months, when they started clearing old fields and preparing new ones. They usually planted corn in March and began cotton planting in April. Once the cotton began to grow, there were regular cycles of hoeing and plowing that continued until the end of July. During the mid-summer, much of the field labor was work in the cornfields.

The vast majority of enslaved antebellum blacks worked on farms and plantations. Some, however, had city-dwelling owners or were rented out to individuals and businesses, usually on an annual basis that began in January. The "temporary" masters of slaves whom they rented were responsible for providing them with food, shelter, clothing, and medical attention. Some urban bondspeople, however, were allowed to seek their own employment, returning the majority of their earnings to their masters. These persons provided their own material support and housing. It was a kind of "freedom" that slaves in the countryside, even skilled rural bondsmen, could only dream of achieving. What work did those who resided and labored in southern cities perform?

The South's cities – Baltimore, Washington, DC, Richmond, Petersburg, Norfolk, Charleston, Savannah, Atlanta, Mobile, New Orleans, Louisville, St Louis, and others, like its countryside, relied on slave labor in many of its economic sectors, but particularly as domestics and day workers assigned "drudgery" duties. Females typically were domestics, although some also worked as seamstresses, midwives, street hawkers, and in the urban sex industry. Men dug ditches, laid roads, and worked in private and municipal construction of all types, as longshoremen, blacksmiths, coopers, firemen, fishermen, oysterers, and watermen of varied occupations. Some worked in tobacco warehouses, cotton gins, textile mills, and nail factories or were employed building railroads, digging coal, and in iron-smelting furnaces.[14] Slave labor remained important to urban life throughout the antebellum era, although the slave population's decided shift to rural cotton-related labor lessened the numbers assigned to cities. So too did the growing fear of an urban slave revolt that ushered in greater restrictions on the "freedoms" of city slaves.

The type of work a slave performed not only affected their internal "status," but also their public, gendered images. Most of the kind of agricultural and skilled labor that slave men performed in the southern antebellum countryside, for example, bolstered images of their "manliness" because it emphasized widely accepted masculine traits of physical strength and endurance. This same type of work, on the other hand, profoundly defeminized women in the eyes of casual observers, owners, and overseers alike. It cast slave women in what became the stereotypical image of the female "workhorse."

Slaveholders relied on this workhorse image to push female laborers inordinately hard, sometimes denying them minimal levels of material support and punishing them severely when women did not, in their estimation, comply. Frederick Law Olmstead's remarks upon seeing a gang of slave women repairing roads in South Carolina are indicative of the grossly negative images of black womanhood that female rural labor routinely inspired. Curiously, nowhere in Olmstead's "observations" does such an "unflattering" view of male laborers emerge. His harshest remarks were reserved for the slave women he encountered. "Clumsy, awkward, gross, elephantine in all their movements; pouting, grinning, and leering at us; sly, sensual, and shameless, in all their expressions and demeanor; I never before had witnessed, I thought, anything more revolting than the whole scene."[15] Olmstead's description was so grotesque that one almost loses the labor context from which he spoke, one in which women, who were in the majority in laboring groups, worked alongside men, filling holes in a muddy, rutted country road with soil that they hand-carted and logs that they cut and hand-laid. In their "prime," slave women such as those Olmstead encountered, did as much labor as, and sometimes more than, slave men. Yet their experiences and images as laborers could be quite different from those of their male counterparts.[16]

4.2 Eli Whitney's cotton gin
Source: Wikimedia Commons

Table 4.1 US antebellum southern slave population, 1820–1860[17]

US States	1820	1830	1840	1850	1860
Alabama	47,449	117,549	253,532	342,844	435,080
Arkansas		4,576	19,935	47,100	111,115
Florida			25,717	39,310	61,745
Georgia	149,656	217,531	280,944	381,682	462,198
Kentucky	126,732	165,213	182,258	210,981	225,438

Table 4.1 (continued)

US States	1820	1830	1840	1850	1860
Louisiana	69,064	109,588	168,452	244,809	331,726
Maryland	107,398	102,994	89,737	90,368	87,189
Mississippi	32,814	65,659	195,211	309,878	436,631
Missouri	10,222	25,096	58,240	87,422	114,931
N. Carolina	205,017	245,601	245,817	288,548	331,059
S. Carolina	251,783	315,401	327,038	384,984	402,406
Tennessee	80,107	141,603	183,059	239,459	275,719
Texas				58,161	182,566

Table 4.2 Percentage of households with slaves, percentage of slaves in population, 1860[18]

State	% Households with Slaves	% Slaves in Population
Mississippi	49	55
South Carolina	46	57
Georgia	37	44
Alabama	35	45
Florida	34	44
Louisiana	29	47
Texas	28	30
North Carolina	28	33
Virginia	26	31
Tennessee	25	25
Kentucky	23	20
Arkansas	20	26
Missouri	13	10
Maryland	12	13
Delaware	3	2

Table 4.3 US cotton prices and production, 1790–1860

Year	Size of Bale (lbs)	Number of Bales[19]	Price[20] (cents)/lb
1790	225	3,135	0.28
1800	225	73,145	0.44
1810	247	177,638	0.155
1820	269	334,378	0.17
1830	308	731,452	0.095
1840	368	1,346,232	0.123
1850	415	2,133,851	0.117
1860	436	3,837,402	0.13

While men and women who were field workers often did the same kinds of work, the workloads of women, the physical and psychological conditions under which they labored, and the rewards for their efforts often differed substantially, sometimes profoundly, from those of men. Moreover, occupational differences outside the field were substantial. A significant minority of females, but many fewer males, were domestics. Large holdings employed both, but antebellum women dominated these positions, especially among smaller slaveholdings. Female domestics were maids, nurses, cooks, seamstresses, spinners, weavers, and midwives, while in southern towns they were also waitresses and washerwomen. Male slaves, on the other hand, had greater opportunity to hold skilled and supervisory positions that privileged their experiences in both rural and urban settings. Men exclusively held the elite occupations of blacksmith, cooper, painter, wheelwright, carpenter, miner, tanner, and joiner and, therefore, had greater opportunity to earn extra cash and to hire themselves out to "temporary masters." They also held leadership positions as drivers, overseers, foremen, and head craftsmen that were extremely rare for women to gain.[21]

Southern female slaves, especially those who were "field" workers, routinely worked longer hours and were responsible for more work – a combination actually of skilled, manual, domestic, and sexual labor – that continued well into the night and during time that male slaves traditionally had "off." The phenomenon of assigning slave women full-time field work, coupled with occasional or even permanent part-time work as domestics or skilled labor, such as weaving, sewing, or midwifery, was especially important on small-to-middling-sized farms or plantations. Fannie Moore in North Carolina, for example, recalled that her mother "work in de fiel' all day 'nd piece and quilt all night. Den she ha' to spin enough thread to make four cuts for de white fo'ks ebber night. Why sometime I nebber go to bed. Had to hold de light for her to see by."[22]

Sara Colquitt's experiences as a slave on a small tobacco farm in Virginia, and later on a large cotton plantation in Alabama, were exemplary. Her Virginia owners were "good" she admitted, but "us had to work hard and late." Sara routinely performed a combination of field and domestic tasks, all the while caring for her infant child. "I worked in de fields every day from 'fore daylight to almost plumb dark," she recalled. "I usta take my littlest baby wid me. I had two chilluns, and I'd tie him up to a tree limb to keep off de ants and bugs whilst I hoed and worked de furrow." Once her field task was completed at the end of the day, she had other labor to undertake. "I was one of de spinners, too, and had to do six cuts to de reel at de time and do hit at night plenty times." "'Sides working de fields and spinning," she concluded, "sometimes I'd hep wid de cooking up at de big House when de real cook was sick or us had a passel of company."[23] Sara's labor routine changed drastically when she was sold in the late 1850s to a planter in Alabama who had enough slaves to relegate her work sphere to that of his home. There she was responsible for most of the housework.[24] Once a slave's status became principally that of a domestic, usually their labor, like that of Sara's in Alabama, was confined to their master's home, barnyard, loom house, kitchen, and gardens, although it was not unusual for slave domestics to be sent to the fields during harvest time.

Female field laborers, even those on large holdings, on the other hand, might be called on for some sort of domestic labor if the master or mistress wanted to fill some temporary void. It was unusual, therefore, except on the especially large plantations, for women to be merely confined to agricultural work for the duration of their "prime" status. Young slave females and elderly women had even more diverse assignments. And it was not that men did more labor in the fields. The farm journals of antebellum southern planters, as well as the diaries of "observers" of slave women's labor, routinely note that women and men performed comparable levels of work in the "field."

Rising early in the morning to the sound of an overseer or driver blowing a horn and working until nightfall for five-and-a-half to six days a week, female laborers stood toe-to-toe with male field workers. Some historians do contend that men did the heaviest and dirtiest work, especially clearing new fields, plowing, and ditching. Throughout the South, however, women were also responsible for this kind of work. Amelia Walker of Virginia, for example, remembered watching her mother working in the fields: "Mama plowed wid three horses – ain't dat somp'n. Thought women was sposed to work 'long wid men, I did."[25] Henrietta McCullers of North Carolina concurred proudly: "I plowed an' dug ditches 'an cleaned new groun' an' hard wuck ain't neber hurted me yit...Dey only had one man, Uncle Mose, an' so, of course, he had to have some help ter ten' bout hundert acres."[26] "Seeing a wench plowing," one Mississippi slavery observer noted, "I asked him [the overseer] if they usually held the plough. He replied that they often did."[27] Frederick Law Olmstead's observations concurred. He not only noted women routinely plowing, hoeing, ditching, and repairing roads, but also involved in the dirty task of fertilizing. "I saw women working again, in large gangs with men," he began one such description. "In one case they were distributing manure...[which] had been...carted into heaps...a number of the women were carrying it in from the heap in baskets, on their heads, and one in her apron, and spreading it with their hands between the ridges on which the cotton grew last year." The remainder, he continued, "followed with great, long handled, heavy, clumsy hoes, and pulled down the ridges over the manure, and so made new ridges for the next planting."[28] Solomon Northup's narrative of his life as a slave in antebellum Louisiana illuminated the work of female domestics in the house, yard, laundry, and barn; but he was especially impressed by the work that enslaved women performed alongside, and instead of, men in the virgin forests and tiresome fields of the rural parish where they resided. He was astonished, for example, by the "large and stout" lumberwomen, Charlotte, Fanny, Cresia, and Nelly, who could fell trees in the forest as efficiently as their male peers; by Patsey's ability to pick 500 pounds of cotton in one day; and by the women on Jim Burns's neighboring sugar and cotton plantation who produced fine harvests without any male assistance. Of the black women he met as a slave, Solomon exclaimed: "they perform their share of all the labor required on the plantation. They plough, drag, drive team, clear wild lands, work on the highway, and so forth."[29]

Male slaves, on the other hand, usually were either responsible for skilled or manual labor, not both. Likewise, comparatively few men routinely worked at night or on Saturday afternoons and Sundays, their traditional "leisure time," which many used instead in self-employment. Moreover, bondsmen received greater rewards for their labor than female slaves – larger food allowances; less responsibility for care of their offspring and home environment; greater social freedom and physical mobility; and more opportunity to move up the occupational ladder to supervisory roles. Of course there were many exceptions in each case, particularly because the size of the slaveholding, the gender ratio of the prime workers, and the kind of major crop being produced had much influence on the slave's experience as a worker. Charlie Hudson recalled, for example, that on his farm both men and women did work at night, after they returned from the fields: "De 'omans cooked supper whilst de mens chopped wood."[30] Still, these broad differences hold more than they collapse.

Motherhood added another dimension to the labor of female slaves. Clearly, slave women were the principal rearers of their children, whether in matrifocal, nuclear, or extended families. As such, they were responsible for their day-to-day care, even when owners provided nurses. Frances Willingham, for one, recalled the work that women did at night while men rested. "When slaves come in from de fields at night de 'omans cleant up deir houses atter dey et, and den washed and got up early next mornin' to put de clothes out to dry." "Mens would eat, set 'round talkin' to other mens and den go to bed."[31] But it was not just the food and clothing preparation, social and skilled instruction, and nurture and discipline of slave children that equaled large amounts of additional work for these women. It was also the labor negotiations with owners, mistresses, overseers, and drivers that mothers reluctantly, but often forcefully, entered into on behalf of their children. They knew only too well the problems their offspring would face once they entered the slave-work world. They also knew that once a slave started to work, it placed a real "value" on him or her, a value that owners did not hesitate to accrue through sale or exchange. Certainly, the large numbers of slave women who headed matrifocal households, or lived with their children while their husbands lived elsewhere, often found themselves in this kind of precarious situation.

Fannie Moore's description of her mother's relationship with their overseer on a South Carolina plantation is instructive. "De ol' overseeah he hate my mammy, case she fight him for beatin' her chillun. Why she git more whuppins for dat den anythin' else. She hab twelve chillun."[32] A slave woman from Georgia uttered similar complaints, but about her mistress. "My marster's wife was very mean to all of us," she explained. "She sold my oldest child to somebody where I couldn't ever see him any more [sic] and kept me...She took my baby child and put her in the house with her to nurse her baby and make fire. And all while she was in the house with her she had to sleep on the floor."[33] Nancy Williams of Yanceville, Virginia recalled the story of "Ant Cissy," a slave woman who called their owner a "mean dirty nigger-trader" when he decided not to keep her daughter Lucy's labor for his own, but to sell her. When her son Hendley died some time later, Cissy refused to publicly acknowledge any grief for her son's death, preferring instead to again take the opportunity to voice her bitter feelings about Lucy's sale. "Ant Cissy ain't sorrored much at the death of her child," Williams concluded. "She went straight up to ole Marsa' an' shouted in his face, 'Praise Gawd, praise Gawd! My little chile is gone to Jesus. That's one chile of mine you never gonna sell.' "[34] Undoubtedly, slave mothers often damaged their own relations with labor supervisors while trying to negotiate the work their children did and the conditions under which they worked.

Likewise, much of the negotiations that slave women had to enter into as laborers themselves was often across gender lines, offering further difficulties. The world in which they lived and worked was not just racist, it was profoundly sexist. To be doubly discriminated against as workers, with virtually no chance of gaining a position of authority at their workplaces, meant that these women had extremely little bargaining power with the men who inevitably had the last say as to their work assignments, conditions, rewards, and punishments. More often than not, slave women must have felt themselves caught between a rock and a hard place as workers. If, on the one hand, they resisted their workloads or conditions too much, their male supervisors might feel especially threatened by the undermining power of those thrice considered their inferiors – as women, blacks, and workers. If, on the other hand, they were submissive or compliant workers, they ran the risk of arousing the sexual attention of those in charge. And then there was always the threat of engendering hostility from fellow workers who might feel betrayed in either instance.

Another important difference between the experiences of slave female and male laborers, perhaps the most significant difference of all, was the sexualized component of women's work. Most male slaves did not face the constant sexual harassment or battery that many slave women confronted and most feared. Indeed, one aspect of female labor that scholars are just beginning to fully recognize as *labor* was the demand that slave girls and women act as sexual outlets for male owners, overseers, drivers, and male slaves as well. The debate over slave breeding rages on, even though there is substantial evidence to document its prevalence throughout the South and across the generations. Yet the use of the slave female body to produce a "new crop" of slave laborers was only one part of the phenomenon of their sexual enslavement. Masters and other males who came in contact with slave women expected, and often demanded, their compliance with requests for sexual favors. It literally became part of their jobs and a source of enormous pain for the enslaved.

Indeed, the sexual abuse of female slaves was one of the most disruptive traumas that slave girls, women, and their families experienced.

Scholars can thank Deborah Gray White for her ground-breaking analysis of the designated personalities of slave women as either "Jezebel" or "Mammy."[35] Indeed, the role of Jezebel in the slaveholder's imagination tells us much about the sexual labor of female slaves. If "Mammy," the popular, endearing image of the older domestic slave female, was the embodiment of the perfect mature woman, maternal and nurturing, pious and selfless, Jezebel, or the sexualized slave woman, was just the opposite.[36] In the apologist myths and minds of white southerners, she came to embody all the dread associated with womanhood from Eve through time – an evil, manipulative temptress who used her insatiable sexual appetite for personal gain. She was seducer, adulteress, whore for hire, all wrapped up in one. Jezebel was the bane of her mistress and the damnation of her master or any man who fell under her spell. Few men could resist her wiles; from presidents to the lowliest overseer, Jezebel had her way with them. "Marse Sid ain't got but one weakness an' dat am pretty yaller gals," Chaney Spell of North Carolina admitted. "He just can't desist [sic] them. Finally Mis' Mary found it out an' it pretty near broke her heart."[37] Slave mistress Mary Chesnutt's statement about slave women is famous enough: "we live surrounded by prostitutes."[38] It reverberated within the complaints of many white women in slaveholding families. Indeed, the presence of Jezebel was the basis for the bitterest denunciation of the institution of slavery by southern white women of that class.

Slaves, especially enslaved women, of course, had a radically different opinion as to the nature of the problem. Rosa Maddox, raised in Mississippi and Louisiana, would have challenged Chesnutt's characterization. In defense of Jezebel, she likely would have replied, as she did to her interviewer when asked to speak on the subject: "a white man laid a nigger gal whenever he wanted her. Seems like some of them had a plumb craving for the other color. Leastways they wanted to start themselves out on the nigger women."[39] "Marsters an' overseers use to make slaves dat wuz wid deir husbands git up, [and] do as they say," one ex-slave noted.

"Send husbands out on de farm, milkin' cows or cuttin' wood. Den he gits in bed wid slave himself. Some women would fight an' tussel. Others would be [h]umble – feared of dat beatin'. What we saw, couldn't do nothing 'bout it," he added. "My blood is b[o]ilin' now [at the] thoughts of dem times. Ef dey told dey husbands he wuz powerless."[40]

The sexual standard of the day rewarded plantation patriarchs with extramarital sexual pleasure, vis-à-vis slave girls and women, leading these men to demand sexual favors as part of these females' duties, their labor.[41] It was a tradition passed down from one generation of slaveholding men to the next. "[Ethel Mae] told me 'bout Marsa bringing his son Levey...down to the cabin," one former slave confessed. "They both took her – the father showing the son what it was all about – and she couldn't do nothing 'bout it."[42]

White patriarchal privilege was only one part of the slaveholder's "reasoning." The commonality of the practice, too, must have numbed some to the moral sting. Ex-slave Jacob Manson, for example, recalled that many of the slaveholding men in his neighborhood had slave women. "Marster had no chilluns by white women," he noted. "He had his sweethearts among his slave women. I ain't no man for tellin' false stories. I tells de truth, an' dat is de truth." Manson stated that his master, Colonel Bun Eden, was so taken with his slave women that he refused to hire white overseers, but used black drivers instead – "he liked some of de nigger women too good to have any uder white man playin' arou' wid 'em." At that time, Manson added, "it wus a hard job to find a marster dat didn't have women 'mong his slaves. Dat wus a ginerel thing 'mong de slave owners."[43]

As a former slave noted above, owners were not the only men who pursued slave women's sexual favors and who responded badly when refused. Overseers also had access to, and power over, slave women that they did not hesitate to use. "Dar was an overseer who use to tie mother up in de barn wid a rope aroun' her arms up over her head, while she stood on a block. Soon as dey got her tied, dis block was moved an' her feet dangled, you know, couldn' tech de flo,'" Minnie Folkes began her story of her mother's abuse. "Dis ole man, now, would start beatin' her nekked 'til the blood run down her back to her heels. I took an' seed de whelps an' scar fer my own self wid dese heah two eyes." He beat her so viciously, Folkes explained, because she "fuse to be wife to dis man." Folkes maintained that her owner never knew the elder Folkes was treated so, for "ef slaves would tell, why dem overseers would kill 'em," or so they feared.[44] Even slave men could rape or harass a slave girl or woman without fear of retribution, that is, unless she was a "favorite" of his owner or overseer, or the sex act was deemed "perverse." The slave man George, for example, was indicted in a Mississippi court in October 1859 for the rape of a female slave child. Although the lower court found him guilty and sentenced him to die, the judgment was reversed on appeal.[45]

The prices of slave women reveal the "value" slaveholders placed on this female "asset." Throughout the South and over the antebellum decades, male slaves generally cost more than females, skilled laborers more than field hands, and the young more than the elderly.[46] The only real exception to these rules of the market was the fancy girl trade and "good breeding" women. "Marie was pretty, dat's why he took her to Richmond to sell her. You see, you could git a powerful lot of money in dose days for a pretty gal," Carol Anna Randall explained of her sister's sale to the Carolinas. Joe Bruin of the Alexandria, Virginia firm of Bruin and Hill placed Emily Russell, a beautiful mulatto whom he planned to sell as a prostitute in New Orleans, on the market for US$1,800. Slave autobiographer James Pennington explained:

> It is under the mildest form of slavery, as it exists in Maryland, Virginia and Kentucky, that the finest specimens of coloured females are reared....for the express purpose of supplying the market [to] a class of economical Louisian and Mississippi gentlemen, who do not wish to incur the expense of rearing legitimate families, they are, nevertheless, on account of their attractions, exposed to the most shameful degradation.[47]

Pennington went on to illustrate his claim by presenting the case of slaves Mary Jane and Emily Catherine Edmondson, ages 14 and 16, priced together at US$2,250. They charged such an exorbitant fee, Pennington asserted, because they intended to sell them as prostitutes in the Deep South.[48]

As the demand for slaves increased over the decades after the legal closing of the international slave trade, many slaveholders resorted to forcing slave women and men to procreate, to produce a "new crop" of laborers that their owners used or, increasingly, sold. The slave's sexual acts were part of the labor that owners demanded to produce additional laborers. The fertility of slave women was routinely a part of the advertisements for slave females and discussed in the negotiations for their sale. Moreover, prospective buyers were allowed to physically examine these women to ascertain their ability to bear children. Closely related to the myth of Jezebel and the reality of her vicious abuse and exploitation as a sex slave, therefore, was that of the slave-breeder woman. Slave testimony is rife with documentation that more than suggests that some slaves were part of breeding experiments, at least during the antebellum era.

"I was about 17 years old when I was given to my young Maser, me and the man that I called my husband," Lizzie Grant of Dunbar, West Virginia explained:

> So our young Maser put us together to raise from just like you would stock today. They never thought anything about it either. They never cared or thought about our feelings in the matter. Of course we got use to one another and never thought anyting about the way they put us to live...Maser made me marry him as we were going to raise him some more slaves. Maser said it was cheaper to raise slaves than it was to buy them...[49]

Josephine Howard described a similar marriage between her parents. "Course mamma an' pap wasn't married like folks is now, 'cause back den de white folks jes' put de slave men an' women together jes' like dey is horses or cattle."[50]

Slave men as well as women were forced to participate.[51] Yet, from the slave's perspective, there were several reasons why the process was much more abusive to women than to men. Certainly, the consequences were greater for the women involved – they had to sustain the pregnancies and raise the children born of these "couplings." Likewise, they risked being repeatedly forced to have sex with other men, whipped severely, or sold if they did not produce the number of children that their owners thought them capable of birthing. Slaveholders rarely blamed a couple's infertility on the male, but rather on the woman's unwillingness to conceive, her secretive use of contraception or abortion, or her physical inability to bear children. "De 'breed woman' always bring mo' money den de res, ebben de men," one ex-slave woman explained. "When dey put her on de block dey put all her chillun aroun' her to show folks how fast she ben hab chillun. When she sold, her family nebber see her agin."[52]

Slave Family Life in the Antebellum South

The thriving domestic slave trade that these women, their partners, and their offspring were more and more a part of during the decades before the Civil War ripped asunder generations-old families and communities as traders forced enslaved men, women, and children from the Upper South to the Deep South frontiers that became Arkansas, Alabama, Mississippi, Louisiana, and Texas. Family, therefore, did not necessarily mean a nuclear family or stability, and community did not always maintain the promise of loyalty and support. Still, the thousands of those in the antebellum generations who composed narratives often spoke about family members, kinship, marriage, communal life, and ideals. Given the violent oppression imposed by owners, overseers, drivers, slave traders, and southern law – which allowed no slave couple to legally marry; denied slaves parental rights; and did not recognize slave men as patriarchal heads of their families, or slave women as feminine dependants worthy of physical and sexual protection and emotional support – those gendered and familial ideals were sometimes impossible to realize and certainly, if ever realized fully, were difficult to sustain.

The auto/biographical documents offered by those persons who were enslaved tell us much about what family was, what it was not and, as far as they were concerned, what it should have been, even though they were enslaved. During the colonial period, authors who had been enslaved and had gained access to the western press, such as Ottobah Cugoano, Olaudah Equiano, and Albert Gronniosaw, as noted in chapter 3, added their voices to the descriptions of family life in Africa before they were enslaved, lending some idea of their ideals. Still, Africa was not so distant in the experiences and imaginations of antebellum slaves (especially those in regions where Africans were still being actively smuggled into) that some creole blacks did not openly demonstrate respect and reverence for those in their communities who retained traditional cultural beliefs, practices, and knowledge.[53] There remained, as well, sometimes the hope, or fantasy, that African kin would arrive from the ancestral home to carry their loved ones back. Shadrack Richard in Georgia, for example, remembered the story of his African grandfather who purportedly traveled to Georgia to buy his son and take him back to West Africa. Both died before they could return.[54] Africa, for many, therefore, continued to be a site of pride as well as familial and communal reference where blacks were powerful, had a social, cultural, and political "place," and had caring kin.

Narrative accounts of antebellum slave family and community life also indicate that these social arenas were the psychological sources of personal strength and group accomplishments that, within the violent, unpredictable world of southern slaves, were nothing short of miraculous. Nat Turner's account of how he came to organize and lead the slave revolt of August 1831 in Southampton County, Virginia, for example, is full of references to his socialization by his parents, his grandmother, and local blacks who, collectively, convinced him that he was intellectually and psychically gifted. "Having soon discovered to be great," Turner noted of his local acclaim, he believed that he "must appear so, and therefore studiously avoided mixing in society, and wrapped myself in mystery, devoting my time to fasting and prayer."[55] The celebrated author and escaped slave Harriet Jacobs, like Nat Turner, also lived in an extended slave family that gave her a sense of exceptionalism, not only because of her own personal traits, but also because her family held all its members to high standards of character and diligence.[56]

For others, family and community, or the lack of this kin/ social network, shaped their lives in equally profound ways. Famed abolitionist, author, and editor Frederick Douglass, for example, raised in Maryland, repeatedly spoke of the absence of familial and communal support in his bestselling *Narrative of the Life of Frederick Douglass*. His mother was, Douglass noted, for all intents and purpose, absent, as was a filial bond between him and his siblings. "My mother and I were separated when I was but an infant," he explained.[57]

Although raised by his grandmother with his siblings, Douglass also asserted "the early separation of us from our mother had well-nigh blotted the fact of our relationship from our memories."[58]

Close blood relationships, nonetheless, mattered, and typically mattered a great deal to the enslaved. Despite the increased experience of familial separation, dispersal and loss as a result of a growing domestic slave trade from the 1820s onward, marriage, children, and extended kin remained central and essential to the identities, psyches, and imaginations of the enslaved, perhaps even more than in earlier periods. Why? The actual demographic possibility for some type of family relations was greatest for slaves in the decades leading up to the Civil War, when men and women of childbearing age were present in equal proportions on large holdings and within walking distance of those in small quarters. Moreover, many southern slaves had families that were generations old by the height of the antebellum era. Memories of families and communities flung across the Atlantic diaspora remained important for some, but most focused their attention on regionally based family near at hand, or at least near in memory. While most had some experience with familial loss, parts of functional slave families and communities still persisted for many.

What were the ideals of family and community life with which antebellum enslaved men and women identified? Within family units, distinct gender roles often held sway, as they had in earlier generations. Husbands expected wives to be supportive and obedient. "A man wid a good wife, one dat pulls wid him," Ezra Adams explained, "can see and feel some pleasure and experience some independence."[59] They, along with their masters, also expected women to provide the domestic labor for their families. One ex-slave remembered how his mother fed her children, even if she went to bed hungry herself, and "treated us with all the tenderness which her own miserable condition would permit."[60] Elizabeth Sparks of Matthews County, Virginia explained that her mother "wuz a house woman" who had to wash her owners' clothes before she could clean those of her family. "Sometimes she'd be washin' clothes way up 'round midnight. No sir, couldn't wash any nigguh's clothes in daytime."[61]

Prime women, like Sparks's mother, obviously could not offer constant care for their young. Some of these childcare tasks went to elderly, very young, or infirm slaves during the working hours of full-time working mothers. Josephine Briston of South Carolina recalled that "De old lady dat looked after us, her name was Mary Novlin. ... [and] she looked after every blessed thing for us all day long en cooked for us right along wid de mindin."[62] Charlie Van Dyke, permanently disabled because of a leg injury, "work[ed] around the yard and look[ed] after his sisters and brothers and also the other slave children" while his mother and other parents worked.[63] Communal expectations of men and women who had medicinal knowledge was that they would treat their kin and others for numerous illnesses, including dropsy, asthma, rheumatism, colds, and consumption. The slave community, and masters, expected elderly slave women who had experience as midwives to assist pregnant women.[64]

Familial expectations were that men and boys would provide physical protection and emotional support too. One former slave recounted stories of the men who kept terrorizing panthers away from the quarters.[65] As a young Virginia slave boy, the famed black leader of the late nineteenth and early twentieth centuries, Booker T. Washington, could rely on his brother John to "break in" his new, rough flax shirt that pierced his skin like "a hundred small pin-points."[66] Mingo, who lost his parents as a small child to sale, honored his father's friend John with the recollection that "My pappy tol' him to take care of me for him," and John's attention on that Alabama plantation was "the only caren'" Mingo remembered.[67] Jacob Branch tried to shield his mother from her mistress' cowhide.[68] Some husbands and fathers, faced with familial separation, escaped only to return and take their kin with them. Celestia Avery, for one, told of her uncle who built a shelter in a cave in the woods of Georgia and then "carried his wife and two children back" to live with him until freedom.[69]

Fathers, brothers, grandfathers, and uncles, when present in families and communities, not only helped to protect and comfort, but also provided their families with food, clothing, recreation, and leadership. Before he ran away, Charles Ball's father would bring food, presents, and entertain his family when he visited.[70] One former bondsman from late antebellum Alabama suggested the importance of food supplements males provided when noting: "The slaves got plenty of coons, rabbits and bear meat, and could go fishing on Sundays, as well as turtle hunting."[71]

Slave Punishment and Material Support

Slaves not only had expectations of kind, even loving, treatment and consideration from their family members and larger slave community, but also believed that their owners should treat them fairly and kindly, given the value of their labor. Nonetheless, former slaves repeatedly testified that antebellum southern owners of even the most compliant bonded persons sometimes would treat them savagely.[72]

Enslaved children were not exempt from owner brutality. It was not unusual, for example, for slaveholding men and women to demand that children work, even if ill; to punish slave youth harshly, sometimes sadistically, when they were unable to perform labor with adult-like skill or stamina; and to sell those thought to be disobedient or if it was fiscally beneficial to do so. Once slave boys and girls began to labor and came under the direct supervision of whites, therefore, they began to suffer psychological and physical abuse similar to that endured by adults. Delia Garlic of Alabama, for example, remembered that, as a child worker, her mistress had run a hot iron up and down her arm because her baby had hurt its hand while playing with the young domestic.[73] The youngster Armaci Adams fainted from the severe beating her owner gave her when someone killed a turkey she was responsible for raising.[74] The persistent fear of sale and subsequent isolation from family and friends was particularly frightening to young slaves because it was common to sell slaves as young adolescents. This too was the age when girls were first subject to sexual abuse, when they were still virgins.[75]

"I now entered on my fifteenth year – a sad epoch in the life of a slave girl," Harriet Jacobs began her tale of sexual harassment. "My master began to whisper foul words in my ear. Young as I was, I could not remain ignorant of their import."[76] "When my sister was 16 years old," Lewis Clark explained, "her master sent for her." It was a meeting that changed the young woman's life, and that of her family's, forever. According to Clark, his sister was "pretty" and near white. "She was whiter than I am, for she took after her father," he explained of his mulatto sibling. "When he sent for her again," Clark continued, "she cried, and didn't want to go." Finally confiding her troubles in their mother, there was little that her female parent, who had gone through the same experience, could advise her except to try to "be decent, and hold up her head above such things, if she could." Their master, enraged that the girl should publicly expose his desire for her and her rejection of him, "sold her right off to Louisiana." "We were told afterwards," Lewis added, that "she died there of hard usage."[77]

Antebellum slaves also testified that they worked for the most minimal, and sometimes wholly inadequate, quotas of food, clothing, medical attention, and shelter.[78] Those who had nutritionally adequate diets and clothing typically worked hard during their "spare" time to provide it for themselves. Slaveholders usually afforded only "mush" for children to eat, a porridge of milk and bread made from corn or wheat. As children aged and became more lucrative workers, masters allocated them small portions of meat, typically fatty pork. They provided adult workers with weekly rations of flour and meat or fish. Many slaves augmented their food allowances with vegetables they grew themselves, or meat and fish that mostly men caught in the forests and nearby streams or rivers.[79]

Clothing allowances were not any better than food. Owners distributed work clothing twice a year, in the fall and late spring. Children wore one-piece shifts made from wool, cotton, or flax. Prime males received long pants and shirts, straw hats for the summer and shoes for the winter. Full-time working females wore dresses or skirts and blouses, along with scarves for their heads, as well as shoes and coats for cold weather wear. Many adolescent girls and women, trained as spinners, weavers, knitters, dyers, quilters, and seamstresses, provided additional clothing and household goods, such as quilts, blankets, and bed coverlets, for themselves and their families from reworking cast-off material, yarn, and clothing. "I could take the wool offen the sheep's back an' kerry it thru ter CLAWTH. Wash it, card it, spin it, weave it, sew it inter clothes – an' (with a laugh) wear it, when I gotter chance," one former slave woman noted.[80]

Most enslaved males built the housing that slaves occupied, as well as some of their sparse furnishings. Antebellum slave housing was usually a small, wooden, one-door, no-windowed cabin comprised of a single room and perhaps a loft and cellar. Married couples, as well as nuclear and matrifocal families, typically lived in separate family shelters, but prime workers who were not married and did not have kin in their quarters – a growing phenomenon as a result of the active, antebellum domestic slave trade – lived with other single workers of the same gender. Domestic and skilled servants sometimes were found living in a segregated quarter closer to their owner's homes. Small children who were domestics, and sometimes adult household workers who served as personal maids and valets, at times slept in the rooms of those whom they served.[81]

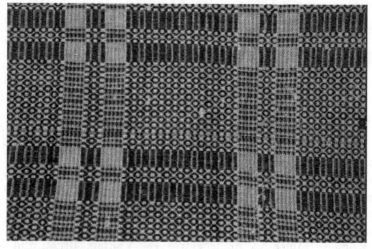

4.3 Partial woven panel, US slave coverlet, cotton, indigo, red natural dye, c. 1840
Source: Cones Collection

Antebellum Slave Resistance

Antebellum slave resistance, of innumerable forms, to individual and kin abuse was palpable. Antebellum resistance strategies mirrored those of the colonial era. Some, like Charles Ball's father in Maryland, ran away after his beloved wife was sold to Georgia and he learned of his own impending sale.[82] Minnie Folkes's mother repeatedly took the whipping that left her bloody, rather than succumb to her overseer's sexual demands, while Sukie Abbott in the Southside of Virginia fought back and was sold.[83] Lulu Wilson's mother "would knock him [her master] down and bloody him up," but he still continued to sell her children when he wanted to do so.[84] Famed seamstress Elizabeth Keckley refused to let the man who rented her beat her, declaring: "No, Mr Bingham, I shall not take down my dress before you. Moreover, you shall not whip me unless you prove the stronger. Nobody has the right to whip me but my own master, and nobody shall do so if I can prevent it."[85] Lucretia Alexander of Arkansas recalled that her father was sold five times rather than submit to physical abuse, while a slave man who worked with W. L. Boost was whipped to death because he refused to work as much as his owner demanded.[86] A former North Carolina bondswoman recalled that her mother turned to prayer: "My mammy she trouble in her heart bout de way they treated. Ever night she pray for de Lawd to git her an' her chillun out ob de place."[87] Some slaves even resorted to suicide as the final resistance effort. One Texas ex-slave explained that an elderly man on her plantation killed himself after being whipped. The next morning they saw "old Beans, what's so old he can't work good no more...hangin' from a tree back of de quarters. He done hang himself to 'scape he mis'ry!"[88] Walter Rimm remembered that "when massa start to whip him [Bob Love] he cuts his throat and dives into de river. He am dat scairt of a whippin' dat he kilt himself."[89]

Slaves also resisted their material deprivation and psychological abuse. They routinely stole food, especially meat, when they were hungry. Others were punished for talking back and other forms of disrespect to whites, stealing clothing, not performing their assigned tasks completely or properly, or sometimes for annoying their master or mistress in some unrecognizable way. Temporary escape to nearby caves and forests provided some relief from those beaten and washed down in brine, while many escaped singularly or in kin and communal groups to free territories, states, and countries.[90] Some left their masters just long enough to find others with whom they felt connected. "Aunt Jane was no kin to me," Charlotte Brooks confessed, "but I felt that she was because she came from my old home."[91]

As in the earlier time periods, antebellum slave men tended to escape permanently and long distance, while women escaped temporarily and over short distances. Of the 562 runaway slaves whom owners advertised for in the Huntsville, Alabama newspapers between 1820 and 1860, for example, 85 percent were men and 15 percent were female.[92] Lavinia Bell was one of the female exceptions who successfully escaped, but not without paying dearly for her efforts. Bell, who was held near Galveston, Texas, repeatedly tried to escape. She eventually made it to Canada, but the toll her resistance took on her was extreme. According to Bell, and Montreal physician John Reddy, the price for freedom that she paid was cut, burnt, broken, and beaten into her body – in her slit ears; broken teeth; broken jaw; skull fractures; large brands on her abdomen and hand; scars and marks covering her back and most of her body; and a finger that had been cut off.[93] Typically, those like Bell who attempted escape and were caught suffered extreme physical brutalization. Adeline Cunningham, for example, recalled that a slave who ran away in Lavaca County, Texas was blinded as a result.[94] Solomon Northup remembered Celeste, the Avoyelles Parish, Louisiana woman who hid in the palmettos and declared that, even though she was ill, she "would rather die in the swamp than be whipped to death by the overseer."[95]

"Routes" that slaves took on the "underground railroad" crisscrossed slave territory, depositing escaped fugitives north (to free northern states and Canada), south (to Mexico) and west (to California and other territories either free or too far away to matter). Basements and barns of farmhouses, churches, shipping companies, and other businesses controlled by secreted abolitionists – Quakers, free blacks, and others – served as "stops" along the way to freedom. Slaves traveled individually, as couples, in family groups, and as communities. Fantastical, but true, stories of escape recall the great, even outrageous, lengths to which slaves went to gain freedom. Henry "Box" Brown managed to escape by being sealed in a crate and shipped north from Virginia. Harriet Tubman, a disabled Maryland slave woman, managed to free herself through escape in 1849, only to return to the South and help more than seventy others to freedom. And spouses Ellen and William Craft, in 1848, disguised themselves as master (light-skinned Ellen cross-dressed as William's ailing owner) and slave to take the train and steamboat to freedom in Philadelphia from Macon, Georgia. They also speak to the significant amount of aid each fugitive had, either in slave territory or once they reached "freedom." Vigilance committees of black and white men and women in Philadelphia, Boston, Albany, and other free regions of the country helped to ferret men and women away from impending danger, provided them with food, clothing, shelter, further transportation, medicine, legal aid, and a means to support themselves.[96]

While slave resistance was present daily and in varied forms, no demonstration of slave dissatisfaction captured the white imagination, ire, and uniformly violent response more than slave revolts. From the colonial period to the end of the antebellum, more than forty revolts occurred, and many other plots in the United States that were not actually executed were discovered. Both slave men and women were implicated in these events. Of those antebellum revolts, that of Nat Turner in Southampton County, Virginia in August 1831, was especially important because of: its location – the state with the largest slave population; its timing – coming two years after David Walker's incendiary *Appeal* and the same year as the launching of the most important national anti-slavery newspaper, William Lloyd Garrison's and Isaac Knapp's *Liberator*; its local impact on whites – the murder of sixty local whites; and the legislative impact in Virginia, that was largely copied throughout slaveholding states and territories – the passing of extensive legal restrictions regarding slave and free black mobility, literacy, occupations, residency, religious practices, and the ability to meet publicly and privately.[97]

Table 4.4 Slave revolts in colonial North America and the United States, 1526–1860[98]

Date (Year)	Name	Location
1526	San Miguel de Guadeloupe Revolt	Sapelo Island, Georgia (Spanish North America)
1691	Mingoe's Revolt	Middlesex and Rappahannock Counties, Virginia
1708	Newton Slave Revolt	Long Island, New York
1711	Sebastian's Revolt	South Carolina
1712	New York Slave Revolt	New York City, New York
1720	Benjamin Cattle Revolt	Charleston, South Carolina
1729	Blue Ridge Mountain Revolt	Maroon colony in Blue Ridge Mountains of Virginia
1730	Williamsburg Revolt	Williamsburg, Virginia
1738	Georgia Revolt	Georgia
1738	Maryland Revolt	Prince George's County, Maryland
1739	Stono Slave Revolt	Stono River area, South Carolina
1740	Charleston Revolt	Charleston, South Carolina
1741	Panic of New York	New York City, New Jersey
1767	Alexandria Revolt	Alexandria, Virginia
1771–1774	Savannah Revolts	Savannah and St Andrews Parish, Georgia
1782	St Malo Revolt	Spanish Louisiana
1791–1792	Point Coupee Slave Revolt	French Louisiana
1795	Point Coupee Revolt	Spanish Louisiana
1792	Northampton Slave Revolt	Northampton County, Virginia
1797	Screven Slave Revolt	Screven County, Georgia
1799	Southampton Slave Revolt	Southampton County, Virginia

Table 4.4 *(continued)*

Date (Year)	Name	Location
1800–1802	Gabriel's Conspiracy	Henrico County, Virginia
1803	York Slave Revolt	York, Pennsylvania
1805	Wayne Slave Revolt	Wayne County, North Carolina
1805	Chatham Manor Revolt	Stafford County, Virginia
1811	Charles Deslondes Uprising	La Place, Louisiana
1817	St Mary's Revolt	St Mary's County, Maryland
1818	Wilmington Revolt	Wilmington, North Carolina
1820	Talbot Island Revolt	Talbot Island, Florida
1822	Denmark Vesey Rebellion	Charleston, South Carolina
1831	Nat Turner Rebellion	Southampton County, Virginia
1831	Seaford Revolt	Seaford, Eastern Shore, Maryland
1835	Brazos Revolt	Brazos, Texas
1837	Alexandria Revolt	Alexandria, Louisiana
1840	Avoyelles, Rapides, Iberville Revolts	Avoyelles, Rapides, Iberville Parishes, Louisiana
1842	Cherokee Nation Slave Revolt	Oklahoma
1845	Maryland Revolts	Rockville and Charles County, Maryland
1848	Doyle Revolt	Fayette County, Kentucky
1856	New Iberia Revolt	New Iberia, Louisiana
1858	Coffeesville Revolt	Coffeesville, Mississippi
1859	John Brown's Raid	Harper's Ferry, Virginia

But it was not just revolts in US slave territory that frightened antebellum southern whites and deepened the resolve of enslaved blacks to fight for freedom. Shipboard slave revolts were still occurring in the Atlantic throughout the era. The US press and public were especially intrigued by the details and outcome of the African rebellion that occurred on the Cuban slaver *La Amistad* in 1839. Brought illegally from Sierra Leone to Havana aboard the Portuguese slaver *Tecora*, and then sold to Spanish planters who intended to sell them elsewhere in the Caribbean, 53 Africans revolted on July 1, 1839, killing most of the crew. They hoped to sail back to Africa, but were seized in US waters on August 24 and imprisoned in New Haven, Connecticut. Very public trials regarding their status as either slave or free, given the end of the legal African slave trade in the United States in 1808 and the illegality of the trade to Spanish colonies as well, ensued over the next two years. The Africans, under the leadership of Singbe (Joseph Cinque), were assisted in their efforts to gain freedom by northern abolitionists. To add to their cause célèbre, former president of the United States John Quincy Adams argued, and won, their case before the US Supreme Court in 1841.[99]

That same year, slaves being shipped from Virginia to New Orleans revolted on the Atlantic coast slaver *Creole*, killing one crew member before arriving in the free British island of Nassau in the Bahamas. The revolt was led by a fugitive slave, Madison Washington, who had been captured after returning to Virginia from Canada to retrieve his wife. Local Nassau residents demanded freedom for the Virginia slaves, based on Britain's 1833 Act of Emancipation. The British government did not return the slaves, allowing them to remain free, but did compensate their owners the hefty sum of US$110,330.[100]

Antebellum Slave Community Life

The actions of the freed British slaves on Nassau who demanded freedom for the fugitives from Virginia suggest an operative black nationalism in the Atlantic world. Locally and in the diaspora as well, however, no family or community was perfect, and certainly antebellum enslaved men and women instigated and endured their share of internal abuses. Some slaves documented incidences of stealing, desertion, and "hitting, fussing, fighting, and rukkussing in the quarters."[101] Anderson Furr of Georgia remembered that, on his farm, slave men sometimes would "get rowdy-lak, drinkin' liquor and fightin."[102] Others would inform on their fellow bondmen or women or assist overseers or owners in beating them.[103] Rose Williams in Texas complained bitterly of forced sexual relations with husband Rufus – forced by her master and Rufus.[104] Others teased or abandoned women forced into concubinage.[105] Some, like Fannie Long from North Carolina, remembered divisions and jealousies among the slaves based on color stratification, noting, for example, "dem yaller wimen wus highfalutin' too, dey thought dey wus better dan de black ones."[106] Disputes over religious beliefs were not uncommon; nor was the fear of victimization by those believed to be endowed with supernatural powers.[107]

Clearly, the gamut of injustices, misunderstandings, jealousies, dishonesties, and downright meanness found in families and communities was no less prevalent among the enslaved than the free. Still, many seemed to have concluded, as Jane Pyatt of Portsmouth, Virginia did, that: "The respect that the slaves had for their owners might have been from fear, but the real character of a slave was brought out by the respect that they had for each other."[108]

Enslaved men and women took the opportunity to express their respect for, and enjoyment of, family and community not only through marriage, childbirth and -rearing, but also through ritualized, and regularized, work, play, and worship. Enslaved people of the antebellum and earlier eras expressed their individuality, as well as familial and communal values, in everyday activities. Music, wordplay, and movement, for example, were as much a part of work routines and religious services as they were a part of the communities' numerous cornshuckings, dances, courtships, weddings, funerals, children's games, storytelling, and quiltings. One former slave from Arkansas explained that in his community "there used to be plenty of colored folk fiddlers. Dancing, candy pulling, quilting – that was about the only fun they would have. Corn shucking, too."[109] A Virginia native recalled that

"We could sing in dar, an' dance ol' squar' dance all us choosed, ha! ha! ha! Lord! Lord! I can see dem gals now on dat flo'; jes skippin' an' a trottin'."[110] Wade Owens, of Alabama, offered rich detail of the extracurricular activities his slave community enjoyed. Adults, Owens noted, would have "dem Saddy night frolics an' dance all night long an' nearly day. At de cornhusking's dey'd sing 'All 'Roun' de Corn Pile Sally,' an' dey had whiskey an' gin." Storytellers enthralled children with "all kinds of ghos' stories 'bout witches gittin' outter dey skins." Sunday church services sometimes followed Saturday night "frolics," but enslaved men and women, particularly those who did not worship with whites or under their watchful eyes, often chose a work night to worship secretly. As one former slave from antebellum Florida recalled, "The slaves went to the white folks' church on Sundays," where the white ministers would tell them to "mind your masters, you owe them your respect," but they also held their own meetings in a designated cabin.[111] At baptism, "dey'd give de water invitation an' den go in water. An' didn't dey come out happy, shouting and praying?" and at the sitting-up rituals before funerals, they would "sing, shout an' holler an' try to preach."[112]

These images of relaxation, recreation, spiritual expression, and even joy documented very limited experiences that occurred sparingly during the work calendar of the enslaved, regardless of one's age, gender, or work status whether skilled, field, domestic, or supervisory. Nonetheless, they were important to their sense of identity, their resistance to dehumanization, the bonds they forged as a community, and their psychological survival. Unfortunately, such experiences were especially difficult to acquire for those who worked on the brutal frontiers of antebellum slavery in the cotton South.

Antebellum Slave Frontiers

Antebellum slavery flourished in the Lower South and Southwest. While the Lower South states of Georgia, Alabama, Louisiana, and Mississippi were the frontier of cotton production during much of the antebellum era, Texas was the new cotton frontier at the close of the era.

Independent Mexico, including the territory of Texas, was poised to emancipate all of its slaves soon after nationhood in 1821. In East Texas, located on the borders of slave states Louisiana and Arkansas, a growing population of white immigrants from the United States struggled to maintain black slavery in order to benefit from cotton production. During the eight years between Mexico's independence and its abolition of slavery in 1829, Moses and Stephen Austin managed to gain permission to settle a colony of US Anglos in Texas.[113] They rushed into Mexico's Texas to claim fertile land and establish plantations.[114] By 1825, there were 444 slaves in Austin's colony alone – 24 percent of that settlement's population.[115] In 1834, reportedly a thousand bondspeople resided in Brazos and another thousand in Nacogdoches.[116] Most worked on farms and plantations that produced cotton, corn, and sugar.

The tension over the ability of US citizens to settle and bring slaves to Mexico's Texas, as well as the right of masters already there to maintain their human property, fueled great political, economic, cultural, and eventually military tension.[117] When the war for Texan independence from Mexico finally broke out in 1835, there seemed little doubt that, if the "Anglo revolutionaries" prevailed, black slavery would be guaranteed. And so it was.[118] Even as the war was being fought, traders were smuggling Africans into Galveston.[119]

Indeed, once Texas became part of the United States in 1848, the rush by new Anglo migrants to purchase slaves to work in the new state boosted their prices greatly, from an average of US$345 in 1845 to approximately US$800 in 1860.[120] Even on the brink of the Civil War, it was still not unheard of for Texas slaveholders to buy prime male hands for US$1,500 or even US$1,800; and prime females for approximately US$800.[121] Autobiographical accounts of former slaves are replete with examples of painful separations related to the developing institution of chattel slavery in Texas; an institution that included only 40,308 slaves in 1848, but that had expanded that population to 169,166 men, women, and children in 1861. Indeed, the number of slaves in Texas increased, on average, by more than 10,000 per year, each year, between 1850 and 1860, rendering Texas the state with the most growth in slaves, by far, in the nation that decade.[122]

Unlike many former Texas slaves who knew, or remembered, little of their family history, Silvia King was certain of her personal history. She had been born in Morocco where she was married and had three children. That was before she was sold as a slave to Bordeaux, France, trained as a chef, and sold again to traders smuggling human cargo into New Orleans. There, a trader going to Texas purchased her.[123] Silvia had to leave her Moroccan family when taken to France; and years later she was forced to separate from what community she had acquired in France. These were the stories of adults. But children too figured in this painful scenario – they were the boys and girls left behind, or who became part of the trade themselves. Tom Robinson of Cass County, Texas recalled: "I can just barely remember my mother. I was not 11 when they sold me away from her."[124] Sarah Ashley recounted that she had been born in Mississippi, but sold as a child to Texas. Her sisters and father were sold in Georgia. "Us family was sep'rated," she explained.[125]

Those persons who come to Texas in the 1840s and 1850s, like those who arrived during the 1830s, mostly settled in the east; but slavery eventually came to flourish in most of the state, particularly in the countryside.[126] As throughout the frontier South and Southwest, the initial economic outlay for the land, slaves, equipment, seed, and work animals in Texas was high. Slaveholders held their black laborers to a rigorous work routine in order to successfully reap fast profits.[127]

The physical and psychological impacts on slave bodies, their families, and communities reflected the frontier-work regimen's harshness. Edgar Bendy recounted that he rarely spent time with his parents since he was hired out as a nurse in town while his parents worked on his master's cotton and sugar plantation.[128] Walter Rimm of San Patricio recalled that his father had to work regardless of illness. "Dey wants you to work if you can or can't," Rimm explained. "My pappy have de back mis'ry and many de time I seed him crawl to de grist mill. Him am buyed 'cause him an de good millhand."[129] Adeline Marshall recalled that her owner and his drivers were relentless, "all de time whippin' and stroppin' de niggers to make dem work harder. Didn't make no difference to Cap'n how little you is, you goes out to de field mos' soon's you can walk."[130]

Owners used powerful incentives to force their slaves to work as intensely, and consistently, as possible. Sarah Ford from West Columbia added that her master ordered their black driver to work and whip his slaves harshly. "Uncle Big Jake sho' work de slaves from early mornin' till night. When you is in de field you better not lag none...Massa Charles run dat plantation jus' like a factory."[131] Slaves not only complained about cruel masters, but also cruel mistresses. Julia Blanks in San Antonio, for one, remembered one mistress who was so awful to a female slave that "she would make the men tie her down, and she had what they called cat-o-nine tail, and after she got the blood to come, she would dip it in salt and pepper and whip her again. Oh, she was mean!"[132]

California remained part of Mexico after Texas withdrew. While few fugitive slaves were able to reach California, the national debate over the soul of the nation hardly was absent there. As residents began to organize for statehood in the late 1840s, many were "free soilers" who wanted no black residents, free or slave. This was especially so since the California Gold Rush of 1849 witnessed hundreds of slaveholding whites hurrying to the California goldfields with their slaves in tow, providing what many believed was unfair competition.[133] Others were either outright abolitionists or proslavery advocates. The first two senators from California typify this divide. One was the famed abolitionist John Fremont, who was the first Republican presidential nominee and the first to emancipate slaves of "rebellious" masters during the Civil War. The other inaugural California senator was William Gwin, a slaveholder, originally from Tennessee, whose slaves actually sued him for reparations. When California finally was admitted to the Union in 1850, it was declared a free state. Still, slavery did not immediately disappear. Many, like Gwin, refused to release their slaves; and bondspersons were still advertised for sale in local newspapers as late as 1853. Some state residents even continued to hope that the state would eventually divide into two separate political entities – one slave and the other free.[134]

Their hopes were encouraged by the audacious plans of William Walker, a Tennessee physician, lawyer, landgrabber, and mercenary leader who attempted to occupy Baja California and Sonora in 1853, where he planned to create an additional US slaveholding state. His attempts failed, but that did not deter Walker who went on to establish himself briefly as the political leader of Nicaragua, where he immediately reinstated slavery (it had been abolished since 1824) and later tried to create slaveholding states in other parts of Central America. Walker's filibustering actions (at war with a country with which the United States was at peace) were supported by pro-slavery southerners and westerners. Even President Franklin Pierce recognized the "legitimacy" of Walker's Nicaraguan government in 1856. Walker eventually was defeated, and returned to the United States. His last attempt to create a US slave state in Central America ended in his death by a Honduran firing squad in 1860.[135]

Despite the continual attempts to divide California and reinstate slavery in its southern region, the state remained free. As a result, some who were brought in as slaves were able to sue, successfully, for their freedom. Arriving as a slave from Mississippi via Utah, famed Angeleno Biddy Mason, for example, sued Robert Marion Smith and was granted her freedom in 1856. Archy Lee stood trial four times in search of his freedom as a California resident and finally gained it in 1858. Others, like George Washington Dennis, were able to buy their freedom.[136] The life that they gained as free blacks, however, was no more "free" than that experienced by free people of color in other parts of the nation. California legislators reduced free black rights tremendously between 1849 and 1860, denying them the franchise and the ability to testify in court or serve on juries. They also banned free blacks from homesteading and forbade them to marry across the color line.[137]

Enslaved men and women continued to try to escape to Mexico once it abolished slavery in 1829. Those who attempted to gain freedom were not just the black slaves of whites. On November 15, 1842, more than twenty black bondspeople belonging to Cherokee citizens of Oklahoma ran away in a bid to reach Mexico and freedom. Before leaving, they raided a local store for food, ammunition, and other supplies and took horses and mules for transportation. Along the way, others joined their escape – some who were the black slaves of Choctaw and Creek Indians. They had been gone for thirteen days when overcome by Cherokee forces. Two managed to evade capture, but the others were returned to their masters and to a way of life not dramatically distinct from blacks owned by whites.[138] Seven years later, however, a group of enslaved blacks of Cherokees and Creeks joined forces with Seminole blacks in Oklahoma and actually managed to escape to Mexico.[139]

Most slaveholders who migrated south and west during the antebellum era, taking their slaves with them, or buying those who had been sold once they reached their designation, did so willingly. Native American masters of black slaves who resided east of the Mississippi River, however, were forced to move from the Lower South to Oklahoma in the 1830s and 1840s during the horrific "Trail of Tears."[140] Consider, for example, the experiences of those enslaved by Cherokees – the largest group of Native American masters of black slaves in the nation.

Although the antebellum slaveholding class among Cherokees was minuscule – only 1.25 percent of Cherokee household heads in 1835 and 1.67 percent in 1860,[141] their use and treatment of slaves, as well as their status within the Cherokee Nation, paralleled that of white, southern slaveholders. Indeed, the success of Cherokee slaveholders is indicative of the success slave labor typically brought to owners in agrarian-based economies of the South and West. Cherokee slaveholders, many of whom were "mixed-blood" European- and Native-descended (78 percent in 1835, for example, as opposed to a 17 percent average for the Cherokee Nation),[142] were the economic and political elite in the Cherokee Nation. Even though slaveholders typically owned an average of seven slaves, there were some who owned substantial numbers. Joseph Vann held 110 slaves in 1835; George Waters, 100; and nineteen others owned between twenty and seventy.[143] By the early 1840s, Vann had approximately 300 slaves.[144] With the help of their black slaves who typically worked in gangs, they dominated the Cherokee agrarian economy. Generally, they cultivated corn, wheat, millet, and other cereal crops for export. Some, such as Joseph Vann's slaves, also grew cotton for export, but never to the same extent as grain crops. Others were skilled artisans or domestics, handled livestock, were employed in salt works, and even served as interpreters. Children and the elderly had other tasks similar to those who worked for whites.[145] The Cherokee slaveholding elite managed to control most of the Nation's farmland, export-crop production, and access to markets. They produced, for example, most of the corn – their most important cash crop – and owned 75 percent of the mills and 42 percent of the ferries.[146] Former slave Chaney McNair noted, for example, that "we raised wheat, corn and Hungarian Millet."[147]

Their wealth, as with other slaveholding southerners, translated into political power. When the Cherokee Nation was formally united under the New Echota Constitution of 1827, eleven of their twelve "founding fathers," or signers of the Constitution, were slaveholders. John Ross, the principal chief of the Cherokee Nation from 1828 to 1866, owned approximately nineteen slaves. John Martin, the Cherokee's Nation's treasurer and first chief justice of its supreme court, owned 100 slaves. Slaveholders also dominated the Cherokee Nation's social life, sponsoring their all-important, annual Green Corn Festival and numerous other balls, dances, picnics, and recreational and cultural events.[148]

Abolition

Mexico, on the southwestern border of the United States, was hardly the only nation in the Americas that had ended the institution by 1830. So too had Haiti (1803), Argentina (1813), Colombia (1814), and Chile (1823). Bolivia soon followed in 1831 and, certainly most importantly, with regard to influence in the United States, Britain passed a gradual emancipation act in 1833 that would end slavery in their expansive empire, including the Caribbean, by 1838. Anti-slavery forces, black and white, male and female, were effectively turning the tide. The institution of slavery in the United States was coming to a close, but not without a mighty struggle that would lead to national division and cataclysmic warfare.

The effort to end slavery, of course, did not begin in the antebellum decades.

It began when the first African challenged his or her enslavement in the Atlantic trade. Long traditions of resistance to enslavement have been documented elsewhere in this text. Without a doubt, Africans and their descendants were

4.4 Abolition time line (The Americas and the Caribbean)[149]

- 1813: Gradual emancipation adopted in Argentina.
- 1814: Gradual emancipation begins in Colombia.
- 1823: Slavery abolished in Chile.
- 1824: Slavery abolished in Central America.
- 1829: Slavery abolished in Mexico.
- 1831: Slavery abolished in Bolivia.
- 1833: Abolition of Slavery Act passed in Britain (gradual).
- 1842: Slavery abolished in Uruguay.
- 1848: Slavery abolished in all French and Danish colonies.
- 1851: Slavery abolished in Ecuador.
- 1854: Slavery abolished in Peru and Venezuela.
- 1863: Emancipation Proclamation issued in the United States.
- 1863: Slavery abolished in all Dutch colonies.
- 1865: Slavery abolished in the United States via the Thirteenth Amendment.
- 1871: Gradual emancipation established in Brazil (an earlier gradual emancipation law of 1850 was largely ignored).
- 1873: Slavery abolished in Puerto Rico.
- 1886: Slavery abolished in Cuba.
- 1888: Slavery abolished in Brazil.

the most important advocates for freedom, but they were not the only ones.

Organized efforts at anti-slavery began during the colonial period, particularly during the era of the American Revolution. These efforts resulted in the end of the legal African slave trade to the United States, the gradual end to black slavery in the Northeast and some western territories, lenient manumission laws in the Upper South, and the founding of the American Colonization Society and the colony of Liberia for freed slaves. Abolitionist efforts, however, stalled somewhat in the face of the increasing, and incredible, profits that short-staple cotton, produced by enslaved black labor, poured into the hands not only of southern slaveholders, but of those, north and west, associated with the numerous industries and services that cotton production mandated. Slave-produced wealth especially bought great political influence and, for the decades preceding the Civil War, political, cultural, and legal battles over the destiny of slavery fought between pro-slavery and anti-slavery camps.

The year 1830 marked the beginning of tremendous efforts on both sides. It was in that year, for example, that forty free black men from eight states met in a convention to consider the condition of African Americans in the nation. One year later, William Lloyd Garrison, who would become the face of radical white abolitionism in the antebellum era, published, along with Isaac Knapp, the first edition of the *Liberator Magazine*, financially backed by a small number of supporters, particularly well-to-do free blacks like James Forten. Garrison was not only a publisher, determined to dedicate his newspaper to the absolute and immediate end to slavery, but also a keen organizer and anti-slavery strategist. On January 6, 1832, he met with eleven other white men in Boston to form the New England Anti-Slavery Society (NEASS). The American Anti-Slavery Society (AASS), a biracial umbrella organization of men and women that encouraged the development of state and local affiliates, was formed in December 1833, with a number of members from the NEASS as well as twenty-one Quakers, three blacks, and four women.[150] Early national leaders included Garrison, but also: New York merchant brothers Arthur and Lewis Tappan; author, editor, and educator Theodore Dwight Weld; biracial entrepreneur Robert Purvis, his sailmaker father-in-law James Forten, and the Reverend James McCrummell, all of Philadelphia; Boston attorney Wendell Phillips; noted poet John Greenleaf Whittier; Ohio editor James G. Birney; activist author and editor Lydia Maria Child; African American brother and sister Charles Lenox Remond and Sarah Parker Remond of Salem; activist Maria Weston Chapman; black editor, author, and Presbyterian minister Samuel T. Cornish; and author, editor, and orator Lucy Stone. Five years after its founding, the AASS could boast of more than 1,350 local auxiliaries and 250,000 members.[151]

Most abolitionists of the post-1830 era did not support efforts of gradual emancipation or colonization. Immediate emancipation became the popular call of abolitionists, black and white, throughout the nation, and certainly in those areas in the Northeast, Midwest, and West where public efforts were centered. These men and women, some of whom were clergy and many of whom were deeply religious, hoped to persuade the nation to abolish slavery through pointing out the moral, social, and cultural damage that the institution was wreaking, not only on the enslaved, but on the nation as a whole. Garrison and his closest followers, therefore, were primarily pacifists who believed in moral suasion and nonviolent protest.

As the antebellum anti-slavery movement grew, however, different factions developed varied strategies. Garrison, for example, was especially opposed to engagement in the political process. He believed that the United States was politically crippled by a morally corrupt federal system that was controlled by a pro-slavery Congress and a pro-slavery Constitution. "A sacred compact, forsooth!" he wrote of the Constitution in 1832. "We pronounce it the most bloody and heaven-daring arrangement ever made by men for the continuance and protection of a system of the most atrocious villainy ever exhibited on earth."[152] Garrison wanted no "union with slaveholders" and believed that the United States would never be morally sound as long as slavery existed on its soil. The Constitution, he insisted, was "a covenant with death" and "an agreement with Hell," as he publicly burned a copy of it at the Fourth of July events sponsored by the Massachusetts Anti-Slavery Society in 1854. One of his great supporters, Wendell Phillips, added that "it is impossible for free and slave States to unite on any terms, without all becoming partners in the guilt and responsible for the sin of slavery."[153]

Many abolitionists, however, considered Garrison's critique of the government too radical and strategically impractical. His stance, along with his liberal embrace of female equal participation in abolitionist organizations, and his criticism of the nation's clergy whom he labeled pro-slavery sympathizers, led to an eventual split in the movement. At the annual meeting of the AASS in 1840, an argument regarding Garrison's support of Abby Kelley for an executive committee position ended with 300 delegates walking out and creating the American and Foreign Anti-slavery Society (AFAS). Its leadership included the Tappans, Weld, Gerrit Smith, James Birney, Cornish, Henry Highland Garnet, and Henry B. Stanton.[154] They published their own newspaper, *The National Anti-Slavery Standard*, and were especially active politically. Many of the AFAS, for example, went on to form the pro-abolitionist Liberty Party in 1840. The Liberty Party, in turn, became instrumental in the development of the Free Soil Party of 1848 and the Republican Party of 1856, both opposed to the expansion of slavery. Abraham Lincoln was the Republican Party's first winning presidential nominee in 1860.[155]

Anti-slavery advocates – black and white, male and female, affiliated with both the AASS and the AFAS – all agreed that the acquisition of free black rights was vital to their abolitionist campaigns. Not to embrace this platform would, they argued, play into the hands of pro-slavery opponents who declared that northern white abolitionists were just as uncomfortable with having blacks as their equals as southerners, *and* that they also viewed blacks as their racial inferiors.[156] Free blacks, who were active participants in every faction of the abolitionist movement, certainly believed they should be equal citizens. Despite the early push to colonize them outside the nation, free people of color were a growing community in antebellum America. Their numbers increased from 313,000 in 1830 to 378,000 ten years later, to 424,000 in 1850, and to 477,000 in 1860.[157]

In order to accomplish their ends, abolitionists used numerous avenues that gained them growing national, and international, attention. One of their most effective resources was newspapers. The most influential dedicated to the cause included, of course, Garrison's *Liberator* (1831–1865) and the *National Anti-Slavery Standard* (1840–1870); the New York State Anti-Slavery Society's *Friend of Man* (1836–1842); and *The National Era* (1847–1855); along with many early black journals, including Samuel Cornish's and John B. Russwurn's *Freedom Journal* (1827–1829); Cornish's *The Colored American* (1837–1841); Martin Delany's *Mystery* (1843–1847); Frederick Douglass's and Delany's *North Star* and Douglass's *Frederick Douglass Paper* (1847–1855); as well as Samuel Ringgold Ward's and Mary Ann Shadd Cary's publication in Canada, *The Provincial Freeman* (1853–1870). Newspapers were believed to be so important to abolition that not a few anti-slavery presses were destroyed, and at least one editor, Elijah P. Lovejoy, lost his life trying to defend his fourth printing press (three others had previously been destroyed by pro-slavery mobs) in Alton, Ohio in 1836.[158] Nothing, however, spoke to a literate audience inclined to anti-slavery sentiment more than the writings of formerly enslaved men and women about their experiences. The most popular of the tens of autobiographical accounts published before the Civil War were those of Frederick Douglass (1845), Solomon Northup (1853), Charles Ball (1837), William Wells Brown (1847), Josiah Henson (1849), Henry Bibb (1849), James Pennington (1849), and Harriet Jacobs (1861).[159]

Anti-slavery activists used every talent available to them to address the subject. Poets, such as John Greenleaf Whittier, published poems that addressed the topic, penning this one, for example, to honor his dear friend:

TO WILLIAM LLOYD GARRISON
Champion of those who groan beneath
Oppression's iron hand:
In view of penury, hate, and death,
I see thee fearless stand.
Still bearing up thy lofty brow,
In the steadfast strength of truth,
In manhood sealing well the vow

And promise of thy youth.
Go on, for thou hast chosen well;
On in the strength of God!
Long as one human heart shall swell
Beneath the tyrant's rod.
Speak in a slumbering nation's ear,
As thou hast ever spoken,
Until the dead in sin shall hear,
The fetter's link be broken!
I love thee with a brother's love,
I feel my pulses thrill,
To mark thy Spirit soar above
The cloud of human ill.[160]

Actors took to the stage to perform anti-slavery plays; and musicians held anti-slavery themed concerts based on music composed specifically for the cause. Songs found in Maria Weston Chapman's *Songs of the Free, and Hymns of Christian Freedom* published by Isaac Knapp in 1836, Jairus Lincoln's *Anti-Slavery Melodies: For the Friends of Freedom* (1843), and William Wells Brown's *The Antislavery Harp* (1848) were sung by the Garrison Juvenile Choir, the Hutchinson Family Singers, and others at anti-slavery audiences throughout the Northeast and Midwest.[161] Some of the songs were meant to deliver a potent, ironic message while amusing singers and audiences alike. Consider, for example, this song sung to the patriotic tune of "My Country 'Tis of Thee":

My country! 'tis of thee,
Stronghold of slavery,
Of thee I sing:
Land where my fathers died,
Where man's rights deride,
From every mountainside,
Thy deeds shall ring.
My native country! thee,
Where all men are born free,
If white their skin:
I love thy hills and dales,
Thy mounts and pleasant vales,
But hate thy negro sales,
As foulest sin.[162]

Writers penned short stories and novels. Certainly, the most popular novel of the era, indeed of the nineteenth century, was Harriet Beecher Stowe's sentimental, anti-slavery drama *Uncle Tom's Cabin*, originally serialized in the abolitionist journal *The National Era* in 1851, but published in 1852 and later translated into sixty languages. The book was so popular that it sold 10,000 copies the first week in the United States, 1.5 million copies in England alone during its first year, and was a bestseller in the United States, Britain, Asia, and Europe.[163]

Anti-slavery authors hoped to affect even the youngest of readers. The Philadelphia Female Anti-Slavery Society, for example, produced an alphabet poem book for children thematically based on abolition that the organization sold, quite successfully, at its fair in 1846. It began:

> Listen, little children, all,
> Listen to our earnest call:
> You are very young, 'tis true,
> But there's much that you can do.
> Even you can plead with men
> That they buy not slaves again,
> And that those they have may be
> Quickly set at liberty...

and continued:

> A is an Abolitionist –
> A man who wants to free
> The wretched slave – and give to all
> An equal liberty.
> B is a Brother with a skin
> Of somewhat darker hue,
> But in our Heavenly Father's sight,
> He is as dear as you.
> C is the Cotton-field, to which
> This injured brother's driven,
> When, as the white-man's *slave*, he toils,
> From early morn till even.... [164]

Those who were not literate could benefit from the scores of anti-slavery lectures annually sponsored by the AASS, its affiliates, and like-minded organizations. Unitarian minister Samuel May, Theodore Dwight Weld, Charles Lenox Remond – who was the first black man hired to lecture for the cause – William Wells Brown, and especially Frederick Douglass were perhaps the most important male lecturers. Maria Stewart, Sarah Remond, and Sojourner Truth helped to explicate the black female perspective. Brown, Douglass, Charles Remond, and William and Ellen Craft lectured across England and some of Europe. The slate of female lecturers also included numerous white women, including former slaveholding sisters Angelina and Sarah Grimke, Lucy Stone, Lucretia Mott, Lydia Maria Child, and Abbey Kelley. These men, and women, sometimes faced violent pro-slavery crowds who threatened, yelled, pushed, pulled, punched, shot at them, and even placed prices on their heads. William Lloyd Garrison was threatened more than once with lynching, and the state of Georgia offered a US$5,000 reward for his capture.[165]

Abolitionists took their message not only to the towns and cities they toured, but to the federal government. They flooded Congress with petitions, devised and distributed by female members, which addressed varied aspects of the institution of slavery, such as: the suspension of slavery and the domestic slave trade in the nation's capital; the repeal of fugitive slave legislation; and opposition to the annexation of Texas and Florida. Their efforts were met by pro-slavery forces in the federal legislature who passed a Gag Law in 1836 to keep their petitions from being read and, therefore, discussed. The AASS's affiliates responded by sending even more – 400,000 alone in 1838![166]

Local anti-slavery societies could differ substantially in membership. Many were segregated by race. African Americans believed that they had the most to gain, or lose, from the movement and, as such, should always be able to articulate an anti-slavery and free black civil rights agenda and plan of action without influence from whites, even like-minded whites. They often found themselves to the "left" of many of their white comrades, even those like Garrison whom most believed to be quite liberal. Free African American men organized themselves into societies, held multi-state conventions, published newspapers, pamphlets, broadsides, biographies, and autobiographies, starred on the lecture circuits at home and abroad, donated funds, and conferred closely with others dedicated to the cause. Some also supported those political parties and activities associated with free soil and anti-slavery. Robert Purvis, men in the Forten family, Theodore S. Wright, William C. Nell, Henry Highland Garnet, Martin Delaney, Samuel Cornish, Charles Lenox Remond, and several others, most especially Frederick Douglass, were at the center of the black male activists' efforts in the Northeast.

The "Negro Convention" movements of the 1830s, 1840s, and 1850s, in particular, were unique sites of black, male anti-slavery strategizing, although a few women always attended.[167] One of the first conventions was held in Philadelphia in 1830 and was presided over by Bishop Richard Allen, co-founder of the Free African Society in 1787 and the Bethel African Methodist Episcopal Church in Philadelphia in 1784. Out of a series of conventions held in Philadelphia afterwards, local activists formed the Moral Reform Society, with wealthy sailmaker James Forten as president. Their mantra was to effect Christian militancy in order to promote freedom, equality, education, temperance, and economy. The organization, which was squarely Garrisonian in outlook, began publishing the *National Reformer* in 1839, but disbanded in 1841.[168] Its members continued to be active in other organizations and influenced the agenda of the conventions that met at least a dozen times in New York, Ohio, and Pennsylvania. In the West, black Californians also organized three Colored Conventions between 1856 and 1858 to address growing discriminatory legislation that targeted free blacks.[169] The Negro Conventions, like those held in San Francisco and Sacramento, typically organized blacks by state and regionally. While their specific agendas changed slightly across time, delegates generally agreed that they should agitate for immediate abolition, equal rights, educational and occupational opportunities, moral uplift, and gendered responsibility.[170] Many also supported the other reform efforts of the day, particularly women's rights. Frederick Douglass, after all, was one of the few men present at Seneca Falls women's convention in 1848.[171]

Some abolitionist organizations also were gender segregated, or comprised mostly of youth. Massachusetts, for example, which could boast 183 local antebellum organizations, included 41 all-female societies and 13 youth groups in this total.[172] Indeed, the organized anti-slavery movement of the 1830s, 1840s, and 1850s gave ample opportunity for women in particular, even married women of middle-class status, to participate in this reform effort, both educating and politicizing them in ways that led to their leadership in nineteenth-century campaigns focused on Native American rights, temperance, gender equality, and social institutional reform (prisons, asylums, libraries, orphanages, and public schools). It was, for the most part, the abolitionist lecture circuit that first brought black and white women to speak before gender-integrated groups. Abolition also was a major instigator of female editorships, publications, and petitions to Congress.[173] As historian Julie Roy Jeffrey notes in her work about women in the movement, Garrison and others were clear about the incredible role that female abolitionists played. "The Anti-Slavery cause," Garrison wrote in 1847, "cannot stop to estimate where the greatest indebtedness lies, but whenever the account is made up, there can be no doubt that the efforts and sacrifices of WOMEN, who helped it, will hold a most honourable and conspicuous position."[174]

As lecturers, petitioners, fundraisers, authors, biographers, editors, artists, sewing-circle participants, fugitive-slave supporters, free-produce advocates, teachers, and letter writers, these women were active in every part of the abolitionist movement except as candidates for political office. They held three biracial conventions of their own, the Anti-Slavery Conventions of American Women, at the end of the 1830s. There they condemned slavery and racial prejudice, encouraged women to sign anti-slavery petitions, financially supported the movement, and criticized churches for not joining the cause.[175] As women, they were particularly aware of the nineteenth-century lens of virtuous/Christian womanhood and responsible motherhood that they could bring to the anti-slavery cause through documenting the sexual abuse of female slaves and the loss of slave children by way of the domestic slave trade. They challenged women to perceive slave females as their "sisters." They especially confronted southern women to take responsibility for the ending of female-slave degradation. Angelina Grimké Weld's lectures and 1836 *An Appeal to the Christian Women of the South* set the stage for white women's appearances before male and female audiences and left nowhere for southern elite women to hide on the topic of slavery. Angelina and her sister Sarah were former "Christian" slaveholding women from Charleston, South Carolina. Their denunciation of the institution and of its treatment of women and families, and their challenge to southern women who stood by and supported it, struck deep. Comparing southern women to those of the Bible who stood up for what was right, as well as to the anti-slavery women of Britain and the North, Grimké asserted:

> Let the Christian women there arise...in the majesty of moral power, and that salvation is certain. Let them embody themselves in societies, and send petitions up to their different legislatures, entreating their husbands, fathers, brothers and sons, to abolish the institution of slavery; no longer to subject *woman* to the scourge and the chain, to mental darkness and moral degradation; no longer to tear husbands from their wives, and children from their parents; no longer to make men, women, and children, work *without wages*; no longer to make their lives bitter in hard bondage; no longer to reduce *American citizens* to the abject condition of *slaves*, of "chattels personal"; no longer to barter the *image of God* in human shambles for corruptible things such as silver and gold.[176]

Antebellum African American free women, like their male and European American counterparts, also invested mightily in the abolition movement. They derived much of their inspiration, strategies, and legitimacy from the legacy of charity, self-help, and self-improvement traditions of the free black and white female communities. Indeed, some of these first black female organizations formed as auxiliaries to male groups, or formed after black men and white female abolitionist groups had either restricted or excluded black women from their organizations because of their race, gender, or both. Sarah Forten famously penned her dismay and disappointment at the unequal embrace of her white abolitionist sisters in her poem "An Appeal to Women," which began:

> Oh, woman, woman in thy brightest hour
> Of conscious worth, of pride, of conscious power
> Oh, nobly dare to act a Christian's part,
> That well befits a lovely woman's heart!

Dare to be good, as thou canst dare be great;
Despise the taunts of envy, scorn and hate;
Our "skins may differ," but from thee we claim
A sister's privilege, in a sister's name.[177]

The efforts of black anti-slavery female activists, like those of others, were folded into the larger agendas of self-help, moral uplift, and literacy for all US persons of African descent, not just slaves. They organized clubs such as the African Female Benevolent Society in Newport, Rhode Island, the Colored Female Religious and Moral Reform Society in Salem, Massachusetts, and the Minerva Literary Society of Philadelphia. They are, indeed, credited with founding the first women's abolition society, the Salem Female Anti-Slavery Society, in 1832. They also helped to found biracial female societies, such as the Philadelphia Female Anti-Slavery Society in 1833 and others in Rochester, New York, and in Lynn and Boston, Massachusetts. Their organizations were located largely in northeastern cities, but also in southern urban centers such as Baltimore, Washington, DC, Richmond, Charleston, and New Orleans. Free women of color used their talents and accomplishments honed in their societies to protest slavery and racial discrimination. Many of the literary texts authored by this first significant generation of African American women authors, for example, promoted abolition. Harriet Wilson, Charlotte and Sarah Forten, Harriet Jacobs, Maria Stewart, Ann Plato, and Frances E. W. Harper were foremost among these literate black female writers. Mary Prince's *The History of Mary Prince, a West Indian Slave*, a brutal documentation of British West Indian slavery published in 1831, was the first slave narrative written by a black woman in the Americas. That same year, Maria Stewart began her lecture series, giving four lectures in two years to audiences in Boston on the causes of abolition and free black and women's rights. Stewart was the first woman of any race to give public lectures to a mixed-gendered audience. The following year, she became the first free African American woman to publish a book of hymns and meditations. Charlotte Forten's anti-slavery writings were published, like Stewart's, in Garrison's *Liberator*, but also in *The Christian Recorder*, *The Anglo-African Magazine*, the *National Anti-Slavery Standard*, and *The Atlantic Monthly*. Mary Ann Shad

Cary, who supported free black migration to Canada, began publishing her own anti-slavery newspaper, the *Provincial Freeman*, in 1853.[178]

Pro-slavery advocates did not sit idly by while abolitionist men and women campaigned for the end of slavery. They did not hesitate to mount an offense in support of their ideas about racial difference and the issue of slavery. Beginning in the 1830s, more and more southerners dedicated speeches and writings in defense of the institution and their treatment of the enslaved. The most important pro-slavery authors included: Thomas R. Dew, Professor of Political Law at the College of William and Mary; noted South Carolina and Missouri jurist and politician William Harper; Baptist minister and Virginia slaveholder Thornton Stringfellow; South Carolinian lawyer, planter, and Congressman James Henry Hammond; Hammond's friend, the South Carolinian physician Josiah C. Nott; law scholar Henry Hughes of Mississippi; US Vice President John C. Calhoun of South Carolina, who had introduced the idea of state nullification of federal law in 1828, an idea that proved to exacerbate growing sectional strife in the nation; and the Virginia lawyer George Fitzhugh. Most couched their arguments in the idea that slavery had existed since the ancient world as part of a natural organization, or hierarchy, of mankind. Not only was slavery natural, they argued, it was the foundation of great societies since it allowed each group, beginning with the lowliest, to contribute appropriate to their abilities. As historian Drew Faust notes, "turning to the past as a catalog of social experiments, slavery's defenders discovered that from the time of Greece and Rome, human bondage had produced the world's greatest civilizations. The peculiar institution, they argued, was not so very peculiar, but had provided the social foundation for man's greatest achievements."[179] The slaves of the South, James Hammond professed, were the "mudsill" of their society:

> In all social systems there must be a class to do the menial duties, to perform the drudgery of life...a class requiring but a low order of intellect and but little skill. Its requisites are vigor, docility, fidelity. Such a class you must have, or you would not have that other class which leads progress, civilization, and refinement. It constitutes the very mud-sill of society.[180]

The South, he continued, has "found a race adapted to that purpose...A race inferior to her own, but eminently qualified in temper, in vigor, in docility, in capacity to stand the climate, to answer all her purposes. We...call them slaves."[181]

Pro-slavery advocates such as John C. Calhoun and George Fitzhugh also spoke of the "positive good" of slavery, due to its "civilizing" and "paternalistic" nature, a paternalism that not only helped black slaves, they insisted, but also made their material and working conditions superior to those of white workingmen of the North.[182] "I hold that in the present state of civilization, where two races of different origin, and distinguished by color, and other physical differences, as well as intellectual, are brought together," Calhoun noted in 1837, "the relation now existing in the slaveholding States between the two, is, instead of an evil, a good – a positive good."[183] Fitzhugh reiterated Calhoun's theme, writing in *Sociology of the South* in 1854, that "The dissociation of labor and disintegration of society, which liberty and free competition occasion, is especially injurious to the poorer class...Slavery relieves our slaves of these cares altogether, and slavery is a form, and the very best form, of socialism."[184]

Pro-slavery advocates, therefore, had an answer for those anti-slavery women who, like Angelina Grimke Weld, addressed their concerns to southern women. Fitzhugh, drawing on the notion of a natural hierarchy, dismissed the intellectual and emotional ability of women altogether, thereby undermining any respect one might have had for their opinions on slavery. "But half of mankind are but grown-up children," he noted, "and liberty is as fatal to them as it would be to children."[185] Thomas R. Dew noted, much earlier in 1832, as part of the debate in the Virginia legislature regarding the fate of slavery in that state, that it was indeed slavery that allowed the white women of the South to be "the delight and charm of every circle she move [sic] in." "We behold," Dew expounded, "the marked efficiency of slavery on the conditions of woman – we find her at once elevated, clothed with all her charms, mingling with and directing the society to which she belongs, no longer the slave..."[186] It was slavery that shielded white women from the status of the slave woman, the negative incentive that kept both white southern women and men pro-slavery. And as for those abolitionist women of the North who would have southern women come over to their side, Julia Gardiner Tyler, wife of President John Tyler of Virginia, had an answer – a woman's role should be confined to the home and to the duties of wife, mother, and mistress, not to the public or to public causes. "Her circle is," Julia Tyler noted in an article in a women's magazine in the mid-1830s, "that of the family... Such is emphatically the case with the women of the Southern states. Do you wish to see them, you must visit their homes."[187]

Despite pro-slavery arguments that centered on the treatment of the slave or the "place" of women in the public sphere, the heart of this national debate and this growing sectional divide was the geospatial destiny of an institution that had proved to be enormously profitable. The nation more than doubled its size with the Louisiana Purchase in 1803. Additional expanses of land were added to the United States as a result of the nation's acquisition of: West Florida in 1810; East Florida and parts of Oregon in 1819; Texas in 1845; the remainder of present-day Oregon in 1846; other western lands that had belonged to Mexico in 1848; and parts of New Mexico and Arizona in 1853. Between 1803 and 1853, therefore, the new nation acquired the land boundaries that still constitute the continental United States. Two burning questions that emerged with each new territorial acquisition was: would slavery, and the wealth that derived from it, be allowed to exist in this new land?

The Missouri statehood question was the first national debate since the era of the Revolution over the location of slavery. State formation meant state representation in Congress. Since slaves counted as three-fifths persons for the apportioning of delegates to the House of Representatives, slavery had great influence on the balance of power in Washington. Neither pro-slavery advocates nor those who were opposed to the institution's spreading wanted the other side to have greater power in Congress, either in the House or in the Senate. As such, moderates often tried to broker a compromise that allowed a "balance" of "slave" and "free" states. The Missouri Compromise of 1820 allowed Maine to enter the nation as a free state, Missouri to enter as a slave state, and stipulated that the remainder of the Louisiana Purchase territories, north of the 36°30′ parallel, remain free.[188] Even though the line was "drawn in the sand," the debate on slavery's expansion continued in the federal government and in the general public.

Thirty years later, the Compromise of 1850 brought California into the Union as a free state, but allowed New Mexico and Utah territory (all land acquired after the Mexican War of 1846–1848) the right of popular sovereignty – those persons who settled there could decide for themselves whether or not slavery would be allowed. The Compromise also offered to pro-slavery supporters a very favorable fugitive slave law and the retention of slavery in the nation's capital, while anti-slavery forces received a ban on the domestic slave trade in Washington, DC.[189]

The question over the admission of Nebraska to the Union brought the issue to a particularly explosive head. Supporters who wanted to develop Nebraska territory for white settlement and provide encouragement for a transcontinental railroad through the region were met with stiff pro-slavery opposition because Nebraska would be free from slavery, given the boundary established by the Missouri Compromise. Senator Stephen A. Douglass of Illinois proposed a compromise – that two territories be organized, Kansas and Nebraska, out of the land and that their settlers determine, through popular vote, whether or not they would allow slavery.[190]

It was almost certain that those who settled in Nebraska would not choose to allow slavery because its locale was too northern to promote an agrarian economy that would benefit from slave labor. Free soilers – those who were opposed to the spread of slavery for various reasons, including opposition to unfair competition by those who held slaves and a desire not to live close to blacks – flocked to Nebraska. Cotton, however, could be grown in Kansas. The race was soon on as to who would predominate settlement – pro-slavery advocates or free soilers. Both sides promoted migration through forming land companies that assisted those who moved. After a series of very heated debates, Senator Douglass's plan passed the House by the closest of votes (113–100) on May 22, 1854, and three days later in the Senate by a vote of 35–13, to become the Kansas–Nebraska Act. Those

who hurried to the region hoped to vote in the state constitutional elections that would either accept or reject slavery.
From Missouri and elsewhere, pro-slavery activists called
Border Ruffians came into Kansas sometimes only to vote
and sway elections in their favor. Anti-slavery fighters, known
as Jayhawkers, arrived for the same purpose. Fighting, often
guerrilla in style and instigated by both sides, repeatedly
broke out in the days and weeks before and after elections.
Opposing sides set up their capitals – Lecompton was controlled by pro-slavery advocates; and Topeka by free soilers
and abolitionists. People were killed in both Osawatomie and
Potawatomie, dubbing the territory "Bleeding Kansas."[191]
Indeed, John Brown, who would plan and execute a rebellion
to free slaves originating in Harper's Ferry, Virginia, in 1859,
was implicated first in the revenge murder of five pro-slavery
farmers in what became known as the Potawatomie Massacre in May 1856. All in all, approximately 56 people died
between 1856 and 1861 in these "civil wars."[192]

But the fighting was not just in Kansas. In Congress as
well, violent debates over the fate of Kansas ensued. Senator
Charles Sumner of Massachusetts, a well-regarded abolitionist, spoke against the attempt to allow slavery in Kansas. In
his "Crime Against Kansas" speech given in May 1856,
Sumner asserted:

> Not in any common lust for power did this uncommon tragedy have
> its origin. It is the rape of a virgin Territory, compelling it to the
> hateful embrace of slavery; and it may be clearly traced to a depraved
> desire for a new Slave State, hideous offspring of such a crime, in
> the hope of adding to the power of slavery in the National
> Government.[193]

Preston Brooks of South Carolina, a member of the House
of Representatives, was so offended by Sumner's speech and
other remarks he believed were insulting to the people of his
home state that he attacked the Senator, bludgeoning his head
with a cane until the cane broke and Massachusetts's legisla-
tor lay unconscious. Anti-slavery activists, and much of the
North, were livid, while the South welcomed Brooks, newly
resigned from Congress as a result of his violent outburst, as
a hero – both reactions further dividing the nation. Suffering
from head trauma, spinal cord damage and post-traumatic

stress disorder, Sumner was unable to resume his duties in Congress for two years.[194]

Meanwhile, in Kansas, the two sides of the contest authored and voted on several territorial constitutions, including: the Topeka Constitution in November 1855 that outlawed slavery; the Lecompton Constitution of November 1857, which proposed popular sovereignty on the issue of slavery; the Leavenworth Constitution of April 1858, which not only forbade slavery but supported women's rights; and the Wyandotte Constitution of July 1859 that forbade slavery. The US Congress accepted the Wyandotte Constitution and voted to admit Kansas into the United States as a free state on January 29, 1861.[195]

The 1850s were the backdrop to other divisive national issues related to the institution. None was more significant than the case of Dred Scott (*Dred Scott v. Sanford*), who sued

SOUTHERN CHIVALRY — ARGUMENT versus CLUB'S.

4.5 "Southern Chivalry – Argument versus Club"; the caning of Senator Charles Sumner by Representative Preston Brooks in Congress, 1856
Source: American Antiquarian Society, Worcester, Massachusetts, USA/Bridgeman Images

for his freedom. Scott was a Virginia-born slave who was taken by his master, Peter Blow, to Alabama and then to Missouri in 1830. Blow died in 1832, and Scott was bought by John Emerson, an army surgeon. Emerson subsequently took Scott to the free state of Illinois and then to Wisconsin territory – also free, given the terms of the Northwest Ordinance of 1787 and the Missouri Compromise of 1821. There, Dred Scott married a slave woman, Harriet Robinson, who was bought by Dr Emerson. Years later, Scott and his wife moved back to slave territory (Louisiana) with Emerson. Scott could have sued for freedom while he was living on free land, but he did not do so. In 1843, however, his owner died. When Dred Scott wished to buy his freedom and that of his wife for US$300 from Emerson's widow, she refused. Scott then decided in 1846 to sue for his freedom in court.[196] Peter Blow's sons, who were close to Scott, helped to pay his legal fees. In 1850, the lower court in St Louis, Missouri (where Mrs Emerson resided and had been hiring out the Scotts), freed Scott, his wife, and their two children based on Mr and Mrs Scott's residence in free territory. The Missouri Supreme Court, however, overturned that decision. The Scotts then sued in the federal court, which upheld the Missouri Supreme Court decision. The case then was heard before the US Supreme Court.[197]

Chief Justice Roger Taney, a known supporter of slavery, delivered the majority decision (7–2) for the Court on March 6, 1857. The Court had found in favor of the earlier decision of the Missouri Supreme Court and ordered the Scotts back to slavery. Taney, mightily aware of the ongoing and intensifying sectional debate on the "place" of slavery and the slave in the United States, wrote a decision that addressed two key questions that the Dred Scott case, and others in the lower courts, elicited. One essential query centered on the citizenship status of black Americans, slave and free. Taney determined that blacks, regardless of their legal status, were not citizens of the United States.[198] As such, the Chief Justice went on to note, Scott had no right to sue in federal court. The court also ruled that the Missouri Compromise was unconstitutional.[199] Despite Taney's decision, however, Dred Scott and his family did receive their freedom – Peter Blow's sons purchased and emancipated them. Eighteen months later, Dred Scott died of tuberculosis. The case, however, was much more significant than determining the status of one family.

Anti-slavery advocates across the nation felt that the ruling of the Scott case by the Supreme Court was a tremendous blow to free black rights and the abolitionist cause. With the Missouri Compromise, and all like laws that might stem the territorial growth of slavery, deemed unconstitutional, there seemed to be no ready way to force the nation to end the institution. It would not be long, however, before the pro-slavery South felt an actual assault in its territory that would end any effort to remain part of the United States. They would soon decide to leave and take slavery, and their slaves, with them.

In early July 1859, John Brown and his two sons, Oliver and Watson, rented a farm on the Potomac in Maryland. Over the next three months, they and others in their camp, with money and support from northern abolitionists, plotted an assault that they hoped would initiate a series of revolts that would end slavery. They planned to raid the federal arsenal at Harper's Ferry, Virginia, and distribute weapons and ammunition to local slaves and other willing residents, setting off a well-armed rebellion. They mounted their attack on the night of October 16 with twenty people – Brown and nineteen other men (fourteen white and five black). Word of the "raid" spread quickly. By the next morning, Colonel Robert E. Lee had arrived with the Marines. When Brown refused to surrender, Lee attacked. The battle was over in a few minutes. Twelve of Brown's men were killed, including his two sons; five others were taken as prisoners. Five local people had died in the fray. On December 2, 1859, John Brown, having been found guilty of treason, was hanged in Charlestown, Virginia.[200]

Less than a year after Harper's Ferry, on November 6, 1860, Abraham Lincoln, the Republican candidate for the presidency, won. His politics surrounding slavery were so offensive to southerners that his name had not appeared on the ballot of two-thirds of southern states. The dye had been cast. South Carolina withdrew from the Union before his inauguration. Three years later, amidst a bloody civil war that was not favoring the Union, Abraham Lincoln's

Emancipation Proclamation went into effect, freeing all slaves in those areas in rebellion against the United States. Another three years passed, witnessing the end of the war, the assassination of Lincoln, and the ratification of the Thirteenth Amendment to the Constitution of the United States on December 6, 1865. The largest slave society in the Americas had come undone. Four million slaves in the United States were finally free.

Further Reading

Camp, Stephanie. *Closer to Freedom: Enslaved Women and Everyday Resistance in the Plantation South*. Chapel Hill, NC: University of North Carolina Press, 2004.

Diouf, Sylviane Anna. *Dreams of Africa in Alabama: The Slave Ship Clotilda and the Story of the Last Africans Brought to America*. New York: Oxford University Press, 2009.

Faust, Drew Gilpin. *The Ideology of Slavery: Proslavery Thought in the Antebellum South, 1830–1860*. Baton Rouge, LA: Louisiana State University Press, 1981.

Fett, Sharla. *Working Cures: Healing, Health and Power on Southern Slave Plantations*. Chapel Hill, NC: University of North Carolina Press, 2002.

Foner, Eric. *The Fiery Trial: Abraham Lincoln and American Slavery*. New York: W. W. Norton, 2011.

Johnson, Michael, and Roark, James L. *Black Masters: A Free Family of Color in the Old South*. New York: W. W. Norton, 1984.

Johnson, Walter. *Soul by Soul: Life Inside the Antebellum Slave Market*. Cambridge, MA: Harvard University Press, 2001.

King, Wilma. *Stolen Childhood: Slave Youth in Nineteenth Century America*. 2nd edn. Bloomington, IN: Indiana University Press, 2011.

Mellon, James. *Bullwhip Days: The Slaves Remember, An Oral History*. New York: Grove Press, 1988.

Stevenson, Brenda E. *Life in Black and White: Family and Community in the Slave South*. New York: Oxford University Press, 1996.

Conclusion

"Neither slavery nor involuntary servitude, except as a punishment for crime whereof the party shall have been duly convicted, shall exist within the United States, or any place subject to their jurisdiction."

The Thirteenth Amendment to the Constitution of the United States[1]

By the time that "freedom" finally did arrive, African American men, women, and children who had been enslaved in the American South had undergone a myriad of experiences as witnesses, actors, victims, and victors in the profound unsettling that the Civil War, and its economic, political, legal, cultural, and social consequences, had engendered.

The South, as enslaved blacks had known it in 1860, was, by 1865, profoundly changed – with a defeated master class, poor as a result of an agrarian-based economy, left in shambles; more than a quarter of a million dead soldiers; leveled cities; torn-up railroads; still sugar mills; empty cotton and tobacco barns; burnt fields; weedy rice swamps; and a scattered black workforce that did not want to return to the plantation. Certainly, everyone remembered for years to come, if not for the remainder of their lives, where they were, what they were doing, and how they felt when they found out that they were free. They all remembered the moment freedom came, even if it took some time to decide exactly what freedom was and how it really would affect their lives. Freedom was defined in federal and state laws in what might have seemed like bold black-and-white terms, but the experiences of those who became "free" made up thousands of gray shades of reality.

Post-Civil War black life, of course, was created, maintained, and lost against the backdrop of three dramatically different federal Reconstruction plans, the beginning and end of the Freedmen's Bureau, and the ratification of three profoundly important amendments to the US Constitution. These laws and institutions led to significant early gains. Black men and women sought, and managed to gain, legal marriage status and reunited families. Some were able to acquire property, work tools, and animals so that they could begin to work *their* family farms on their own terms. Many, particularly the younger generations of those freed, gained a modicum of literacy. Some were even able to attend newly created colleges and become teachers, preachers, physicians, and other professionals. Many skilled craftsmen, especially in southern cities, set up their own shops alongside those of small businessmen and -women. A black male electorate participated in the southern body politic and sent representatives to local, state, and federal office.

Black freedom, however, was soon challenged, customarily and legally, with the imposition of discriminatory Black Laws, mob rule, Jim Crow, and disenfranchisement. Racial segregation and discrimination, backed by domestic terrorism, were meant to snap blacks back into a place of inferiority, submission, and dependency not unlike the status they held as slaves. Indeed, it would be another hundred years before the Reconstruction amendments would have significant meaning for many African Americans. Even today, the legacies of inequality as victims and defendants in the criminal justice system, and via educational exclusion, economic marginalization, medical experimentation, social isolation, and cultural denunciation – all characteristics of life under slavery – still remain as markers of black life for far too many. So too remains the determination of the descendants of slaves to resist this dehumanization and to insist, instead, on equality.

What is slavery? Slavery in the past, as today, is an institution that supports mythologies of privilege, superiority, and power. It is created and sustained by hierarchies that victimize persons who many are socialized to believe should live on the margins of our societies because of their gender, poverty, youth, color, religion, sexual orientation, military status, physical and mental disabilities, and so on. If this were not true, how could there still be 20 million slaves and counting in the world today? What is freedom? Freedom is breaking away from our tacit acceptance of inequality. Resistance was one legacy of slavery, routinely, and often dramatically, employed by Africans and their enslaved descendants throughout the Americas, that actually is worth retaining and supporting.

Notes

Introduction: What is Slavery?

1 Thomas Jefferson, *Notes on the state of Virginia* (Virginia: the author, 1787), Kindle Edition, location 2510.
2 Quoted in Robert Morgan, "The 'Great Emancipator' and the Issue of Race: Abraham Lincoln's Program of Black Resettlement," *The Journal of Historical Review* 13(5) (Sept.–Oct. 1993): 6, http://www.ihr.org/jhr/v13/v13n5p-4_Morgan.html.
3 Lisa A. Lindsay, *Captives as Commodities: The Transatlantic Slave Trade* (Upper Saddle River, NJ: Pearson/Prentice Hall, 2008), 44.
4 Delia Garlic, *When I Was a Slave: Memoirs from the Slave Narrative Collection*, ed. Norman Yetman (New York: Courier Dover Publications, 2012), 43.
5 Nell I. Painter, *Soul Murder and Slavery* (Waco, TX: Baylor University Press, 1995).
6 An often-cited source on the debate on slave agency is Walter Johnson, "On Agency," *Journal of Social History* 37(1) (Fall 2003):113–24,https://muse.jhu.edu/journals/journal_of_social_history/v037/37.1johnson.html.

Chapter 1 Slavery Across Time and Place Before the Atlantic Slave Trade

1 David Brion Davis, *Inhuman Bondage: The Rise and Fall of Slavery in the New World* (New York: Oxford University Press, 2006), 32.

2 Mark Chavalas, "Mesopotamia," in *The Historical Encyclopedia of World Slavery*, vols 1–2, ed. Junius P. Rodriguez (Santa Barbara, CA: ABC-CLIO, Inc., 1997), vol. 2, 430.

3 Jerise Fogel, "Roman Republic," in Rodriguez, *The Historical Encyclopedia of World Slavery*, vol. 2, 551–3.

4 Walter Scheidel, "The Roman Slave Supply" (Working Papers, *Princeton/Stanford Working Papers in the Classics*, Stanford University, Stanford, CA, May 2007), 4–5, https://www.princeton.edu/~pswpc/pdfs/scheidel/050704.pdf.

5 Catherine Hezser, *Jewish Slavery in Antiquity* (2005; repr. New York: Oxford University Press, 2010), 202–16, Oxford Scholarship Online, doi: 10.1093/acprof:oso/9780199280865.001.0001.

6 Ibid., 13–14.

7 Ibid., 69–82.

8 Jerise Fogel, "Roman Republic," in Rodriguez, *The Historical Encyclopedia of World Slavery*, vol. 2, 551–3.

9 Hezser, *Jewish Slavery in Antiquity*, 83–104.

10 Ibid., 202–16.

11 Ibid., 105–20.

12 Ibid., 123–48.

13 Benjamin Lawrence, "Greece," in Rodriguez, *The Historical Encyclopedia of World Slavery*, vol. 1, 312–14.

14 See, for example, *Spartacus and the Slave Wars: A Brief History with Documents*, ed. Brent D. Shaw (Boston, MA: Bedford/St Martin's, 2001).

15 See, for example, Keith Bradley, "Resisting Slavery in Ancient Rome," BBC History, February 17, 2011, http://www.bbc.co.uk/history/ancient/romans/slavery_01.shtml.

16 Frederico Poole, "Egypt, Condition of Slaves in," in Rodriguez, *The Historical Encyclopedia of World Slavery*, vol. 1, 241–2; Eckhard Eicler, "Egypt, Slavery in Ancient," in Rodriguez, *The Historical Encyclopedia of World Slavery*, vol. 1, 243–5.

17 "Ancient Egypt: The Will of Amonkhau in Favor of His Second Wife, c. 1100 BCE," last modified January 2004, in André Dollinger, *An Introduction to the History and Culture of Pharaonic Egypt*, http://www.reshafim.org.il/ad/egypt/texts/amonkhau.htm.

18 Jennifer Margulis, "Arab World," in *Chronology of World Slavery*, ed. Junius P. Rodriguez (Santa Barbara, CA: ABC-CLIO, Inc., 1999), 102–3.

19 Paul Lovejoy, *Transformations in Slavery: A History of Slavery in Africa*, 3rd edn (Cambridge: Cambridge University Press, 2011), Kindle Edition, location ch. 1, 916.

20 James D. Medler, "Central Asia," in Rodriguez, *Chronology of World Slavery*, 104.

21 Hyong-In Kim, "East Asia," in Rodriguez, *The Historical Encyclopedia of World Slavery*, vol. 1, 240–1.

22 Rodriguez, *Chronology of World Slavery*, 93–101.

23 Egypt is referred to as part of both the Middle East and Africa in this text.

24 Chou Ch'u-fei, "Document 7: Description of East Africa (1178)," in Rodriguez, *Chronology of World Slavery*, 396.

25 Timothy Insoll, "East Africa," in Rodriguez, *The Historical Encyclopedia of World Slavery*, vol. 1, 239.

26 James Walvin, *Atlas of Slavery* (Harlow, England: Pearson/ Longman, 2006), 23.

27 Justin Corfield, "Settlement Patterns in Medieval Africa," in *Encyclopedia of Society and Culture in the Medieval World*, ed. Pam J. Crabtree (New York: Facts On File, Inc., 2008), *Ancient and Medieval History Online*, Facts On File, Inc., http://www.fofweb.com/activelink2.asp?ItemID=WE49 &iPin=ESCMW500&SingleRecord=True; Walvin, *Atlas of Slavery*, 11.

28 Gwendolyn Midlo Hall, *Slavery and African Ethnicities in the Americas: Restoring the Links* (Chapel Hill, NC: The University of North Carolina Press, 2005), 2.

29 Timothy Insoll, "Timbuktu," in Rodriguez, *The Historical Encyclopedia of World Slavery*, vol. 2, 636.

30 Linda Heywood, "Slavery and Its Transformation in the Kingdom of Kongo, 1491–1800," *Journal of African History* 50(1) (2009): 3, doi: http://dx.doi.org/10.1017/S0021853709 004228.

31 Heidi J. Nast, "Islam, Gender, and Slavery in West Africa Circa 1500: A Spatial Archaeology of the Kano Palace, Northern Nigeria," *Annals of the Association of American Geographers* 86(1) (Mar. 1996): 44–77, http://www.jstor.org/ stable/2563946.

32 John Oriji, "Igboland, Slavery and the Drums of War and Heroism," in *Fighting the Slave Trade: West African Strategies*, ed. Sylviane A. Diouf (Athens, OH: Ohio University Press, 2003), 121–31.

33 John Thornton, *Africa and Africans in the Making of the Atlantic World, 1400–1680* (Cambridge: Cambridge University Press, 1992), 74–5, 85–100.

34 Ibid., 88.

35 Joseph Miller, "Introduction," in *Women and Slavery: Africa, the Indian Ocean World, and the Medieval North Atlantic*, vol. 1, ed. Gwyn Campbell, Suzanne Miers, and Joseph Miller (Athens, OH: Ohio University Press, 2007), 11.

36 Miller, "Introduction," in Campbell, Miers, and Miller, *Women and Slavery*, 11–13.

37 Claire Robertson, "Women as Slaveholders, Africa," in Rodriguez, *The Historical Encyclopedia of World Slavery*, vol. 2, 700–1.

38 Miller, "Introduction," in Campbell, Miers, and Miller, *Women and Slavery*, 21–2; Philip J. Havik, "From Pariahs to Patriots: Women Slavers in Nineteenth-Century 'Portuguese' Guinea," in Campbell, Miers, and Miller, *Women and Slavery*, 309–21.

39 Walvin, *Atlas of Slavery*, 27–8.

40 Ibid., 28.

41 Jane Hathaway, "Ottoman Empire," in Rodriguez, *The Historical Encyclopedia of World Slavery*, vol. 2, 483–4.

42 Helene N. Turkewicz-Sanko, "Ukraine," in Rodriguez, *The Historical Encyclopedia of World Slavery*, vol. 2, 659–60.

43 Daniel Boxberger, "Amerindian Slavery, Pacific Northwest," in Rodriguez, *The Historical Encyclopedia of World Slavery*, vol. 1, 36.

44 Leland Donald, "Slavery in Indigenous North America," in *The Cambridge World History of Slavery, Vol. 3: 1420–1804*, ed. David Eltis and Stanley Engerman (Cambridge, UK: Cambridge University Press, 2011), 246.

45 Patricia Kilroe, "Amerindian Slavery, Plains" in Rodriguez, *The Historical Encyclopedia of World Slavery*, vol. 1, 37.

46 Donald, "Slavery in Indigenous North America," in Eltis and Engerman, *The Cambridge World History of Slavery*, 219.

47 Theda Perdue, *Slavery and the Evolution of Cherokee Society, 1540–1866* (Knoxville, TN: University of Tennessee Press, 1979), 4.

48 Ibid., 11–15.

49 "Aztec Social Structure," in "Aztec and Maya Law," Tarlton Law Library and the Benson Latin American Collection at The University of Texas, http://tarlton.law.utexas.edu/exhibits/aztec/aztec_social.html.

50 Neil Whitehead, "Indigenous Slavery in South America, 1492–1820," in Eltis and Engerman, *The Cambridge World History of Slavery*, 248.

51 Ibid., 252.

52 Ibid., 254.

53 Ibid.

Chapter 2 African Beginnings and the Atlantic Slave Trade

1 "Narrative of the Enslavement of Ottobah Cugoano, a Native of Africa; Published by Himself in the Year 1787," in *The Negro's Memorial; or, Abolitionist's Catechism; by an Abolitionist*, ed. Thomas Fisher (London: Hatchard and Co., 1825), 120–7, electronic edn, The University of North Carolina at Chapel Hill, 1st edn, 1999, http://docsouth.unc.edu/neh/cugoano/cugoano.html.

2 Historians have not settled completely on the number of Africans who arrived. See: Lindsay, *Captives as Commodities*, 4; Lovejoy, *Transformations in Slavery*, Kindle location ch. 1, 948.

3 See the section "How Many Were Enslaved" in *The Atlantic Slave Trace*, ed. David Northrup (Lexington, MA: D.C. Heath and Company, 1994), 37–66.

4 Walvin, *Atlas of Slavery*, 31–6; Kate Lowe, "The Lives of African Slaves and People of African Descent in Renaissance Europe," in Joaneath Spicer (ed.), *Revealing the African Presence in Renaissance Europe* (Baltimore, MD: Walters Art Museum, 2012), 19; Allison Blakeley, "Problems in Studying the Roles of Blacks in Europe," *Perspectives on History*, May 1997, http://www.historians.org/publications-and-directories/perspectives-on-history/may-1997/problems-in-studying-the-role-of-blacks-in-europe.

5 Lindsay, *Captives as Commodities*, 34–5.

6 Lovejoy, *Transformations in Slavery*, Kindle location ch. 1, 967; David Eltis, *The Rise of African Slavery in the Americas* (Cambridge, UK: Cambridge University Press, 2000), 244–50.

7 Ibid.

8 Ibid.

9 Walvin, *Atlas of Slavery*, 55.

10 Ibid., 56–7.

11 Richard L. Garner, "Long-Term Silver Mining Trends in Spanish America: A Comparative Analysis of Peru and Mexico," *The American Historical Review* 93(4) (Oct. 1988): 898–935, http://www.jstor.org/stable/1863529.

12 Paul Lovejoy, *Transformations in Slavery: A History of Slavery in Africa*, 7th edn. (Cambridge: Cambridge University Press, 1998), 44–50.

13 Lovejoy, *Transformations in Slavery*, Kindle location ch. 3, 1692.

14   Thornton argues that the vast majority were Kimbundu speakers, with some Kikongo. Engel Sluiter, "New Light on the '20. and Odd Negroes' Arriving in Virginia, August 1619," *William and Mary Quarterly*, 3rd series, 54(2) (April 1997): 396–8, http://www.jstor.org/stable/2953279; John K. Thornton, "Notes and Documents: The African Experience of the '20 and Odd Negroes' Arriving in Virginia in 1619," *William and Mary Quarterly*, 3rd series, 55(3) (July 1998): 421–34, http://www.jstor.org/stable/2674531; William Thorndale, "The Virginia Census of 1619," *Magazine of Virginia Genealogy* 33 (1995): 155–70.

15   Lovejoy, *Transformations in Slavery*, Kindle location ch. 3, 1730.

16   Ibid., ch. 3, 1750.

17   Ibid., ch. 3, 1810–1820.

18   Ibid., ch. 3, 1780.

19   Ibid., ch. 3, 1535–1947, passim.

20   Ibid., ch. 5 , 2791; Walvin, *Atlas of Slavery*, 45–6.

21   Walvin, *Atlas of Slavery*, 54; Ottobah Cugoano, "Thoughts and Sentiments on the Evil and Wicked Traffic of the Slavery and Commerce of the Human Species," in *Pioneers of the Black Atlantic: Five Slave Narratives from the Enlightenment, 1772–1815*, ed. Henry Louis Gates and William L. Andrews (Washington, DC: Counterpoint, 1998), 94; Olaudah Equiano, *The Interesting Narrative of the Life of Olaudah Equiano*, in Gates and Andrews, *Pioneers of the Black Atlantic*, 211–17. Some historians have challenged the validity of the Equiano text, suggesting that Equiano may have been born in South Carolina. This author, however, finds the text extremely useful given that Equiano, no doubt, received firsthand accounts from others as validated by like texts published during this era. Vincent Carretta, *Equiano, The African: Biography of a Self-Made Man* (Athens, GA: University of Georgia Press, 2005), passim.

22   Regarding the profitability of the slave trade, see Milton Meltzer, *Slavery: A World History* (South Boston, MA: De Capo Press, 1993), 41, 43, 45.

23   Alexander Ives Bortolot, "Trade Relations among European and African Nations," in *Heilbrunn Timeline of Art History* (New York: The Metropolitan Museum of Art, 2000–2014), http://www.metmuseum.org/toah/hd/aftr/hd_aftr.htm.

24   Lovejoy, *Transformations in Slavery*, Kindle location ch. 3, 1642.

25   Ibid., Kindle location ch. 3, 1649.

26   Hall, *Slavery and African Ethnicities in the Americas*, 15.

27 *"A Narrative of the Most Remarkable Particulars in the Life of James Albert Ukawsaw Gronniosaw, An African Prince, As Related by Himself* (1770)," in Gates and Andrews, *Pioneers of the Black Atlantic*, 40.

28 Cugoano, "Thoughts and Sentiments on the Evil and Wicked Traffic," in Gates and Andrews, *Pioneers of the Black Atlantic*, 94.

29 "Joseph Wright of the Egba [originally named 'The Life of Joseph Wright: A Native of Ackoo (1839)],'" in *Africa Remembered: Narratives by West Africans from the Era of the Slave Trade*, ed. Philip D. Curtin (Madison, WI: The University of Wisconsin Press, 1967) 326–7.

30 Ibid., 330.

31 Cugoano, "Thoughts and Sentiments on the Evil and Wicked Traffic," in Gates and Andrews, *Pioneers of the Black Atlantic*, 94.

32 *The Interesting Narrative of the Life of Olaudah Equiano, or Gustavus Vassa, the African. Written by Himself.*, Vol. I: (London: printed for and sold by the author, 1789), 48–70, electronic edn, The University of North Carolina at Chapel Hill, 1st edn, 2001, http://docsouth.unc.edu/neh/equiano1/equiano1.html.

33 The term Maafa is the Kiswahili term for disaster. It is used interchangeably in this text with the more traditional term Middle Passage. Marimba Ani, *Let the Circle Be Unbroken: The Implications of African Spirituality in the Diaspora* (New York: Nkonimfo Publications, 1988), passim.

34 Stephanie Smallwood, *Saltwater Slavery: A Middle Passage from Africa to American Diaspora* (Cambridge: Harvard University Press, 2007), 70–1.

35 Nigel Tattersfield, *The Forgotten Trade: Comprising the Log of the Daniel and Henry of 1700 and Accounts of the Slave Trade from the Minor Ports of England, 1698–1725* (London: Jonathan Cape, 1991), 141–2.

36 Walvin, *Atlas of Slavery*, 65–6.

37 "Joseph Wright of the Egba," in Curtin, *Africa Remembered*, 331–2.

38 Lindsay, *Captives as Commodities*, 95.

39 Ibid., 90.

40 See, for example: James Walvin, *The Zong: A Massacre, the Law and the End of Slavery* (New Haven, CT: Yale University Press, 2011).

41 "Thoughts and Sentiments on the Evil of Slavery," in Gates and Andrews, *Pioneers of the Black Atlantic*, 94.

42 "The Interesting Narrative of the Life of Olaudah Equiano," in Gates and Andrews, *Pioneers of the Black Atlantic*, 217–18.
43 Ibid., 220.
44 Eric Robert Taylor, *If We Must Die: Shipboard Insurrections in the Era of the Atlantic Slave Trade* (Baton Rouge, LA, Louisiana State University Press, 2006).
45 Pascoe G. Hill, *Fifty Days on board a Slave Vessel* (Baltimore, MD: Black Classic Press, 1993), 24–5, 48–9. First published 1844 by J. Winchester, New World Press.

Chapter 3 African People in the Colonial World of North America

1 This enslaved man actually arrived in the United States after the colonial period. His experience of capture, sale, travel to and sale in Charleston, however, mirrors well the experiences of African slaves arriving in the colonial era. Omar ibn Said, "Autobiography of Omar ibn Said, Slave in North Carolina, 1831," ed. John Franklin Jameson, *The American Historical Review* 30(4) (July 1925): 787–95, electronic edn, http://docsouth.unc.edu/nc/omarsaid/omarsaid.html.
2 Richard R. Wright, "Negro Companions of the Spanish Explorers," in *The Making of Black America: Essays in Negro Life and History. Vol. 1, The Origins of Black Americans*, ed. August Meier and Elliott Rudwick (New York: Atheneum, 1974).
3 Charles A. Grymes, "The Spanish in Virginia before Jamestown," in Virginia Places (Geography of Virginia), http://www.virginiaplaces.org/settleland/spanish.html. Also see Clifford Lewis and Alfred Loomie, *The Spanish Jesuit Mission in Virginia* (Chapel Hill, NC: The University of North Carolina Press, 1953).
4 Paul Hoffman, "Legend, Religious Idealism, and Colonies: The Point of Santa Elena in History, 1552–66," *The South Carolina Historical Magazine* 84(2) (Apr. 1983): 59–71, http://www.jstor.org/stable/27563624. Spain and Portugal were united between 1580 and 1640.
5 Ronald Wayne Childers, "The Presidio System in Spanish Florida 1565–1763," in "Presidios of the North American Spanish Borderlands," ed. Judith A. Bense, Special Issue, *Historical Archaeology* 38(3) (2004): 26–8, http://www.jstor.org/stable/25617178.
6 Jane Landers, "Black Frontier Settlements in Spanish Colonial Florida," in "The Frontier," ed. Pat Anderson, Special Issue, *OAH Magazine of History* 3(2) (Spring 1988): 28–9, doi: 10.1093/maghis/3.2.28.

7 Alejandra Dubcovsky, "The Testimony of Thomás de la Torre, a Spanish Slave," *The William and Mary Quarterly* 70(3) (July 2013): 559–80, http://www.jstor.org/stable/10.5309/willmary quar.70.3.0559.

8 Jane Landers, "Gracia Real de Santa Teresa de Mose: A Free Black Town in Spanish Colonial Florida," *The American Historical Review* 95(1) (Feb. 1990): 15, http://www.jstor.org/ stable/2162952.

9 J. B. Davis, "Slavery in the Cherokee Nation," *Chronicles of Oklahoma* 11(4) (Dec. 1933): 1057, http://digital.library. okstate.edu/CHRONICLES/v011/v011p1056.html.

10 Susan R. Parker, "A St. Augustine Timeline: Important Historical Events for the Nation's Oldest City," *St. Augustine Historical Society* online, February 1, 2011, http://www.stau gustinehistoricalsociety.org/timeline.pdf.

11 Jane G. Landers, *Atlantic Creoles in the Age of Revolutions* (Cambridge, MA: Harvard University Press, 2010), Kindle Edition, location ch. 4, 1512, Appendix 2, 2145–51.

12 Randolph B. Campbell, *An Empire for Slavery: A Peculiar Institution in Texas, 1821–1865* (Baton Rouge, LA: Louisiana State University Press, 1991), 10; Donald E. Chipman, "Estavanico," *Handbook of Texas* Online, Texas State Historical Association, last modified November 5, 2013, http:// www.tshaonline.org/handbook/online/articles/fes08; "Estavanico, The Black Conquistador," Oregon Public Broadcasting and *PBS Online*, http://www.pbs.org/opb/conquistadors/namerica/adventure2/a10.htm.

13 It is not certain if there were enslaved blacks who participated in Rene Robert Cavelier, sieur de La Salle's failed attempt to establish a French colony on what is today Inez, Texas from 1685 to 1688. See, for example, *The Journeys of Rene Robert Cavelier, sieur de La Salle, Published in 2 volumes*, ed. Isaac Cox, vol. 2 (New York: Allerton Book Company, 1905), also available online, University of North Texas Libraries, http:// texashistory.unt.edu/ark:/67531/metapth6103/.

14 Campbell, *An Empire for Slavery*, 11.

15 Herman Bennett, *Africans in Colonial Mexico: Absolutism, Christianity and Afro-Creole Consciousness, 1570–1640* (Bloomington, IN: Indiana University Press, 2003), 27. M. Malowist, "The Struggle for International Trade and Its Implications for Africa," in *General History of Africa, Vol. V: Africa from the Sixteenth to the Eighteenth Century*, ed. B. A. Ogot (Berkeley: University of California Press, 1992), 8–9; J. E. Inikori, "Africa in World History: The Export Slave Trade from Africa and the Emergence of the Atlantic Economic Order," in Ogot, *General History of Africa*, 106; Douglas W.

Richmond, "Africa's Initial Encounter with Texas: The Significance of Afro-Tejanos in Colonial Tejas, 1528–1821," *Bulletin of Latin American Research* 26(2) (April 2007): 224–6, doi: 10.1111/j.1470-9856.2007.00220.x; Lorena Madrigal, "The African Slave Trade and the Caribbean," in *Human Biology of the Afro-Caribbean Populations* (Cambridge, MA: Cambridge University Press, 2006), 3, available online http://dx.doi.org/10.1017/CBO9780511542497.002.

16 Inikori, "Africa in World History," in Ogot, *General History of Africa*, 81.

17 Bennett estimates that 151,018 blacks lived in New Spain in 1646. Bennett, *Africans in Colonial Mexico*, 19; Inikori, "African in World History," in Ogot, *General History of Africa*, 96, 103–4.

18 Campbell, *An Empire for Slavery*, 11.

19 Bennett, *Africans in Colonial Mexico*, 17–19; Matthew Restall, "Manuel's Worlds: Black Yucatan and the Colonial Caribbean," in *Slaves, Subjects, and Subversives: Blacks in Colonial Latin America*, ed. Jane Landers and Barry M. Robinson (Albuquerque, NM: University of New Mexico Press, 2006), 147–74 passim.

20 Lovejoy, *Transformations in Slavery*, 107–10; Robin Law, *The Slave Coast of West Africa, 1550–1750: The Impact of the Atlantic Slave Trade on an African Society* (Oxford, UK: Oxford University Press, 1990), 45–58; Inikori, "Africa in World History," in Ogot, *General History of Africa*, 106.

21 Peter Boyd-Bowman, "Negro Slaves in Early Colonial Mexico," *The Americas* 26(2) (Oct. 1969): 134, http://www.latinamericanstudies.org/slavery/TA-1969.pdf.

22 Gwendolyn Midlo Hall, *Africans in Colonial Louisiana: The Development of Afro-Creole Culture in the Eighteenth Century* (Baton Rouge, LA: Louisiana State University, 1992), 29, 61; Peter Caron, " 'Of a Nation the Others Do Not Understand': Bambara Slaves and African Ethnicity in Colonial Louisiana, 1718–1760," *Slavery & Abolition* 18(1) (April 1997): 98–121.

23 Garrigus, John, trans., "The 'Code Noir' (1685)" (Paris: Prault, 1767; repr. Societé, d'Histoire de la Guadeloupe, 1980), https://directory.vancouver.wsu.edu/sites/directory.vancouver.wsu.edu/files/inserted_files/webintern02/code%20noir.pdf.

24 Carl A. Brasseaux, "The Administration of Slave Regulations in French Louisiana, 1724–1766," *Louisiana History: The Journal of the Louisiana Historical Association* 21(2) (Spring 1980): 144, http://www.jstor.org/stable/4231984.

25 Ibid., 143.

26 Charley Richard, "200 Years of Progress in the Louisiana Sugar Industry: A Brief History," American Sugar Cane League, http://www.assct.org/louisiana/progress.pdf.

27 Ira Berlin, *Many Thousands Gone: The First Two Centuries of Slavery in North America* (Cambridge, MA: Belknap Press of Harvard University Press, 1998), 370, Table 1.

28 "A Brief History of New Sweden in America," The Swedish Colonial Society, http://colonialswedes.net/History/History.html.

29 Oscar Williams, *African Americans and Colonial Legislation in the Middle Colonies* (New York: Garland Publishing, Inc., 1998), 4–5.

30 Quoted in ibid., 6.

31 Ibid., 8–9.

32 Quoted in ibid., 14–16; also see Thelma Willis Foote, *Black and White Manhattan: The History of Racial Formation in Colonial New York City* (New York: Oxford University Press, 2004), 38–40.

33 Williams, *African Americans and Colonial Legislation in the Middle Colonies*, 25.

34 Russell Thornton, *American Indian Holocaust and Survival: A Population History Since 1492* (Norman, OK: University of Oklahoma Press, 1987); Russell Thornton, "Population History of Native North Americans," in *A Population History of North America*, ed. Michael R. Haines and Richard Hall Steckel (Cambridge, MA: Cambridge University Press, 2000), 13.

35 Roberta Jestes, "Indian Slaves in Virginia and Maryland," *Native Heritage Project*, June 27, 2012, http://nativeheritage-project.com/2012/06/27/indian-slaves-in-maryland-and-virginia/. Virginia outlawed Indian slavery in 1705, but it was only after 1777 that the state legislature acted to enforce this law. Most still had to sue to receive freedom.

36 Sluiter, "New Light on the '20. and Odd Negroes,'" 396–8; Thornton, "The African Experience," 421–34; Thorndale, "The Virginia Census of 1619," 155–70.

37 Thornton, "The African Experience," 432–4; John K. Thornton, "African Dimension of the Stono Rebellion," *American Historical Review* 96(4) (Oct. 1991): 1101–13, http://www.jstor.org/stable/2164997; Anne Hilton, *The Kingdom of Kongo* (Oxford: Clarendon Press, 1985), 90–103; Annette Laing, "'Heathens and Infidels'? African Christianization and Anglicanism in the South Carolina Low Country, 1700–1750," *Religion and American Culture* 12(2) (Summer

2002): 199–200, 206–9, 211–12, http://www.jstor.org/stable/ 1123898.

38 Thornton, "The African Experience," 431–4; James Deetz, *Flowerdew Hundred: The Archaeology of a Virginia Plantation, 1619–1864* (Charlottesville: University Press of Virginia, 1993), 20–2.

39 Thornton, "The African Experience," 431–4; Deetz, *Flowerdew Hundred*, 20–2.

40 Thornton, "The African Experience," 431–4; *The Negro in Virginia, Compiled by Workers of the Writers' Program of the Work Projects Administration in the State of Virginia* (New York: Hastings House, 1940), 10.

41 Edward Barlett Rugemer, "Making Slavery English: Comprehensive Slave Codes in the Greater Caribbean during the Seventeenth Century," 1–4, http://barbadoscarolinas.org/PDF/ Making%20Slavery%20English%20by%20Rugemer.pdf.

42 Berlin, *Many Thousands Gone*, 369, Table 1.

43 Karl Watson, "Slavery and Economy in Barbados," *BBC History* online, last modified February 17, 2011, http://www. bbc.co.uk/history/british/empire_seapower/barbados_01. shtml.

44 Berlin, *Many Thousands Gone*, 369, Table 1.

45 Foote, *Black and White Manhattan*, 40.

46 Berlin, *Many Thousands Gone*, 369, Table 1.

47 "The Colonial Laws of New York from the Year 1664 to the Revolution," in *The Documentary History of the State of New-York*, vol. 1, ed. E. B. O'Callaghan (Albany, NY: Charles Van Benthysen, 1851), 519–21, under "1702: An Act for Regulating Slaves," http://people.hofstra.edu/alan_j_singer/ Gateway%20Slavery%20Guide%20PDF%20Files/3.%20 British%20Colony,%201664-1783/6.%20Documents/1702. %20Regulating%20Slaves.pdf.

48 Dennis O. Linder, "New York Slave Laws: Colonial Period," in "Famous Trials: The 'Negro Plot' Trials (1741)," 2009, University of Missouri, Kansas City School of Law, http:// law2.umkc.edu/faculty/projects/ftrials/negroplot/slavelaws. html.

49 Douglas Harper, "Slavery in Pennsylvania," in *Slavery in the North*, 2003, http://slavenorth.com/pennsylvania.htm.

50 Edward Raymond Turner, *The Negro in Pennsylvania: Slavery–Servitude–Freedom, 1639–1861* (Washington, DC: American Historical Association, 1911), 17–36.

51 Lorenzo Greene, *The Negro in Colonial New England, 1620–1776*, 3rd edn (New York: Atheneum, 1968), 319.

52 Timothy Fitch to Capt. William Ellery, January 14, 1759, online as "Voyage one by Capt. William Ellery on behalf of

Timothy Fitch," in "The Medford Slave Trade Letters, 1759–1765," Medford Historical Society, http://www.medfordhis torical.org/collections/slave-trade-letters/voyage-one-capt -william-ellery-behalf-timothy-fitch/.

53 Greene, *The Negro in Colonial New England*, 28–9, 58–9, 70, 106, 292.

54 Edward Raymond Turner, "Slavery in Colonial Pennsylvania," *The Pennsylvania Magazine of History and Biography* 35(2) (1911): 143–4 (quoted in the *Pennsylvannia Gazette*, 4 September 1740), http://www.jstor.org/stable/20085542.

55 "Colonial Era: Runaway Slave Advertisements," *African American History Website*, Radford University, http://www. radford.edu/~shepburn/web/Runaway%20Slave%20Adver tisements.htm.

56 Foote, *Black and White Manhattan*, 70–2.

57 "Growing Food," Plimoth Plantation, http://www.plimoth. org/learn/just-kids/homework-help/growing-food.

58 Paul Davis, "Plantations in the North: The Narragansett Planters," in "The Unrighteous Traffick: Rhode Island's Slave History," *Providence Journal*, March 13, 2006, http://res. providencejournal.com/hercules/extra/2006/slavery/day2/.

59 "Agriculture in New York," in *Readings in the Economic History of the United States*, ed. Ernest Ludlow Bogart and Charles Manfred Thompson (New York: Longmans, Green and Co., 1917), 32–4.

60 John Munroe, *History of Delaware* (Newark, DE: University of Delaware Press, 1975), 60.

61 John Jea, "The Life, History, and Unparalleled Sufferings of John Jea, the African Preacher" in Gates and Andrews, *The Pioneers of the Black Atlantic*, 369.

62 Turner, *The Negro in Pennsylvania*, 41; "Slaves in New England," Medford History, Medford Historical Society, http://www.medfordhistorical.org/medford-history/africa-to -medford/slaves-in-new-england/.

63 Foote, *Black and White Manhattan*, 72–5.

64 The dates from 1720, 1750, and 1770 are found in: Ira Berlin, *Generations of Captivity: A History of African-American Slaves* (Cambridge, MA: Belknap/Harvard Press, 2003), 274, Table I. The first designation for Louisiana is 1726, not 1720.

65 Landers, "Black Frontier Settlements in Spanish Colonial Florida," 28–9.

66 Berlin, *Many Thousands Gone*, 370, Table 1. The actual date of the statistic is 1774.

67 Jane Landers, *Black Society in Spanish Florida* (Urbana, IL: University of Illinois Press, 1999), 117. The actual date of the statistic is 1788.

68 Unless otherwise noted, this data is assembled from Berlin, *Many Thousands Gone*, 369–70, Table 1.

69 Much of this discussion of the ethnicities of Africans in colonial North America first appeared in Brenda E. Stevenson, "The Question of the Female Slave Community and Culture in the American South: Methodological and Ideological Approaches," *The Journal of African American History* 92(1) (Winter 2007): 74–95, http://www.jstor.org/stable/20064155.

70 Hall, *Slavery and African Ethnicities in the Americas*, 127–31.

71 Joseph Thérèse Agbasiere, *Women in Igbo Life and Thought* (New York: Routledge, 2000), 29.

72 Allan Kulikoff, *Tobacco and Slaves: The Development of Southern Cultures in the Chesapeake, 1680–1800* (Chapel Hill, NC: University of North Carolina Press, 1986), 322; Douglas B. Chambers, *Murder at Montpelier: Igbo Africans in Virginia* (Oxford, MS: University Press of Mississippi, 2009), 161–2; David Geggus, "Sex Ratio, Age and Ethnicity in the Atlantic Slave Trade: Data from French Shipping and Plantation Records," *Journal of African History* 20(1) (1989): 36n52, http://www.jstor.org/stable/182693.

73 Hall, *Slavery and African Ethnicities in the Americas*, 94–5.

74 Philip Morgan, *Slave Counterpoint: Black Culture in the Eighteenth Century Chesapeake and Low Country* (Chapel Hill, NC: University of North Carolina Press, 1998), 64.

75 James Horn, "Leaving England: The Social Background of Indentured Servants in the Seventeenth Century," *Virtual Jamestown*, Virginia Center for Digital History, University of Virginia, http://www.virtualjamestown.org/essays/horn_essay.html.

76 Ibid.

77 Brendan Wolfe and Martha McCartney, "Indentured Servants in Colonial Virginia," *Encyclopedia Virginia*, Virginia Foundation for the Humanities, last modified December 6, 2012, http://www.encyclopediavirginia.org/Indentured_Servants_in_Colonial_Virginia#start_entry.

78 Morgan, *Slave Counterpoint*, 478.

79 Indian slave trade and slavery in Gallay, *The Indian Slave Trade: The Rise of the English Empire in the American South, 1670–1717* (New Haven, CT: Yale University Press, 2002). Numbers of Indian slaves and their origins are found in ibid., 299, 312, Table 2.

80 Laurence Foster, *Negro–Indian Relationships in the Southeast* (Philadelphia, PA: University of Pennsylvania Press, 1935), 19.

81 Morgan, *Slave Counterpoint*, 478.

82 Peter Wood, *Black Majority: Negroes in Colonial South Carolina from 1670 through the Stono Rebellion* (New York: Norton Press, 1974), 13.

83 Wood, *Black Majority*, 18–19; "The Fundamental Constitutions of Carolina: March 1, 1669," *The Avalon Project: Documents in Law, History and Diplomacy*, Lillian Goldman Law Library, Yale University, 2008, http://avalon.law.yale. edu/17th_century/nc05.asp.

84 Wood, *Black Majority*, 25.

85 Watson, "Slavery and Economy in Barbados," n.p.

86 Wood, *Black Majority*, 29–31.

87 Rugemer, "Making Slavery English," 9–14.

88 Ibid., 2.

89 Ibid., 21–3.

90 Eltis, *The Rise of African Slavery in the Americas*, 105, Table 4-4.

91 Geggus, "Sex Ratio, Age and Ethnicity in the Atlantic Slave Trade:" 23–44, 34, Table 5.

92 Judith Carney, *Black Rice: The African Origins of Rice Cultivation in the Americas* (Cambridge: Harvard University Press), 48–68; David Richardson, "The British Slave Trade to Colonial South Carolina," *Slavery and Abolition* 12 (1991): 125–72 passim.

93 Geggus, "Sex Ratio, Age and Ethnicity in the Atlantic Slave Trade," 35, Table 4; Michael A. Gomez, *Exchanging Our Country Marks: The Transformations of African Identities in the Colonial and Antebellum South* (Chapel Hill, NC: University of North Carolina Press, 1998), 151.

94 Melville J. Herskovits, *The Myth of the Negro Past* (Boston: Beacon Press, 1958). First published by Harper and Brothers in 1941.

95 Sidney W. Mintz and Richard Price, *The Birth of African-American Culture: An Anthropological Perspective* (Boston: Beacon Press, 1992), 1.

96 Kulikoff, *Tobacco and Slaves*; Darrett B. Rutman and Anita H. Rutman, *A Place in Time: Middlesex County, Virginia, 1650–1750* (New York: W. W. Norton and Co., 1984); Berlin, *Many Thousands Gone*; Morgan, *Slave Counterpoint*; Russell R. Menard, "The Maryland Slave Population, 1658 to 1730: A Demographic Profile in Four Counties," *William and Mary Quarterly* 32(1) (Jan. 1975): 29–54, http://www.jstor.org/stable/1922593; Lorena S. Walsh, *From Calabar to Carter's Grove: A History of a Virginia Slave Community* (Charlottesville, VA: University Press of Virginia, 1997).

97 Mechal Sobel, *The World They Made Together: Black and White Values in Eighteenth-Century Virginia* (Princeton, NJ: Princeton University Press, 1987); Charles Joyner, *Down By the Riverside: A South Carolina Slave Community* (Urbana, IL: University of Illinois Press, 1984); Daniel C. Littlefield, *Rice and Slaves: Ethnicity and the Slave Trade in Colonial South Carolina* (Urbana, IL: University of Illinois Press, 1991); Wood, *Black Majority*; Margaret Washington Creel, *"A Peculiar People:" Slave Religion and Community Culture among the Gullahs* (New York: New York University Press, 1988); Joseph E. Holloway, ed., *Africanisms in American Culture* (Bloomington, IN: Indiana University Press, 1990); Hall, *Slavery and African Ethnicities in the Americas*; Chambers, *Murder at Montpelier*.

98 Gomez, *Exchanging our Country Marks*, 6–15.

99 Ibid.

100 Janheinz Jahn, *Muntu: African Culture and the Western World*, trans. Marjorie Greene (New York: Grove/Atlantic, 1991), 35–59; João José Reis, "Batuque: African Drumming and Dance between Repression and Concession, Bahia, 1800–1855," *Bulletin of Latin American Research* 24(2) (April 2005): 201–14, http://www.jstor.org/stable/27733744.

101 Claire C. Robertson and Martin A. Klein, "Women's Importance in African Slave Systems," in *Women and Slavery in Africa*, ed. Claire C. Robertson and Martin A. Klein (Madison, WI: University of Wisconsin, 1983), 9–10.

102 See, for example, the discussion of Hall, *Slavery and African Ethnicities in the Americas*, 66–79 passim.

103 For some discussion of the cultural change or acculturation of slaves in West Africa, see Martin A. Klein, *Slavery and Colonial Rule in French West Africa* (New York: Cambridge University Press, 1998), 10.

104 Hall, *Slavery and African Ethnicities in the Americas*; Gomez, *Exchanging our Country Marks*; Chambers, *Murder at Montpelier*; John W. Blassingame, *The Slave Community: Plantation Life in the Antebellum South* (New York: Oxford University Press, 1979), 25–76.

105 Joseph A. Opala, "Introduction," *The Gullah: Rice, Slavery and the Sierra Leone-American Connection*, Yale University, http://www.yale.edu/glc/gullah/.

106 Kulikoff, *Tobacco and Slaves*, 32.

107 Emily Jones Salmon and John Salmon, "Tobacco in Colonial Virginia," *Encyclopedia Virginia*, Virginia Foundation for the Humanities, Jan. 29, 2013. http://www.encyclopediavirginia.org/Tobacco_in_Colonial Virginia.

108 George Washington quote from, *The Papers of George Washington: Presidential Series*, 6 vols, ed. N. W. Abbot (Charlottesville, VA: 1987–), 1: 223, quoted in Berlin, *Many Thousands Gone*, 268.

109 U. B. Phillips, *American Negro Slavery: A Survey of the Supply, Employment and Control of Negro Labor as Determined by the Plantation Regime*, paperback edn (Baton Rouge, LA: Louisiana State University Press, 1966), 84.

110 Brenda E. Stevenson, *Life in Black and White: Family and Community in the Slave South* (New York: Oxford University Press, 1996), 329, appendix A.

111 Morgan, *Slave Counterpoint*, 179–80.

112 Carney, *Black Rice*, 69–93; Ulrich Bonnell Phillips, *Life and Labor in the Old South* (Boston, MA: Little, Brown and Company, 1946), 115–16; Morgan, *Slave Counterpoint*, 149–54.

113 Morgan, *Slave Counterpoint*, 159.

114 Ibid., 160–1.

115 Philips, *Life and Labor in the Old South*, 118–19.

116 Thomas Bluett, *Some Memoirs of the Life of Job, The Son of Solomon the High Priest of Boonda in Africa; Who was a Slave about Two Years in Maryland; and Afterwards Being Brought to England, was Set Free, and Sent to His Native Land in the Year 1734* (London: Printed for Richard Ford, 1734), 14–16, 40–2, electronic edn, The University of North Carolina at Chapel Hill, 1st edn, 1999, http://docsouth.unc.edu/neh/bluett/bluett.html. For further discussion of Job Ben Solomon's family and community life, see Brenda Stevenson, "Family and Community in Slave Narratives," in *The Oxford Handbook of the African American Slave Narrative*, ed. John Ernest (New York: Oxford University Press, 2014), 277–97.

117 James A. U. Gronniosaw, *A Narrative of the Most Remarkable Particulars in the Life of James Albert Ukawsaw Gronniosaw, an African Prince, As Related by Himself*, in Gates and Andrews, *Pioneers of the Black Atlantic*, 37.

118 Kulikoff, *Tobacco and Slaves*, 330.

119 Regarding the numbers of African imports to South Carolina and Virginia from 1700 through the 1780s, see Morgan, *Slave Counterpoint*, 59.

120 Federal Writers' Project of the Works Progress Administration, "Slave Narratives: Charley Barber," in *Slave Narratives: A Folk History of Slavery in the United States From Interviews with Former Slaves*, Library of Congress, Manuscript Division, South Carolina Narratives, vol. 14, pt 1, 498–503.

121   Charles Ball, *Fifty Years in Chains; or, The Life of an American Slave* (New York: H. Dayton, 1860), Kindle Edition location, 12.

122   Ibid., 68.

123   Stevenson, *Life in Black and White*, 169–70.

124   "Will of John Andrew, Jr," Charleston County, South Carolina Probate Records, Will Book 1740–1747, 282, *USGenWeb Archives*, http://files.usgwarchives.net/sc/colonial/colleton/wills/andrew03.txt.

125   "Slaves Named in Wills," *Halifax County, North Carolina Will Book, 1758–1774*, vol. 1, March 15, 1761, 31, http://www.freeafricanamericans.com/halifax.htm.

126   "Will of Thomas Potts," Craven County, South Carolina Probate Records, Will Book 1760–1767, 388, http://files.usgwarchives.net/sc/colonial/craven/wills/potts05.txt.

127   David George, "An Account of Life of Mr. David George from S. L. A. Given by Himself," *Black Loyalists: Our History, Our People and Canada's Digital Collection*, http://blackloyalist.com/cdc/documents/diaries/george_a_life.htm.

128   "Two Views of the Stono Slave Rebellion, South Carolina, 1739," in "Becoming American: The British Atlantic Colonies, 1690–1763," National Humanities Center, 2009, http://nationalhumanitiescenter.org/pds/becomingamer/peoples/text4/stonorebellion.pdf.

129   M. Watt Espy and John Ortiz Smykla, "Executions in the U.S.: The Espy File, 1608 to 2002," Death Penalty Information Center, http://www.deathpenaltyinfo.org/documents/ESPYyear.pdf.

130   Stevenson, *Life in Black and White*, 169–70; Ira Berlin, "Time, Space, and the Evolution of Afro-American Society on British Mainland North America," *The American Historical Review* 85(1) (Feb. 1980): 56, http://www.jstor.org/stable/1853424.

131   J. William Harris, *The Hanging of Thomas Jeremiah: A Free Black Man's Encounter with Liberty* (New Haven: Yale University Press, 2009); *The Trial of William Weems, James Hartegan, Wiliam McCauley, Hugh White, Matthew Kilroy, William Warren, John Carrol, and Hugh Montgomery for the Murders of Crispus Attucks, Samuel Gray, Samuel Maverick, James Caldwell, and Patrick Carr*, in "The Murder of Crispus Attucks," American Treasures of the Library of Congress, July 27, 2010, http://www.loc.gov/exhibits/treasures/trr046.html.

132   Department of Defense, "Black Americans in Defense of Our Nation," 1985, http://www.shsu.edu/~his_ncp/AfrAmer.html.

133   Mary V. Thompson, "George Washington and Slavery," *George Washington's Mount Vernon (The Library)* online, http://www.mountvernon.org/research-collections/digital-

encyclopedia/article/george-washington-and-slavery/. Stevenson, *Life in Black and White*, 209–10.

134 Paul Finkleman, "Thomas Jefferson and Antislavery: The Myth Goes On," *The Virginia Magazine of History and Biography* 102(2) (Apr. 1994): 203–5, http://www.jstor.org/stable/4249430.

135 J. Kent McGaughy, *Richard Henry Lee of Virginia: A Portrait of an American Revolutionary* (Lanham, MD: Rowman & Littlefield Publishers, Inc., 2004), 61.

136 Whitney Petrey, "Slaves in Revolutionary America: Plantation Slaves in Virginia and the Charleston Slave Trade," East Carolina University Maritime History and Nautical Archaeology, December 2009, https://www.academia.edu/1701748/Slaves _in_Revolutionary_America_Plantation_Slaves_in_Virginia _and_the_Charleston_Slave_Trade.

137 Esther Pavao, "Skirmish at Kemp's Landing," *Revolutionary-War.net*, http://www.revoultionary-war.net/skirmish-at-kemps -landing.html; John Earl of Dunmore, "Lord Dunmore's Proclamation," November 7, 1775, *LEARN NC*, UNC School of Education, http://www.learnnc.org/lp/editions/nchist-revo lution/4238.

138 "The Phillipsburg Proclamation," *Black Loyalists: Our History, Our People and Canada's Digital Collection*, http:// blackloyalist.com/cdc/story/revolution/philipsburg.htm.

139 Peter Kolchin, *American Slavery, 1619–1877* (New York: Hill and Wang, 1993), 70–3.

140 Alan Gilbert, *Black Patriots and Loyalists: Fighting for Emancipation in the War for Independence* (Chicago, IL: University of Chicago Press, 2012), 142.

141 Boston King, "Boston King, a Black Loyalist, Seeks Freedom Behind British Lines," in *African American Voices: A Documentary Reader, 1619–1877*, 4th edn, ed. Steven Mintz (Malden, MA: Blackwell Publishing, 2009), 82–3.

142 "James Armistead (Lafayette) Bibliography: Warrior, Spy, Military Leader (c. 1748–c. 1830)," Bio, A&E Television Networks, 2014, http://www.biography.com/people/james -armistead-537566; James W. St. G. Walker, "KING, BOSTON," in *Dictionary of Canadian Biography*, vol. 5, University of Toronto, 2003, http://www.biographi.ca/en/bio/king_boston_5E.html.

143 "Shelburne Riot," *Black Loyalists: Our History, Our People and Canada's Digital Collection*, http://blackloyalist.com/cdc/story/prejudice/riot.htm.

144 Elise A. Guyette, "The American Republic, 1760–1870: Abolition Timeline," *Flow of History*, http://flowofhistory.org/themes/american_republic/abolition_timeline.php.

145   Boston King, "Memoirs of Boston King," June 4, 1796, *Black Loyalists: Our History, Our People and Canada's Digital Collection*, http://blackloyalist.com/cdc/documents/diaries/king-memoirs.htm.

146   See, for example, excerpts from the 1814 account of the peopling of Sierra Leone via the Company found in: Maureen James, "John Clarkson & the Sierra Leone Company," *Telling History*, 2011, http://www.tellinghistory.co.uk/clarkson-john.

147   Douglas Harper, "Emancipation in New York," in "Slavery in the North," http://slavenorth.com/nyemancip.htm.

148   Douglas Harper, "Slavery in the North," 2003, http://slave north.com/slavenorth.htm; "The Slave Trade and the Revolution," *The Abolition of the Slave Trade*, The Schomburg Center for Research in Black Culture, http://abolition.nypl. org/essays/us_constitution/2/; Steven Deyle, *Carry Me Back: The Domestic Slave Trade in American Life* (New York: Oxford University Press, 2005), Kindle Edition, Kindle location ch. 2, 293.

149   " 'Natural and Inalienable Right to Freedom': Slaves' Petition for Freedom to the Massachusetts Legislature, 1777," in *Collections of the Massachusetts Historical Society*, 5th series, vol. 3 (Boston, 1877), 436–7, *History Matters*, http://historymatters.gmu.edu/d/6237.

150   Douglas Harper, "Slavery in the North," *Slavery in the North*, 2003, http://slavenorth.com/slavenorth.htm. Catherine Adams and Elizabeth H. Pleck, *Love of Freedom: Black Women in Colonial and Revolutionary New England* (New York: Oxford University Press, 2010), 128.

151   Roberta Jestes, "Indian Slaves in Maryland and Virginia."

152   See, for example, Barbara Krauthamer, *Black Slaves, Indian Masters: Slavery, Emancipation and Citizenship in the Native American South* (Chapel Hill, NC: University of North Carolina Press, 2013).

153   Quote from Michael Donald Roethler, "Negro Slavery among the Cherokee Indians, 1540–1866" (PhD diss., Fordham University, 1964), 57–8. Also see R. Halliburton, Jr, *Red Over Black: Black Slavery Among the Cherokee Indians* (Westport, CT: Greenwood Press, 1977), 9–11.

154   Philip J. Schwartz, *Slave Laws in Virginia* (Athens, GA: University of Georgia Press, 1996), 54–5.

155   "Maryland Acts Regarding Slaves and Free Blacks," *Legacy of Slavery in Maryland*, Maryland State Archives, http://slavery.msa.maryland.gov/html/research/slaves_free.html.

156   "George Washington's 1799 Will and Testament," July 9, 1799, *George Washington's Mount Vernon (The*

Library) online, http://www.mountvernon.org/educational-resources/encyclopedia/last-will-and-testament.

157 "Timeline of Slavery in Maryland," Slavery in Maryland research guide, University of Maryland Libraries, August 14, 2014, http://lib.guides.umd.edu/marylandslavery.

158 Stevenson, *Life in Black and White*, 175, 409n22.

159 Leon F. Litwack, *North of Slavery: The Negro in the Free States, 1790–1860* (Chicago, IL: University of Chicago Press, 1965), Kindle location, ch. 1; US Census Bureau, "Total Slave Population in the United States 1790–1860, by State," in Matthew D. Parker, *American Civil War*, http://thomaslegion.net/totalslaveslaverypopulationinunitedstates17901860bystate.html; Erin Bradford, "Free African American Population in the US, 1790–1860, compiled in 2008, University of Virginia Library, http://www.freeaainnc.com/censusstats1790-1860.pdf.

160 US Articles of Confederation art. 4, § 2, art. 9, § 5, pp. 4, 7–8, respectively, *American Memory: A Century of Lawmaking for New Nation*, Library of Congress, http://memory.loc.gov/cgi-bin/ampage?collId=llsl&fileName=001/llsl001.db&recNum=132.

161 US Const. art. IV, § 2, "Constitution of the United States: A Transcription," *The Charters of Freedom*, http://www.archives.gov/exhibits/charters/constitution_transcript.html.

162 Northwest Ordinance, July 13, 1787, National Archives Microfilm Publication M332, roll 9, Miscellaneous Papers of the Continental Congress, 1774–1789, Records of the Continental and Confederation Congresses and the Constitutional Convention, 1774–1789, Record Group 360, http://www.ourdocuments.gov/doc.php?flash=true&doc=8.

163 "Article 4, Section 2, Clause 3," *The Founders Constitution*, ed. Philip B. Kurland and Ralph Lerner (Chicago, IL: University of Chicago Press and the Liberty Fund, 2000), http://press-pubs.uchicago.edu/founders/documents/a4_2_3s6.html.

164 "Regulating the Trade," *The Abolition of the Slave Trade*, The Schomburg Center for Research in Black Culture and the New York Public Library, 2012, http://abolition.nypl.org/essays/us_constitution/4/.

165 Berlin, *Many Thousands Gone*, 308–9; Kolchin, *American Slavery*, 79; Jeff McDonough, "Slave trade was Rhode Island's 'Number One Financial Activity,'" *The Jamestown Press Online*, March 19, 2009, 1, http://www.jamestownpress.com/news/2009-03-19/front_page/003.html.

166 Paul Finkleman, "US Constitution and Acts," *The Abolition of the Slave Trade*, The Schomburg Center for Research in Black Culture and the New York Public Library, 2007, http://abolition.nypl.org/print/us_constitution/.

167 Sylviane Anna Diouf, *Dreams of Africa in Alabama: The Slave Ship Clotilda and the Story of the Last Africans Brought to America* (New York: Oxford University Press, 2009), especially 72–89.

168 "The Clotilda: A Finding Aid," The National Archives at Atlanta, http://www.archives.gov/atlanta/finding-aids/clotilda.pdf.

169 See Douglas R. Egerton, *Gabriel's Rebellion: The Virginia Slave Conspiracies of 1800 and 1802* (Chapel Hill, NC: University of North Carolina Press, 1993).

170 Egerton, *Gabriel's Rebellion*, 21–2; Kolchin, *American Slavery*, 78–81.

171 US Census Bureau, "Total Slave Population in the United States 1790–1860"; regarding cotton production, see Table 6.

172 Litwack, *North of Slavery*, 32; Litwack also notes that there was a brief allusion to free men of color seamen as "citizens" in 1803, Kindle location ch. 2, 303–5.

173 Ibid., ch. 3, 718–21, 764–5.

174 Solomon Northup, *Twelve Years a Slave: Narrative of Solomon Northup, a Citizen of New-York, Kidnapped in Washington City in 1841, and Rescued in 1853* (Auburn, NY: Derby and Miller, 1853), 19, electronic edn, University of North Carolina at Chapel Hill, 1997, http://docsouth.unc.edu/fpn/northup/northup.html.

175 Litwack, *North of Slavery*, Kindle location ch. 1, 172.

176 Ibid., ch. 2, 590–2.

177 Ibid., ch. 3, 694.

178 Ibid., ch. 3, 880–1.

179 Ibid., ch. 3, 892–923.

180 Ibid., ch. 3, 895, 910–12.

181 Ibid., ch. 3, 919–26.

182 Ibid., ch. 4, 1074–89.

183 Ibid., ch. 4, 1197.

184 Ibid., ch. 4, 1305–13.

185 Ibid., ch. 5, 1436–45.

186 Ibid., ch. 4, 1192–1233.

187 Ibid., 698–703, 951–8.

188 Ibid., ch. 3, 932–6, 941.

189 Ibid., ch. 2, 490; Stevenson, *Life in Black and White*, 264, 275.

190 "Charles Deslondes Revolt, 1811," *The Louisiana Gazette and New Orleans Daily Advertiser*, January 10, 1811, *The*

Slave Rebellion Web Site, 2010, http://slaverebellion.org/index.php?page=newspaper-report-of-the-charles-des londe-1811.

191 Stevenson, *Life in Black and White*, 275–6, 290–1.
192 Ibid.
193 Michael Johnson and James L. Roark, *Black Masters: A Free Family of Color in the Old South* (New York: W. W. Norton and Company, 1984), Kindle Edition location ch. 5, 3243.
194 Whittington B. Johnson, "Free African-American Women in Savannah, 1800–1860: Affluence and Autonomy amid Adversity," *The Georgia Historical Quarterly* 76(2) (Summer 1992): 265, http://www.jstor.org/stable/40582536.
195 Ibid.
196 Ibid., 266–7.
197 Johnson and Roark, *Black Masters*, Kindle location ch. 5, 3229–33.
198 Tara Fields, "A Brief Timeline of Georgia Laws Relating to Slaves, Nominal Slaves and Free Persons of Color," February 14, 2004, Rootsweb.com, http://www.rootsweb.ancestry.com/~gacamden/slave_timeline.pdf.
199 Larry Koger, *Black Slaveowners: Free Black Slave Masters in South Carolina, 1790–1860* (Columbia, SC: University of South Carolina, 1995), 1.
200 Ibid.
201 David Lightner and Alexander Ragan, "Were African Americans Slaveholders Benevolent or Exploitative? A Quantitative Approach," *The Journal of Southern History* 71 (3) (Aug. 2005): 539–40, http://www.jstor.org/stable/27648819; Koger, *Black Slaveowners*, 1.
202 Stevenson, *Life in Black and White*, 277.
203 Ibid.
204 "History of Liberia: A Timeline," *American Memory: A Century of Lawmaking for New Nation*, Library of Congress, October 19, 1998, http://memory.loc.gov/ammem/gmdhtml/libhtml/liberia.html.
205 For a discussion of Paul Cuffee's life and colonizationist efforts, see Lamont D. Thomas, *Paul Cuffee: Black Entrepreneur and Pan-Africanist (Blacks in the New World)* (Urbana, IL: University of Illinois Press, 1988).
206 Litwack, *North of Slavery*, Kindle location ch. 1, 249.
207 Forten's quote found at "Historical Document: Forten Letter to Cuffee, 1817," *Africans in America*, WGBH and PBS Online, 1998, http://www.pbs.org/wgbh/aia/part3/3h484.html.
208 Quoted in Litwack, *North of Slavery*, Kindle location ch. 1, 252–4.

209 Ibid., ch. 1, 263; Nemata Blyden, "The Colonization of Liberia," *Colonization and Emigration*, Schomburg Center for Research in Black Culture and The New York Public Library, 2005, http://www.inmotionaame.org/migra tions/topic.cfm;jsessionid=f8301223841402508011132?migr ation=4&topic=4&bhcp=1.
210 See John McNish Weiss, *The Merikens: Free Black American Settlers in Trinidad, 1815–16*, 2nd edn (London: McNeish and Weiss, 2002); and Alan Taylor, *The Internal Enemy: Slavery and War in Virginia, 1772–1832* (New York: W. W. Norton, 2013).

Chapter 4 Slavery and Anti-Slavery in Antebellum America

1 Dora Franks, *Voices from Slavery, 100 Authentic Slave Narratives*, ed. Norman Yetman (Minola, NY: Dover Publications, 2000), 128.
2 Morton Rothstein, "Antebellum Wheat and Cotton Exports: A Contrast in Marketing Organization and Economic Development," *Agricultural History* 40(2) (April 1966): 91, http://www.jstor.org/stable/3741087.
3 James H. Tuten, "Chapter 1: A Brief History of Rice Culture to the 1870s," in *Lowcountry Time and Tide: The Fall of the South Carolina Rice Kingdom* (Columbia, SC: University of South Carolina Press, 2010), 24, available online, http://www.sc.edu/uscpress/books/2010/3926x.pdf.
4 Deyle, *Carry Me Back*, Kindle location ch. 2, 657.
5 Ibid.
6 Ibid, ch. 2, 670.
7 United States Works Projects Administration (WPA), ed., "Vol. 2, Arkansas Narratives, Part 2," in *Slave Narratives: A Folk History of Slavery in the United States from Interviews with Former Slaves* (Washington, DC: Federal Writers' Project, 1941), Kindle Edition, "Mattie Fannen."
8 WPA, "Vol. 16, Texas Narratives, Part 3," in *Slave Narratives*, "Mariah Robinson."
9 WPA, "Vol. 2, Arkansas Narratives, Part 6," in *Slave Narratives*, "Henrietta Ralls."
10 WPA, "Vol. 16, Texas Narratives, Part 4," in *Slave Narratives*, "Ben Simpson."
11 Mattie Mooreman quoted in *Bullwhip Days: The Slaves Remember, An Oral History*, ed. James Mellon (New York: Grove Press, 1988), 136–8.

12 Rosa Starke quoted in Mellon, *Bullwhip Days*, 136.

13 Knut Oyangen, "The Cotton Economy of the Old South," *American Agricultural History Primer*, Iowa State University Center for Agricultural History and Rural Studies, http://rick woten.com/CottonEconomy.html.

14 Richard C. Wade, *Slavery in the Cities: The South 1820–1860* (New York: Oxford University Press, 1967), 4–8; Stevenson, *Life in Black and White*, 185–6; Keith S. Hébert, "Slavery," *Encyclopedia of Alabama*, last modified November 15, 2012, http://www.encyclopediaofalabama.org/face/Article. jsp?id=h-2369.

15 Frederick Law Olmstead, *The Cotton Kingdom: A Traveller's Observations on Cotton and Slavery in the American Slave States, 1853–1861*, ed. Arthur M. Schlesinger (New York: De Capo Press, 1996), 162.

16 Regarding the labor of slave women, see the following: Deborah Grey White, *Ar'n't I a Woman? Female Slaves in the Plantation South* (New York: W. W. Norton Press, 1985), passim; Jacqueline Jones, *Labor of Love, Labor of Sorrow: Black Women, Work and the Family, From Slavery to the Present* (New York: Basic Books, 1985), 11–43 passim; Virginia Meacham Gould, " 'If I Can't Have My Rights, I Can Have My Pleasures, And If They Won't Give Me Wages, I Can Take Them': Gender and Slave Labor in Antebellum New Orleans," in *Discovering the Women in Slavery: Emancipating Perspectives on the American Past*, ed. Patricia Morton (Athens: University of Georgia Press, 1996), 179–201; Wilma King, "The Mistress and Her Maids: White and Black Women in a Louisiana Household, 1858–1868," in Morton, *Discovering the Women in Slavery*, 82–106; Stevenson, *Life in Black and White*, Kindle location ch. 6.

17 *Historical Census Browser*, Geospatial and Statistical Data Center, University of Virginia Library, 2004, http://mapserver. lib.virginia.edu/.

18 Michel Frosch, "Results of the 1860 Census," *The Civil War Homepage*, last updated 2009, http://www.civil-war.net/ pages/1860_census.html.

19 Lewis Cecil Gray and Esther Kathrine Thompson, *History of Agriculture in the Southern United States until 1860* (Washington, DC: The Carnegie Institute of Washington, 1973), 1026, Table 40.

20 Gene Dattel, *Cotton and Race in the Making of America: The Human Costs of Economic Power* (Lanham, MD: Ivan R. Dee, 2009), Kindle Edition, "Appendix: 1, 6366. Cotton Prices in Cents per Pound, Weighted Average, 1800–1860."

21 For the best discussion of gender and slave labor in the ante-bellum South, see Jones, *Labor of Love, Labor of Sorrow*, 14–29; and Julie A. Matthaei, *An Economic History of Women in America: Women's Work, the Sexual Division of Labor, and the Development of Capitalism* (New York: Schocken Books, 1982), 74–97.

22 Fannie Moore quoted in *The American Slave: A Composite Autobiography*, vol. 15, ed. George P. Rawick, North Carolina Narratives, pt. 2 (1941, repr. Westport, CT: Greenwood Publishing, 1979), 129.

23 Sara Colquitt quoted in Rawick, *The American Slave*, vol. 6, Alabama and Indiana Narratives, 87–8.

24 Ibid.

25 Amelia Walker quoted in Charles L. Perdue, Jr, Thomas E. Barden, and Robert K. Phillips, eds, *Weevils in the Wheat: Interviews with Virginia Ex-Slaves* (Charlottesville, VA: University Press of Virginia, 1976), 292.

26 Henrietta McCullers quoted in Rawick, *The American Slave*, vol. 15, North Carolina Narratives, pt. 2, 74.

27 Charles Sackett Sydnor, *Slavery in Mississippi* (1933; repr. Gloucester, MA: Peter Smith, 1965), 10n47.

28 Olmstead, *The Cotton Kingdom*, 168

29 Northup, *Twelve Years a Slave*, 156.

30 Charlie Hudson quoted in Mellon, *Bullwhip Days*, 141.

31 Frances Willingham quoted in Rawick, *The American Slave*, vol. 13, Georgia Narratives, pt. 4, 157.

32 Fannie Moore quoted in Rawick, *The American Slave*, vol. 15, North Carolina Narratives, pt. 2, 130.

33 Quoted in "Compilation Richmond County Ex-Slave Interviews: Mistreatment of Slaves," in Rawick, *The American Slave*, vol. 13, Georgia Narratives, pt. 4, 299.

34 Nancy Williams quoted in Perdue, Barden, and Phillips, *Weevils in the Wheat*, 322–3.

35 White, *Ar'n't I a Woman?*, 27–61.

36 Ibid.

37 Chaney Spell quoted in Rawick, *The American Slave*, vol. 15, North Carolina Narratives, pt. 2, 308.

38 Mary Chesnut quoted in C. Vann Woodward, ed., *Mary Chesnut's Civil War* (New Haven, 1981), in Kolchin, *American Slavery*, 124.

39 Rosa Maddox quoted in Mellon, *Bullwhip Days*, 122.

40 Rev. Ishrael Massie quoted in Perdue, Barden, and Phillips, *Weevils in the Wheat*, 207.

41 William Forbes to George Carter, 20 May 1805, Carter Family Papers, Virginia Historical Society, Richmond; George Carter

to Sophia Carter, 20 June 1816, George Carter Letter Book, Virginia Historical Society, Richmond.

42 Mrs Bird Walton, quoted in Perdue, Barden, and Phillips, *Weevils in the Wheat*, 300–1.

43 Jacob Manson quoted in Mellon, *Bullwhip Days*, 219–20.

44 Minnie Folkes quoted in Perdue, Barden, and Phillips, *Weevils in the Wheat*, 92–3.

45 Helen T. Catterall, ed., *Judicial Cases Concerning American Slavery and the Negro*, vol. 3 (Washington, DC: Carnegie, 1929), 363.

46 Inventory of Adam Shover's Estate, October 13, 1817, Shover Family Papers, Virginia State Library, Richmond; Promissory note, Samuel DeButts, October 29, 1838, DeButts Family Papers, Virginia Historical Society, Richmond; Benjamin Drew, ed., *A North-Side View of Slavery: The Refugee, or the Narratives of Fugitive Slaves in Canada* (Boston, MA: John P. Jewett and Co., 1856), 74; Charles Preston Poland, *From Frontier to Suburbia* (Loudoun Co., VA: Walsworth Publishing Co., 1976), 139.

47 *The Fugitive Blacksmith; on, Events in the History of James W. C. Pennington*, 3rd edn (1849, repr. Westport, CN: Negro Universities Press, 1971), v–vi.

48 Dorothy Sterling, ed., *We Are Your Sisters: Black Women in the Nineteenth Century* (New York: W. W. Norton and Co., 1984), 48. Pennington, *The Fugitive Blacksmith*, v–x; "Carol Anna Randall" in Perdue, Barden, and Phillips, *Weevils in the Wheat*, 236.

49 Lizzie Grant quoted in Rawick, *The American Slave (Supplement, Series II)*, vol. 5, Texas narratives, pt. 4, 1556.

50 Josephine Howard quoted in Rawick, *The American Slave*, vol. 4, Texas Narratives, pt. 2, 163.

51 See for example, "West Turner" in Perdue, Barden, and Phillips, *Weevils in the Wheat*, 291.

52 Fannie Moore quoted in Rawick, vol. 15, *The American Slave*, North Carolina Narratives, pt. 2, 131.

53 See, for example, WPA, "Georgia Narratives, Part 1," in *Slave Narratives*, "Rias Body."

54 WPA, "Georgia Narratives, Part 3," in *Slave Narratives*, "Shade Richards."

55 "*The Confessions of Nat Turner; Leader of the Late Insurrection in Southampton, VA. As Fully and Voluntarily Made to Thos. R. Gray, in the Prison Where He Was Confined, and Acknowledged by Him to Be Such, When Read Before the Court of Southampton, Convened at Jerusalem, November 5, 1831, for His Trial*," transcribed by Thomas R. Gray, in *The*

Confessions of Nat Turner and Related Documents, ed. Kenneth S. Greenberg (Boston, MA: Bedford/St Martins, 1996), 44–5. Also see Stevenson, "Family and Community in Slave Narratives," 277–97.

56 Harriet Jacobs, *Incidents in the Life of a Slave Girl*, ed. Valerie Smith (New York: Oxford University Press, 1988), 87–9.

57 *Narrative of the Life of Frederick Douglass, An American Slave: Written by Himself*, 6th edn (London: H. G. Collins, 1851), 4, https://play.google.com/books/reader?id=U69bAAA AQAAJ&printsec=frontcover&output=reader&authuser=0& hl=en.

58 Ibid., 25.

59 WPA, "Vol. 15, South Carolina Narratives, Pt. 1," in *Slave Narratives*, "Ezra Adams."

60 Ball, *Fifty Years in Chains*, 12.

61 WPA, "Vol. 17, Virginia Narratives," in *Slave Narratives*, "Elizabeth Sparks."

62 WPA, "Vol. 2, South Carolina Narratives, Pt. 1," in *Slave Narratives*, "Josephine Bristow."

63 WPA, "Vol. 1, Alabama Narratives," in *Slave Narratives*, "Charlie Van Dyke."

64 Julia Brown, interview with Geneva Tonsill, Atlanta, Georgia, in Yetman, *Voices from Slavery*, 47–8.

65 See, for example, WPA, "Vol. 12, Georgia Narratives, Pt. 1," in *Slave Narratives*, "Callie Elder."

66 Booker T. Washington, *Up from Slavery: An Autobiography* (Garden City, NY: Doubleday and Co., Inc., 1901), Project Gutenberg eBook, 2008, last modified 2011, ch. 1.

67 WPA, "Vol. 6, Alabama Narratives," in *Slave Narratives*, "Mingo White."

68 Jacob Branch, interview with unknown, Double Bayou Settlement, Texas, in Yetman, *Voices from Slavery*, 40.

69 WPA, "Vol. 12, Georgia Narratives, Pt. 1," in *Slave Narratives*, "Celestia Avery."

70 Ball, *Fifty Years in Chains*, 9–10.

71 WPA, "Vol. 6, Alabama Narratives," in *Slave Narratives*, "Janie Scott."

72 See, for example, *Louisa Picquet, the Octoroon: or Inside Views of Southern Domestic Life*, ed. Hiram Mattison (New York: Hiram Mattison, 1861), electronic edn, University of North Carolina at Chapel Hill, 2003, http://docsouth.unc.edu/neh/picquet/picquet.html; and Jacobs, *Incidents in the Life of a Slave Girl*.

73 Delia Garlic quoted in Rawick, *The American Slave*, vol. 6, Alabama and Indiana Slave Narratives, 130.

74 "Mrs. Armaci Adams" in Perdue, Barden, and Phillips, *Weevils in the Wheat*, 3–4.

75 See, for example, Brenda E. Stevenson, " 'What's Love Got to Do with It?': Concubinage and Enslaved Black Women and Girls in the Antebellum South," in "Women, Slavery, and the Atlantic World," Special Issue, *Journal of African American History* 98(1) (Winter 2013): 99–125, http://www.jstor.org/stable/10.5323/jafriamerhist.98.1.0099.

76 Jacobs, *Incidents in the Life of a Slave Girl*, 44.

77 Narrative of Lewis Clark, *National Anti-Slavery Standard*, 1842, recorded by Lydia Maria Child and found in John W. Blassingame, ed., *Slave Testimony: Two Centuries of Letters, Speeches, Interviews and Autobiographies* (Baton Rouge: Louisiana State University Press, 1977), 156. Also see Stevenson, " 'What's Love Got to Do with It?' " 99–125.

78 The information from this section is taken from Stevenson, *Life in Black and White*, 188–90, 193, 209.

79 Ibid., 188–9.

80 Ibid., 235.

81 See, for example, Stevenson, *Life in Black and White*, 202.

82 Ball, *Fifty Years in Chains*, 9–11.

83 WPA, "Vol. 17, Virginia Narratives," in *Slave Narratives*, "Minnie Folkes" and "Fannie Berry," respectively.

84 Lulu Wilson, interviewed by unknown, Dallas, TX, in Yetman, *Voices from Slavery*, 323.

85 Elizabeth Keckley, *Behind the Scenes. Or, Thirty Years a Slave, and Four Years in the White House* (New York: Oxford University Press, 1988), 33.

86 Yetman, *Voices from Slavery*, 11, 37.

87 WPA, "Vol. 15, North Carolina Narratives, Pt. 2," in *Slave Narratives*, "Fannie Moore."

88 WPA, "Vol. 5, Texas Narratives, Pt. 3" in *Slave Narratives*, "Adeline Marshall."

89 Ibid., "Walter Rimm."

90 Yetman, *Voices from Slavery*, 41; William Still, ed., *Underground Railroad. A Record of Facts, Authentic Narratives, Letters, &c., Narrating the Hardships, Hair-Breadth Escapes and Death Struggles of the Slaves and Their Efforts of Freedoms, as Related by Themselves and Others, or Witnessed by the Author* (Philadelphia, PA: Porter and Coates, 1872), Kindle Edition, "Letter from Miss G.A. Lewis"; Brenda Stevenson, "Slavery," in *Black Women in America: An Historical Encyclopedia*, vol. 2, Darlene Clark Hine, ed. (Brooklyn, NY: Carlson Publishing, Inc., 1993), 1058–9.

91 Octavia V. Rogers Albert, *The House of Bondage, or Charlotte Brooks and Other Slaves* (New York: Oxford University Press, 1988), 9.
92 Campbell, *An Empire for Slavery*, 106.
93 Blassingame, *Slave Testimony*, 341–3.
94 WPA "Vol. 4, Texas Narratives, Pts. 1 and 2," in *Slave Narratives*, "Adeline Cunningham."
95 Northup, *Twelve Years a Slave*, 245.
96 Still, *Underground Railroad*; *Running a Thousand Miles For Freedom; or the Escape of William and Ellen Craft from Slavery* (London, UK: William Tweedie, 1860), electronic edn, University of North Carolina at Chapel Hill, 2001, http://docsouth.unc.edu/neh/craft/craft.html; Catherine Clinton, *Harriet Tubman: The Road to Freedom* (Boston, MA: Back Bay Books, 2005).
97 Stevenson, *Life in Black and White*, 275.
98 Compiled from Joseph E. Holloway, "Slave Insurrections in the United States, An Overview," *The Slave Rebellion Web Site*, 2010, http://slaverebellion.org/index.php?page=united-states-insurrections. Those revolts included in this table are those that actually occurred. Holloway lists many more conspiracies and plots that were discovered before executed.
99 Howard Jones, *Mutiny on the Amistad*, rev. edn (New York: Oxford University Press, 1988), 7, 12–13, 15–16.
100 Jones, *Mutiny on the Amistad*, 208–9; Howard Jones, "The Peculiar Institution and National Honor: The Case of the Creole Slave Revolt," *Civil War History* 21(1) (March 1975): 28–50, doi: 10.1353/cwh.1975.0036.
101 Yetman, *Voices from Slavery*, 13, 134; WPA, "Vol. 12, Georgia Narratives, Pt. 1" in *Slave Narratives*, "Rev. W. B. Allen."
102 Ibid., "Anderson Furr."
103 Yetman, *Voices from Slavery*, 13.
104 Patrick Minges, ed., *Far More Terrible For Women: Personal Accounts of Women in Slavery* (Winston-Salem, NC: John F. Blair, Publisher, 2006), 14.
105 See, for example, Blassingame, *Slave Testimony*, 156; Jacobs, *Incidents in the Life of a Slave Girl*, 87–8; and Picquet, *Louisa Picquet, The Octoroon*, 6, 20–1.
106 WPA, "Vol. 14, North Carolina Narratives, Pt. 1," in *Slave Narratives*, "Mattie Curtis."
107 Albert, *The House of Bondage*, 7–11.
108 Jane Pyatt quoted in Perdue, Barden, and Phillips, *Weevils in the Wheat*, 235.
109 WPA, "Vol. 9, Arkansas Narratives, Pt. 3," in *Slave Narratives*, "H.B. Holloway."

110 WPA, "Vol. 16, Virginia Narratives," in *Slave Narratives*, "Fannie Berry."

111 WPA, "Vol. 17, Florida Narratives," in *Slave Narratives*, "Mary Minus Biddie."

112 WPA, "Vol. 6, Alabama Narratives," in *Slave Narratives*, "Wade Owens."

113 Sean Kelley, " 'Mexico in his Head': Slavery and the Texas-Mexico Border," *Journal of Social History* 37(3) (Spring 2004): 711–13, http://www.jstor.org/stable/3790160.

114 Campbell, *An Empire for Slavery*, 12–25; Kelley, " 'Mexico in His Head,' " 713.

115 Campbell, *An Empire for Slavery*, 19.

116 Some estimate slaves were 20 percent of the population. Ibid., 31, 33.

117 Ibid., 10–34; Kelley, " 'Mexico in his Head:' " 713–17; Paul D. Lack, "Slavery and the Texas Revolution," *Southwestern Historical Quarterly* 89(2) (Oct. 1985): 181–202, http://www.jstor.org/stable/30239908; Eugene C. Barker, "The Influence of Slavery in the Colonization of Texas," *Southwestern Historical Quarterly* 28(1) (July 1924): 1–33, http://www.jstor.org/stable/30234905.

118 The Texas Constitution of 1836 allowed slavery. Campbell, *An Empire for Slavery*, 46–7.

119 Ibid., 46; Also see Kelley, " 'Mexico in his Head,' " 710, regarding the price of Texas slaves during this era.

120 Campbell, *An Empire for Slavery*, 71, Table 2.

121 Ibid., 72–3, Table 4; Samuel H. Williamson and Louis P. Cain, "Measuring Slavery in 2011 Dollars," *MeasuringWorth*, 2013, http://www.measuringworth.com/slavery.php; Robert Evans, Jr "The Economics of American Negro Slavery, 1830–1860," in *The Aspects of Labor Economics*, ed. Harold M. Groves (Princeton, NJ: Princeton University Press, 1962), 212, http://www.nber.org/chapters/c0606.

122 Campbell, *An Empire for Slavery*, 56, Table 1.

123 WPA, "Vol. 4, Texas Narratives, Pt. 2," in *Slave Narratives*, "Silvia King."

124 WPA, "Vol. 10, Arkansas Narratives, Pt. 5," in *Slave Narratives*, "Tom Robinson."

125 "Texas Slave Narrative: Sarah Ashley," transcribed by Eleanor Wyatt, Rootsweb.com, 2000, http://freepages.genealogy.rootsweb.ancestry.com/~ewyatt/_borders/Texas%20Slave%20Narratives/Ashely,%20Sarah.html.

126 Campbell, *An Empire for Slavery*, 57–8.

127 Ibid., 95.

128 WPA, "Vol. 4, Texas Narratives, Pt. 1," in *Slave Narratives*, "Edgar Bendy."

129 WPA, "Vol. 6, Texas Narratives, Pt. 3," in *Slave Narratives*, "Walter Rimm."

130 WPA, "Vol. 5, Texas Narratives, Pt. 3," in *Slave Narratives*, "Adeline Marshall."

131 WPA, "Vol. 4, Texas Narratives, Pt. 2," in *Slave Narratives*, "Sarah Ford."

132 WPA, "Vol. 4, Texas Narratives, Pt. 1," in *Slave Narratives*, "Julia Blanks."

133 Lawrence B. De Graaf and Quintard Taylor, "Introduction: African Americans in California History, California in African American History," in *Seeking El Dorado: African Americans in California*, ed. Lawrence B. De Graaf, Kevin Mulroy, and Quintard Taylor (Seattle, WA: University of Washington Press, 2001), 9.

134 Gerald Stanley, "Senator William Gwin: Moderate or Racist?," *California Historical Quarterly* 50(3) (September 1971): 243–55, http://www.jstor.org/stable/25157333.

135 Brady Harrison, *Agent of Empire: William Walker and the Imperial Self in American Literature* (Athens, GA: University of Georgia Press, 2004).

136 Willi Coleman, "African American Women and Community Development in California, 1848–1900," in De Graaf, Mulroy, and Taylor, *Seeking El Dorado*, 103; De Graaf and Taylor, "Introduction," 9.

137 De Graaf and Taylor, "Introduction," 9–10.

138 Daniel F. Littlefield, Jr and Lonnie E. Underhill, "Slave 'Revolt' in the Cherokee Nation, 1842," *American Indian Quarterly* 3(2) (Summer 1977): 121–6, http://www.jstor.org/stable/1184177.

139 Ibid., 128.

140 Ethan Davis, "An Administrative Trail of Tears: Indian Removal," *The American Journal of Legal History* 50(1) (Jan. 2008–2010): 49–100, http://www.jstor.org/stable/25664483; Wilcomb E. Washburn, "Indian Removal Policy: Administrative, Historical and Moral Criteria for Judging Its Success or Failure," *Ethnohistory* 12(3) (Summer 1965): 274–8, http://www.jstor.org/stable/480522; Mary Hershberger, "Mobilizing Women, Anticipating Abolition: The Struggle against Indian Removal in the 1830s," *The Journal of American History* 86(1) (June 1999): 15–40, http://www.jstor.org/stable/2567405.

141 Halliburton, *Red Over Black*, 192, appendix B; Arthur L. Tolson, *Black Oklahomans: A History, 1541–1972* (New Orleans, LA: Edwards Printing Company, 1972), 26–7.

142 Perdue, *Slavery and the Evolution of Cherokee Society*, 60.

143 Halliburton, *Red Over Black*, 192, appendix B.
144 Littlefield and Underhill, "Slave 'Revolt' in the Cherokee Nation," 127.
145 Rawick, *The American Slave* (Supplement, Series 1), vol. 12, Oklahoma Narratives, 203, 206, 296, 251, 310, 321, 344; Rawick, *The American Slave*, vol. 7, Oklahoma and Mississippi Narratives, 266, 237, 286, 345.
146 Perdue, *Slavery and the Evolution of Cherokee Society*, 60.
147 Chaney McNair quoted in Rawick, *The American Slave (Supplement, Series I)*, vol. 12, Oklahoma Narratives, 222.
148 Rachel Caroline Eaton, *John Ross and the Cherokee Indians* (Chicago, IL: University of Chicago Press, 1921), 1–2; Roethler, "Negro Slavery among the Cherokee Indians," 122; Halliburton, *Red Over Black*, 27.
149 Guyette, "The American Republic: 1760–1870."
150 Mark L. Kamrath, "American Anti-Slavery Society," in *Slavery in the United States: A Social, Political, and Historical Encyclopedia*, vol. 2, ed. Junius P. Rodriguez (Santa Barbara: ABC-Clio, Inc, 2007), 161–2.
151 Ibid. Drescher had smaller numbers for affiliates and members. Seymour Drescher, *Abolition: A History of Slavery and Antislavery* (Cambridge, UK: Cambridge University Press, 2009), 304.
152 William Lloyd Garrison, "On the Constitution and the Union," in "The Great Crisis!," *The Liberator* 2(52) (December 29, 1832), http://fair-use.org/the-liberator/1832/12/29/on-the-constitution-and-the-union.
153 Garrison and Phillips quotes from Paul Finkelman, "Garrison's Constitution: The Covenant with Death and How it was Made," *Prologue Magazine* 32(4) (Winter 2000), http://www.archives.gov/publications/prologue/2000/winter/garrisons-constitution-1.html; also see "No Slavery! Fourth of July! The Managers of the Mass. Anti-Slavery Soc'y ...," *Massachusetts Historical Society* online, http://www.masshist.org/database/431.
154 Kamrath, "American Anti-Slavery Society," 161–2.
155 Eric Foner, *Free Soil, Free Labor, Free Men: The Ideology of the Republican Party before the Civil War* (New York: Oxford University Press, 1995), passim.
156 Litwack, *North of Slavery*, Kindle location ch. 7, 2202–14.
157 Bradford, "Free African American Population in the U.S., 1790–1860."
158 Tunde Adeleke, "Lovejoy, Elijah P. (1802–1837)," in Rodriguez, *The Historical Encyclopedia of World Slavery*, vol. 2, 420–1.

159 "Slave Narratives and *Uncle Tom's Cabin*, 1845–1862," *Africans in America*, WGBH and PBS Online, 1998, http://www. pbs.org/wgbh/aia/part4/4p2958.html; David W. Blight, "The Slave Narrative: A Genre and a Source," Gilder Lehrman Institute of American History, https://www.gilderlehrman.org/ history-by-era/literature-and-language-arts/essays/slave-narra tives-genre-and-source; Pennington, *The Fugitive Blacksmith*; *The Narrative of William W. Brown, a Fugitive Slave. Written by Himself* (Boston, MA: Anti-Slavery Office, 1847), electronic edn, University of North Carolina at Chapel Hill, 2001, http://docsouth.unc.edu/neh/brown47/brown47.html; Douglass, *Narrative of the Life of Frederick Douglass*; Ball, *Fifty Years in Chains*; *The Life of Josiah Henson: Formerly a Slave, Now an Inhabitant of Canada, as Narrated by Himself* (Boston, MA: Arthur D. Phelps, 1849), electronic edn, University of North Carolina at Chapel Hill, 2001, http://doc south.unc.edu/neh/henson49/henson49.html; *Narrative of the Life and Adventures of Henry Bibb, an American Slave, Written by Himself* (New York: The Author, 1849), electronic edn, University of North Carolina at Chapel Hill, 2000, http:// docsouth.unc.edu/neh/bibb/bibb.html; and Jacobs, *Incidents in the Life of a Slave Girl.*

160 "To William Lloyd Garrison," in John Greenleaf Whittier, *Anti-Slavery Poems: Songs of Labor and Reform* (New York: Houghton, Mifflin, and Co., 1888), 9–10, American Verse Project, University of Michigan Humanities Text Initiative, 1997, http://quod.lib.umich.edu/a/amverse/BAE00 44.0001.001/1:4.1?rgn=div2;view=fulltext.

161 "Antislavery Ensemble," *Antislavery Literature Project*, Arizona State University and Iowa State University, 2006, http://antislavery.eserver.org/video/antislavery-ensemble. html/.

162 Jarius Lincoln, "Hymn 17," in *Antislavery Melodies: for The Friends of Freedom* (Hingham, MA: Elijah B. Gill, 1843), 28–9, https://archive.org/details/antislaverymelod1843linc.

163 "Uncle Tom's Cabin," *Harriet Beecher Stowe Center*, https:// www.harrietbeecherstowecenter.org/utc/.

164 "The Anti-Slavery Alphabet: A Pamphlet from 1846," *Jubilo! The Emancipation Century*, May 11, 2011, http://jubiloeman cipationcentury.wordpress.com/2011/05/11/the-anti-slavery -alphabet-a-pamphlet-from-1846/.

165 Jarold D. Tallant, "Garrison, William Lloyd (1805–1879)," in Rodriguez, *The Historical Encyclopedia of World Slavery*, vol. 1, 296–7.

166 Julie Roy Jeffrey, *The Great Silent Army of Abolitionism: Ordinary Women in the Antislavery Movement* (Chapel Hill, NC: University of North Carolina Press, 1998), 86–92.

167 Joel Schor, "The Rivalry between Frederick Douglass and Henry Highland Garnet," *The Journal of Negro History* 64(1) (Winter 1979): 30–8, http://www.jstor.org/stable/2717124; Litwack, *North of Slavery*, location ch. 7.

168 Howard H. Bell, "The American Moral Reform Society, 1836–1841," *The Journal of Negro Education* 27(1) (Winter 1958): 34–40, http://www.jstor.org/stable/2293690.

169 De Graaf and Taylor, "Introduction," 10.

170 Ibid.

171 "(1888) Frederick Douglass on Women's Suffrage," *Woman's Journal*, April 14, 1888, Blackpast.org, http://www.blackpast. org/1888-frederick-douglass-woman-suffrage.

172 Drescher, *Abolition*, 304.

173 See, for example, Jeffrey, *The Great Silent Army of Abolitionism*.

174 William Lloyd Garrison quoted in ibid., 1.

175 Ibid., 93–4.

176 Angelina Emily Grimké, *Appeal to the Christian Women of the South* (New York: American Antislavery Society, 1836), *Uncle Tom's Cabin and American Culture*, Steven Railton and the University of Virginia, http://utc.iath.virginia.edu/abolitn/ abesaegat.html.

177 Ada Sarah Louisa Forten, "An Appeal to Women," in *She Wields a Pen: American Women Poets of the Nineteenth Century*, ed. Janet Gray (Iowa City, IA: University of Iowa Press, 1997), *Poetry Foundation*, http://www.poetryfounda tion.org/poem/182815.

178 Brenda E. Stevenson, "Abolition," in Hine, *Black Women in America*, vol. 1, 1–7.

179 Drew Gilpin Faust, *The Ideology of Slavery: Proslavery Thought in the Antebellum South, 1830–1860* (Baton Rouge, LA: Louisiana State University Press, 1981), Kindle location, 12.

180 " 'The "Mudsill" Theory,' by James Henry Hammond," *Africans in America*, WGBH and PBS Online, 1998, http://www. pbs.org/wgbh/aia/part4/4h3439t.html.

181 Ibid.

182 Faust, *Ideology of Slavery*, 273.

183 John C. Calhoun, "Slavery as a Positive Good," February 6, 1837, TeachingAmericanHistory.org, http://teachingameri canhistory.org/library/document/slavery-a-positive-good/.

184 George Fitzhugh, *Sociology of the South: or Failure of Free Society* (Richmond, VA: A. Morris, 1854), 27–8, electronic edn, University of North Carolina at Chapel Hill, 1998, http://docsouth.unc.edu/southlit/fitzhughsoc/fitzhugh.html.

185 George Fitzhugh, "Sociology for the South," in *Slavery Defended: The Voices of the Old South*, ed. Eric McKitrick (Englewood Cliffs, NJ: Prentice-Hall, 1963), 37–8, quoted in Stevenson, *Life in Black and White*, 42.

186 Thomas R. Dew quoted in Rollin G. Osterweis, *Romanticism and Nationalism in the Old South* (Gloucester, MA: L. Peter Smith, 1964), quoted in Stevenson, *Life in Black in White*, 42.

187 Julia Gardiner Tyler quoted in Ernest R. Groves, *The American Woman: The Feminine Side of a Masculine Civilization* (New York: Greenberg, 1937), 162.

188 Foner, *Free Soil, Free Labor, Free Men*, 89.

189 "Popular Sovereignty," in Rodriguez, *Chronology of World Slavery*, 315.

190 Kansas Historical Society, "Bleeding Kansas," *Kansapedia*, April 2010, last modified September 2011, http://www.kshs.org/kansapedia/bleeding-kansas/15145.

191 Ibid.

192 Ibid.

193 Hon. Charles Sumner, "The Crime Against Kansas: The Apologies for the Crime; The True Remedy Delivered to the United States Senate, 19–20 May 1856," in *The Works of Charles Sumner, vol. IV* (Boston: Lee and Shepard, 1870–1873), 125–249, in John C. Willis, *America's Civil War Documents*, http://www.sewanee.edu/faculty/willis/Civil_War/documents/Crime.html.

194 David Herbert Donald, *Charles Sumner and the Coming Civil War* (New York: Alfred A. Knopf, 1960), 291–6.

195 Kansas Historical Society, "Kansas Constitution," *Kansapedia*, February 2011, last modified September 2012, http://www.kshs.org/kansapedia/kansas-constitutions/16532; Mandi Barnard, "Wyandotte Constitution, Kansas Historical Society," *Kansapedia*, April 2010, modified August 2012, http://www.kshs.org/kansapedia/wyandotte-constitution/13884.

196 "Dred Scott, 150 Years Ago," *The Journal of Blacks in Higher Education* 55 (Spring 2007): 19, http://www.jstor.org/stable/25073625.

197 Walter Ehrlich, "The Origins of the Dred Scott Case," *The Journal of Negro History* 59(2) (Apr. 1974): 132–3, http://www.jstor.org/stable/2717325.

198 Litwack, *North of Slavery*, Kindle location ch. 2, 294–8.
199 Walter Ehrlich, "Was the Dred Scott Case Valid?," *The Journal of American History* 55(2) (September 1968): 256–65, http://www.jstor.org/stable/1899556.
200 Stevenson, *Life in Black and White*, 320–1.

Conclusion

1 "13th Amendment to the United States Constitution," *Primary Documents in American History*, Library of Congress, April 10, 2014, http://www.loc.gov/rr/program/bib/ourdocs/13thamendment.html.

Index